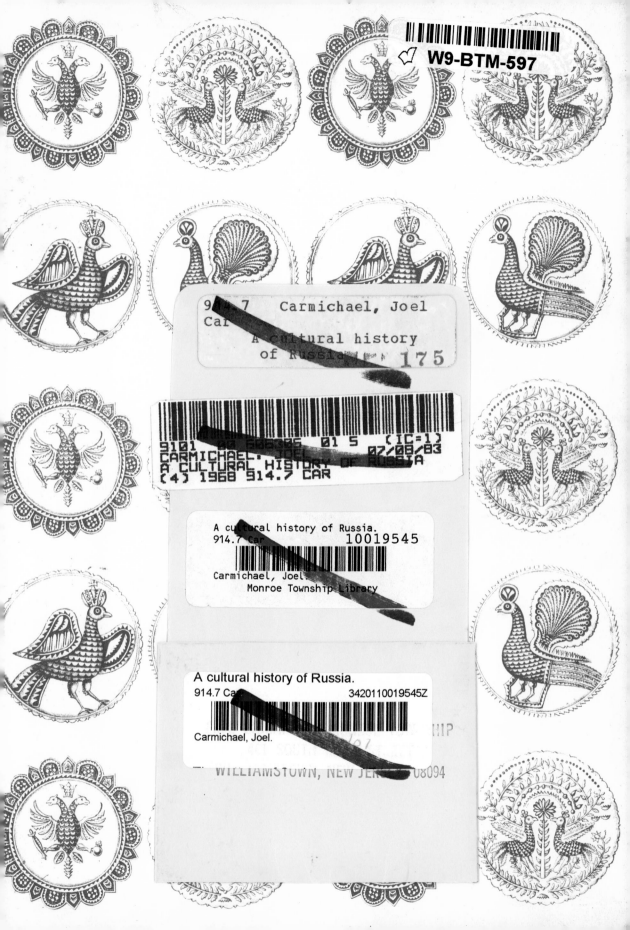

# A Cultural History of RUSSIA

# A Cultural History

# of RUSSIA

JOEL CARMICHAEL

## Weybright and Talley

NEW YORK

*Published in the United States by*
WEYBRIGHT AND TALLEY, INC.
*3 East 54th Street,*
*New York, New York 10022.*


*Library of Congress Catalog Card No. 68–31242*

Printed in Great Britain

# Contents

# Illustrations

A. Rubler: 'The Old Testament Trinity' (*Tretyakov Gallery*) (photo: Deutsche Fotothek)

Fifteenth-century overdoor with representation of the Eucharist (*Tretyakov Gallery*) (photo: Royal Academy of Arts)

'St George and the Dragon': late fifteenth-century icon of the Novgorod School (*Tretyakov Gallery*) (photo: Royal Academy of Arts)

'Boris and Gleb': fourteenth-century icon; Moscow School (*Tretyakov Gallery*)

S. S. Kolmogretz (Yaroslav School): seventeenth-century icon (*District Museum of Art, Yaroslav*) (photo: Royal Academy of Arts)

P. Chirin (Strogonov School): early seventeenth-century icon (*Tretyakov Gallery*) (photo: Royal Academy of Arts)

Illumination from a ms. of *The Tale of the Bloody Encounter with Mamai*, early fifteenth-century (*British Museum*)

Three pages from the *Radziwill Chronicle*, fifteenth-century ms. of *The Tale of Bygone Years, c.* 1113 (*Library of the Academy of Sciences of the USSR*) (photo: John Freeman, from facsimile copy in the British Museum)

Map of Moscow and view of Novgorod from Peter van der Aa's *Agreeable Gallery of the World,* 1719

The largest bell in the world; from Korb's *Diarium Itineris in Moscoviam,* 1700 (*British Museum*) (photo: J. Freeman)

Archangel Cathedral Moscow, 1505–09

Annunciation Cathedral, Kremlin, 1482–90

Assumption Cathedral, Moscow, 1475–9

The Church of the Transfiguration, Kizhi, 1714 (photo: Novosti)

## The Aristocratic Prism I (*pages* 81 *to* 88)

Frontispiece of *The Acts of the Apostles,* 1564 (*Gonville and Caius College, Cambridge*)

Frontispiece and first page of Aesop's Fables, St Petersburg, 1700 (*British Museum*) (photo: John Freeman)

Engraved title-page from a Bible printed in Moscow in 1663 (*University Library, Cambridge*)

Peter the Great Monument in Leningrad by Falcoret, erected in 1782 by Catherine II (photo: Camera Press)

Workmen moving the granite block forming the base of the memorial: engraving dated 1770 (*British Museum*) (photo: John Freeman)

D. G. Levitsky: Portrait of Count Y. E. Sievers, 1779 (*Tretyakov Gallery*) (photo: Royal Academy of Arts)

I. P. Argunov: Portrait of Peasant Woman in Russian Costume, 1784 (*Tretyakov Gallery*) (photo: Royal Academy of Arts)

V. L. Borovikovsky: Portrait of V. I. Arseneyeva' *c.* 1790–1800 (*Russian Museum, Leningrad*) (photo: Royal Academy of Arts)

D. G. Levitsky: Portrait of H. N. Novikov (*Tretyakov Gallery*) (photo: Royal Academy of Arts)

F. A. Alexeyev: View of the Palace Quay from the Peter and Paul Fortress, St Petersburg, 1794 (*Tretyakov Gallery*) (photo: Royal Academy of Arts)

D. G. Levitsky: Portrait of Catherine II (*Tretyakov Gallery*)

D. G. Levitsky: Portrait of two Smolny Pupils, 1773 (*Russian Museum, Leningrad*) (photo: Royal Academy of Arts)

Mantelpiece and chair in cut steel, Tula Foundry, eighteenth century (*Victoria and Albert Museum*)

Wooden gingerbread form, 1776

Woodcut from Prologue to *The Parable of the Prodigal Son*, 1685 (*Library of the Academy of Sciences of the USSR*)
Two scenes from ms. King's 191, eighteenth century (*British Museum*)


## The Aristocratic Prism II (*pages* 105 *to* 112)

Stage design for masquerade at the court of Anna Ivanovna (*School of Slavonic and East European Studies*) (photo: John Freeman)
View of Podnovinsky Square, Moscow, by H. Guttenberg (*Metropolitan Museum of Art*)
View along the River Neva, engraving by Makhaev
View towards the Peter and Paul Fortress, engraving by Makhaev
View of the old Winter Palace, engraving by Makhaev
The Summer Palace, engraving by Makhaev (*School of Slavonic and East European Studies*)
View of the magazine court provisions on the Fontacka River, anon. (*Metropolitan Museum of Art*)
The Ekaterinsky Palace after restoration (photo: B. Utkin, Novosti)
The Ekaterinsky Palace at Tsarskoe Selo, engraving by Makhaev (Metropolitan Museum of Art)
The Peterhof Palace and the cascades (photo: J. Allan Cash)
The Peterhof Palace; contemporary engraving (*British Museum*) (photo: John Freeman)
The Catherine Palace, showing the park and the pond (photo: Camera Press)
The Smolny Convent, by Rastrelli, 1748–64 (photo: J. Allan Cash)
The Winter Palace, Leningrad, begun by Rastrelli, 1754–62 (photo: V. Malyshev, Novosti)
The Hermitage, seen through the arch of the General Staff building (photo: J. Allan Cash)
The interior of the church of the Peter and Paul Fortress, built by Trezzini, 1712–33 (photo: Camera Press)
The Old University of Moscow: exterior and Great Hall (*British Museum*) (photos: John Freeman)


## The Modern Age Takes Root (*pages* 161–176)

O. Kiprensky: Portrait of Pushkin, 1827 (*Tretyakov Gallery*) (photo: Society for Cultural Relations with the USSR)
F. A. Moller: Portrait of Gogol, 1841 (photo: Society for Cultural Relations with the USSR)
Two Manuscript pages from 'Death of a Poet', 1837, and *Vadim*, 1833–4, by Lermontov (*Literary Museum, Moscow*)
Sketch by Gogol for *The Revizor* (*Literary Museum, Moscow, from the facsimile copy of the original in Kiev*)
Portrait of Tolstoy (*Tretyakov Gallery*) (photo: Royal Academy of Arts, London)
Portrait of Belinsky (photo: Society for Cultural Relations with the USSR)
Portrait of Turgenev (photo: Radio Times Hulton Picture Library)
Portrait of Dostoyevsky, by V. Perov, 1872 (*Tretyakov Gallery*) (photo: Royal Academy of Arts)
View of the Kremlin, by R. Bowyder, 1815 (*British Museum*) (photo: John Freeman)
Public Festival in St Petersburg, by J. A. Atkinson, 1812 (*British Museum*) (photo: John Freeman)

V. A. Serov: 'Delegates from the Villages visiting Lenin during the Revolution', 1950 (*Lenin Museum, Moscow*) (photo: Royal Academy of Arts)

The Grand Kremlin Palace, 1961 (photo: Novosti)

Rabin: 'Church of Ivan the Terrible', 1964 (*Grosvenor Gallery, London*)

Serge Soudekine: 'Song of the Workers' Association', stage design, *c.* 1925 (*Collection Riabov*) (photo: G.R.)

E. Neizvestny: 'Suicide', bronze sculpture (*Grosvenor Gallery, London*)

V. Tatlin: design for a Monument to the Third International (photo: G.R.)

A. A. Plastov: 'Collective Farm Threshing', 1949 (*Russian Museum of Art, Kiev*) (photo: Royal Academy of Arts)

Two views of Moscow's underground railway, constructed in the 'thirties (photos: Novosti)

Ernst Neizvestny: pen and ink sketch for 'Figure of Man' (*Grosvenor Gallery, London*)


The author and publishers would like to thank all the individuals and institutions referred to in the above list for most kindly giving permission to reproduce illustrations or for providing photographs.


The picture research was undertaken initially in New York by Jill Weldon under the supervision of Alexis Gregory and later in London by Georgina Brückner.


The layout of the illustrations is by Jane Mackay.

# Chapter 1

# The Misty Beginnings

Every people has a culture, though not every culture is worth writing about. In the case of Russia, which for a couple of generations has loomed so large in world affairs, what is perhaps most striking is the contrast between its importance today and the slowness with which it got started.

Distinguished for centuries by a notorious backwardness, the Russian people was late in taking shape; the culture by which it has expressed itself came still later. Historical origins are bound to be misty: history even in the full light of day is generally enigmatic. The genesis of the Russian people is mistier than most. And while its dim beginnings extend into the past for not much more than a millennium – a brief span, compared with the great societies of the East, of the Mediterranean, and even of Western Europe – its cultural history proper has been of general significance for a matter of five centuries at most.

Yet those five centuries, too, have a background. The cultural monuments that began to evolve a thousand years ago in the great plain of Russia were themselves shaped by preceding movements whose turbulence we can only guess at.

Perhaps the fundamental agency in the shaping of what came to be Russian society may be detected in the interaction between the geography of the great western and central plains, framed by the great river complexes, and the momentous fact that the initial civilizing influences underlying Russian culture emanated from the eastern Christian civilization of Byzantium.

The physical background of Russian history is easily described: a land area consisting of some nine million square miles, or a sixth of the planet's land surface, and a population in our day of more than two hundred million people, three-quarters of them Slavs and comprising all in all more than sixty different nationalities. The land itself is a vast plain, for all practical purposes unbroken, stretching from the Baltic Sea and the Carpathians all the way to the Pacific Ocean across Siberia. There is a small mountain chain, the Urals, which serves as a conventional line of demarcation between Europe and Asia, but as a natural barrier it is negligible: the average altitude does not exceed five thousand feet. In fact the Urals have never impeded the incessant movement from Asia into Europe and back that has been a constant feature of the natural environment of Russia for centuries.

The gradations of climate and vegetation throughout this seemingly endless terrain are slight; on both sides of the Urals the natural environment is the same, and through the gaping southern passage between the Caspian Sea and the low mountain barrier there has been a constant flood of folk migrations across the treeless steppelands that are the cardinal physical feature of the country as a whole.

This bird's-eye view of the area helps one to understand what has doubtless been man's outstanding reaction to this extensive expanse of substantially identical terrain – a desire to fill it. In fact the social history of Russia may be conceived of as a permanent attempt to fill its vast areas with people, and the natural reservoir for this since time immemorial has been the inexhaustible human supplies of central Asia. Beginning with an incessant trek in the immense vacuum of Russian space, the ancestors of the Russians colonized a greater and greater area until their ultimate limits were reached. Instead of shipping surplus population overseas, the proto-Russians simply overflowed into neighbouring territories.

This immense terrain is divided, to be sure, into zonal strips stretching from the Baltic Sea to the Pacific Ocean. The tundra in the north shades into the great forest belt, which in its turn dwindles away into first fertile steppelands such as the gigantic bread-basket of the Ukraine, and then, finally, the desert steppes of southern central Asia. The only direction in which the folk-migration of the Russians' ancestors did not simply come up against an immovable geographical boundary was the west, where the surging of the ethnic overflow collided with the eastward thrust of peoples rooted in central and southern central Europe. Because of this fundamental collision between peoples the western boundary of Russia has always been unstable and indeed fluid, a factor of turbulence for many centuries.

In the west, the Russian landscape is celebrated for its characteristic combination of coniferous trees and birch. The central deciduous forests merge with the tillable zone of steppeland to form a vast belt of country that is both wooded and open – the physical background of Russian society.

This interaction between forest and steppeland, with an ancient polarity between attempts to till the soil and constant interruptions by pastoral peoples roaming the steppes, may be taken as an unchanging background to Russian evolution. There has always been a conflict between settled cultivation of the soil and the persistent depredations, or danger of depredations originating in the limitless steppelands.

These steppelands facilitated movement outside the forest belt, and this movement was helped not only by the flatness of the land but also by the great complex of rivers that encompass and shape European Russia. Broad and slow-moving, with countless tributaries, they penetrate forest and steppeland alike, but without ending up in an open sea. The great river system was a natural means of transport, and in fact marks the tidal flow of Russian migration. The Dnieper that flows into the Black Sea, the upper Volga River, 'Mother of Russia', flowing further east, and the great river-complex of the Western Dvina and the Volkhov taking a northerly course into the Baltic Sea provided the various eastern Slav tribes with labyrinthine water-routes that enabled them to fan out across the great plains.

These tortuous and extended river-routes contributed to the genesis of Russian statehood, for it was they that attracted the scattered bands of Scandinavian adventurers, bandits, and businessmen who laid the foundations of Russian society. The very name 'Russia' is generally agreed to have been one of the names these Scandinavians (known in

Western Europe as 'Vikings') bore when they surged south along the great waterways into the Russian plain.

Thus the history of Russia as a self-conscious political formation, as a country, in short, is taken to have begun sometime in the ninth century AD with, as the traditional Russian chronicle puts it, 'the advent of the Varangians' (=Vikings). This seems to mark the culmination of a gradual, spasmodic and doubtless unorganized movement of buccaneering and commerce that had been making itself felt along the great river-routes of Russia for a couple of centuries. The major goal of these roving Viking businessmen and pirates came to be Islam, the great and busy world that lay even beyond Byzantium. By the eighth and ninth centuries Islam had established itself in a vast and cosmopolitan empire that spanned the Middle East, east and south of Byzantium, and spread along North Africa into Spain. Baghdad, which was to become the capital of the Islamic Empire, was a potent magnet for the Viking traders; vast hoards of Muslim coins unearthed in Scandinavia in modern times bear witness to the liveliness of the commerce that linked the capital of the Muslim Empire with the far north of Europe.

It was this commerce that brought in the organized Viking bands to control and milk the Slav communities that had made their first appearance in history some four centuries before, as subjects of the most successful and powerful wave of nomadic invaders from the Asiatic steppe – the Huns. The collapse of the Hunnish realm with the death of its greatest ruler, Attila, whose name was to become a byword, churned up the countless peoples that had come under its rule, including Slavdom. This dissolution of the Hunnish Empire scattered the proto-Slavs, and brought about the fateful division of Slavdom into east, west and south Slavs. The cultural split between these great branches of Slavdom set its stamp on world history, for it was the east Slavs who were to father the congeries of 'Russian' peoples, while the Slav tribes of the west became Poles, Czechs and Slovaks.

By the accident of being in the east at a time when Byzantium was hard pressed by the extremely rapid expansion of Islam after the death of Muhammad, the east Slavs were to pass under the influence of the eastern branch of Christianity, with a direct link to Greek-speaking

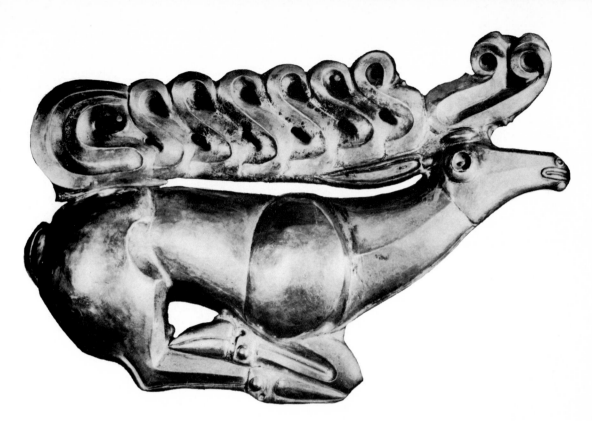

## The Misty Beginnings

Metal objects found in early graves:
(*above*) Relief of the fourth century
BC showing a deerhunt; found
near Kostromkoj.
(*below*) Fifth-century comb with battle
scene; found at Kuriana Solono.

Christ with attendant angels from the Eucharist mosaic in the Church
of the Archangel Michael, Kiev, *c.* 1108.

Holy women, a detail from a fresco in the Cathedral of St Dmitri,
Vladimir, *c.* 1200.

Mosaic from the central dome of the
Cathedral of St Sophia, Kiev, 1043–6;
the photograph on the left is a detail
showing the head of the Pantokrator.

The Rostov-Veliki monasteries, built in the twelfth century.

(*opposite below*) The Cathedral of St Dmitri in Vladimir (1194–7).

Byzantine gold dove of the eleventh century with cloisonné enamel.

175

(*opposite*) Two thirteenth-century icons of the Novgorod School: 'The Dormition of the Virgin' and 'The Descent into Hell'.

The Assumption Cathedral in Vladimir was built from 1158 to 1161.

The St George Cathedral at Yuriev Polsky in the Vladimir region, built in 1234; the detail shows a capital on the northern façade.

St Sophia Cathedral, Novgorod.

Byzantium and thus to the Hellenistic heritage of the Middle East. The Slav tribes of the west consolidated the cleavage in Slavdom by being drawn into the orbit of the Roman Catholic Church, while the Slavs of the south, by drifting into the maelstrom of the Balkan Peninsula, formed part of the mishmash it is characterized by – the Croats becoming Roman Catholics, for instance, and the Serbs turning to the Greek Orthodox Church.

Thus the split in Christendom that was later to become fateful was reflected in the very body politic of Slavdom; the Russians, by becoming the greatest and most powerful peoples speaking Indo-European languages, were to create a framework for an indigenous Russian development of Greek Orthodox culture.

It was perhaps the decay of one of the early Asiatic nomadic empires, the *Khazars*, who probably included both Hunnish elements and tribes from around the Caucasus, that provided the initial attraction for the Viking adventurers. The Khazars, though basically nomads, also tilled the soil and kept cattle; perhaps the major concentration of their society was on commerce: Muslims and Jews had settled among them – indeed, the Khazar rulers were converted to Judaism – and the east Slavs seem to have been allied with Khazars in a variety of enterprises. The pagan Slavs were thus more than mere subjects of the Khazars, and, as their allies, began to need other props when the Khazar power began to be eroded by the expansion of Islam in the south and south-east. Thus the traditional Russian explanation of the 'advent of the Varangians', to the effect that the tribal leaders of the Slavs had turned to the Vikings for succour, may be rooted in historical fact.

As the Khazar power declined, the Vikings multiplied steadily along the great river road leading from Novgorod, along the Volkhov River in the north, to the great centre of Kiev on the Dnieper in the south. The armed Viking businessmen, after being called in to give the pagan Slavs succour, naturally took advantage of the situation to exact tributes and to launch business expeditions of their own, aiming at the opulent markets of the south, from Constantinople to Baghdad.

The formal date assigned in Russian tradition to the acceptance by Russians of the *Vikings' dominion* is AD 862, when the Vikings, in a

2

riposte to the Khazar attempt to bar the trade routes to Constantinople, set out across the Baltic Sea with the aim of reopening those trade-routes. Thus began the career of the forefather of Russian statehood – Rurik, a Danish prince who founded the first dynasty of Russian rulers, and laid the foundations of the first of the Russias, the Russia of Kiev, the first of the trio of cities whose names encompass the broad outlines of all Russian history – Kiev, Moscow, and St Petersburg (now Leningrad).

Kiev, celebrated as 'the mother of Russian cities', was to become the hub of the Slav tribes scattered alongside the great river of the southern steppe, and to provide a matrix for the first efflorescence of Russian culture.

So little is known about *Kievan Russia* that it has been easy to surround it with the glamour of mystery and opulence. It is true that Russian life, to the extent that any generalizations about it have meaning, centred in Kiev for centuries; it was in fact more than three and a half centuries between the advent of the Scandinavian Varangians and the far more important, enduring and fateful inundation of all Russia by the great Mongol conquests of the twelfth century. Yet the word 'Kievan' itself is merely a handy catchword to cover our basic ignorance, still further heightened by the tendentious approach to the question on the part of practically all historical sources.

Perhaps the most definite thing that can be said of Kievan Russian civilization is that it led to the introduction of Christianity, in its eastern branch, promoted the creation of a literary language and engendered the first fruit of Russian art, which at this stage may justly be called a branch of Byzantine art. It need hardly be said that the last two events were above all a reflection of the same primordial socio-historical factor – the introduction of Byzantine Christendom among the pagan barbarians of the south Russian steppe. From a political point of view Kiev was to prove a blind alley; the sovereignty of its grand dukes evaporated well in advance of the Mongol invasions, and it would be impossible, indeed, to speak of a genuine unification even of the territories the Grand Dukes of Kiev laid claim to. However, in the spiritual realm it cannot be denied that Kiev laid the foundations of a culture that was later to be reflected in the authentic movement for the centralization of Russia that was to be linked to the names of Moscow and St Petersburg.

Kiev itself seems, in the eleventh and twelfth centuries, to have excelled any city in Western Europe both in size and splendour; its great stone churches were celebrated, and as a hive of commerce it exercised a magnetic effect on all the other trading centres of the scattered Slav communities.

It is trade, indeed, that explains the abrupt introduction of Greek Christianity into Kievan Russia. For in the close business relations between Kiev and Constantinople, slaves were the most important commodity taken to Constantinople by the early Kievan princes: indeed, the very word 'slave' comes from the word 'Slav'. The slaves of the Kiev princes were a lucrative source of revenue from both Constantinople and the great markets of the Muslim east. The source of the slaves was the unflagging internecine warfare between the princes themselves, and even though the Kiev trade in the west increased and agriculture kept growing substantially throughout the forest areas, the slave trade remained the most important branch of the Kiev economy. Although the Grand Duke of Kiev never imposed his power on the other princes in this period, he did manage to achieve a position of primacy; it was the support of the Greek Orthodox Church that gave this sovereign position of the Grand Duke of Kiev its theoretical justification. The aspect of Byzantine Christianity that found full expression in the earliest political theory of Kievan Russia was the idea of the divine right of rulers; this idea struck firm roots in Kievan Russia, though local conditions made it impossible to force its acceptance down the throats of fractious princelets. Under the Mongol invasion, with the example of the Mongol rulers to fortify it, and still more under the extravagant centralization of State power that characterized the late Moscow period of Russian statehood that was to follow the Mongols and to achieve its greatest expression under the Bolshevik dictatorship, the theory of the untrammelled right of Russian rulers to rule became the cornerstone of the State.

Byzantine political theory was firmly anchored in Russian life even before the formal conversion of the heads of state to Byzantine Christianity at the end of the tenth century, and this theory was more influential in its effects on government than the spiritual content or the immensely complex ceremonial and ritual of the Church. It was the Byzantine principle of the prince anointed of God and unhampered by all human agency that was to become the model for Russian government, in contradistinction to the easy give-and-take of the pagan custom, in which the military leader, whoever he was, was considered to be the natural ruler.

Christian notions began penetrating Kievan Russia as early as the ninth century, as far as we can tell, but not much headway was made against the unorganized mass of pagan Slavdom, which was enthralled by the usual pantheon of countless local deities. These were personifications of the vegetative cycles and the power of nature on which man has always been dependent, and resembled various pagan creeds that Christianity in its day had digested, streamlined, dramatized, and organized.

Kievan Russia comes to us through the slightly misty medium of the ecclesiastical chronicles compiled centuries afterwards in churches and monasteries, largely in the fifteenth and sixteenth centuries; these chronicles claim to be based on an earlier and more basic chronicle, itself composed, however, in the twelfth century. It seems likely that against a background of primitive coarseness and cruelty the early Church exercised a somewhat civilizing and softening influence. Wedded to a theory of the rule of law, and based on a training in letters, however primitive it may seem to us, the Orthodox Church provided Russia, in its Kievan beginnings, with a standard.

Yet the fact that Russia was to receive much of its civilizing material from Greek sources had a fateful effect on its destinies. By selecting the idiom of Church Slavonic – a Bulgarian dialect made current throughout Greek Orthodox Slavdom by two Greek brothers, Cyril, after whom the Russian, Bulgarian and Serbian alphabets still current are named, and Methodius, the 'apostles of the Slavs' – the religious leaders made Russian expression wholly dependent on Greek sources, that is, the Greek scriptures and liturgies that were to underlie the native product that evolved with painful sluggishness.

At the same time these Greek sources, by being embodied in the constricting idiom of Church Slavonic, were transmitted without the saving grace of the Greek language itself, which would at least have provided a channel to antiquity that might have proved fruitful later on, when some educated people could have taken advantage of it. Thus what might have been a channel of culture was both suffocatingly narrow and exotically dislocated: the general effect of this on the growth of Russian culture must be called disastrous.

Kievan Russia, fundamentally empty of people and on the lowest possible cultural level, was altogether dependent for its intellectual life on the Church, the sources of both letters and arts. After the rulers had accepted Christianity in a formal way by the end of the tenth century, the population of the cities and towns was forced or persuaded into baptism. Though the overwhelming majority of the people was illiterate, and was to remain so for almost a millennium, some preachers, generally monks, were trained in the few clerical schools that gradually grew up. Though armed with no more than a smattering of memorized information, they were able to act as educators for the masses, whose paganism was not touched, to be sure, for a very long time to come.

The Russian conversion to Christianity was bound to be basically no more than nominal after all; it would have been too much to expect, even of the higher clergy, any real grounding in Christian dogma. The introduction of Church Slavonic, while useful as a scholarly language, meant that any intellectual expression in it was bound to be quite unintelligible to the masses. It was, perhaps, another form of the external ornamentation that, together with the mumbo-jumbo of an unintelligible ritual and the theatrical dress of the clergy, gave the Church its hold over the people. The threat of eternal damnation, one of the cornerstones of doctrine in this period of Christianity, also helped rivet the people both to their condition in life and to the authority of the Church.

Yet the backwardness of society as a whole, which is so easy to make light of, did not act as a brake on individual talent, and indeed genius. Byzantine tradition inspired great numbers of painters of frescoes and icons, makers of jewellery, and creators of resplendent mosaics; immense originality was attained in the art of enamel-working especially. None of this was merely handed down lifelessly; it was reshaped in accordance with the taste of the artist and of the audience. The result was an unmistakable flavour in the arts of Kievan Russia. In the beginning especially, while the craftsmen and artists were still carrying on their work under the direct influence of original Greek and Italian models, the achievements of Kievan Russia were marked by technical finesse, artistic originality and an overflowing liveliness. It was not until later, after the Church had finally consolidated its paramount position in Russian society, that the liveliness of its first period of efflorescence was ironed out of Kievan art, and it achieved the museum-like, motionless quality it was to become known for after ecclesiastical homogeneity had managed to standardize the expression of the artistic impulse.

The primary form of artistic expression in Russia at this time was doubtless the sacred images. These were not, of course, mere portraits, but, in accordance with the perhaps universal initial impulses of art, were objects whose veneration was meant to have a magical or semi-magical effect. These icons evolved into works of art only because of a battle that had been fought some centuries before in Byzantium, between the champions and opponents of icons; after the puritanical iconoclastic party was defeated in Constantinople, in the middle of the ninth century, the way was clear for a development of the icon form into a high art, perhaps the flower of Russian artistic inspiration of the period.

Iconic art was merely one expression of the new religious faith that flooded Kievan Russia after the conversion to Christianity; the torrential effect of Byzantine Christianity on the primitive society of Kievan Russia can scarcely be overestimated. Kievan Russia, precisely because of its neophyte's ardour, was even more dogmatic and uncompromising on orthodox claims than Constantinople itself. Since the faith had been transmitted not to broad masses of more or less cultivated people, but to a tiny layer of half-educated sectarians, the confidence in the all-inclusive quality of Orthodox Christianity, the simple-minded belief in it as a universal panacea for thought and action, was far more firmly rooted in Kievan Russia than it ever was in Byzantium itself. The Russian word used to translate the Greek '*orthodoxos*' means, significantly enough, 'right praising'; for the Apostolic Church this was a monolithic answer to all questions.

Greek Orthodoxy had separated from the Roman Catholic Church in the eleventh century, in a quarrel over a phrase added by the Roman church to the Nicene Creed. Where the traditional formula read that the Holy Spirit proceeds 'from God the Father' the Roman Church insisted on adding the phrase 'and from the Son', and it was on this question of principle that the mighty schism – still in effect today! – arose between the two great Roman Catholic and Greek Orthodox branches of Christianity.

The Russian Church showed immense single-mindedness, not to say fanaticism, in defending the original formula. One of the features of the transplantation of Christianity to the soil of Russia was, in fact, just this fanatical insistence on external, lapidary formulae that in Byzantium itself had been arrived at only after long-drawn-out debates marked by a maximum of subtle ratiocination. Russia, perhaps partly to make up for its tardy acceptance of Christianity, simply discarded the ratiocination and clung to the formulae. In this way, what was taken over from Byzantium was in fact the results of centuries of philosophical and literary activity, boiled down to a few calcified expressions. Thus the Orthodox definitions of truth as well as the Byzantine forms of art were taken over wholesale, but the actual experimentation, the philosophizing and writing that underlay them, proved indigestible.

Kievan Russia was to import more or less *en bloc* the high stylization and the ornateness of Byzantium, which influenced both the architecture of Russia and its literary and philosophical achievements. From the very beginning Byzantine influence was overwhelming: the early emissaries sent by the Kievan princes to bring back Christianity were bowled over by the splendours of Constantinople's houses of worship, and it was apparently as a direct result of the deep impression made on the perhaps simple-minded barbarians from Kievan Russia that wholly Byzantine churches and cathedrals began springing up in every important eastern Slav centre.

In an attempt to convey in the palpable reality of their churches the simple mythology underlying primitive Christianity, the eastern Slavs represented the firmament as concretely as they could, by a central dome overarching the image of the Celestial Creator of heaven and earth. The

Virgin Mother was a paramount motif of the mosaic and frescoed representations embellishing the inside of the walls and the domes. An extravagance of embellishment, indeed, was perhaps the outstanding single feature of the Russian adaptation of Byzantine art, itself remarkably ornate. In the Kievan period there was a uniform concentration on the beautification of the cathedrals; even though an extreme form of asceticism was to come to prominence in Russian religious life later on, there is not one example of ascetic sparseness in the churches and cathedrals of the Kievan period. The chroniclers of the period, partly, perhaps, because of their exiguous literary ability, harp endlessly on the mere luxury of decoration. An incredible amount of attention seems to have been lavished on precious metals, gems, silks and embroideries; cathedrals were meant to be stunningly gorgeous.

This obsession with fixed external forms is also seen in the function in Kievan Russia of art and letters, which like the icons and buildings were modelled very closely on Byzantium. Here, too, the Greek gift for analysis and speculation was totally obliterated; it was tradition that occupied the paramount place in the attitude of Kievan Russia toward the world at large. There was no occasion for understanding or explaining anything; the collective desire of the intellectual *élite* was simply to pass on all the traditional forms of praise and worship: a theoretical defence of this might have been that it was a chance to acquire some vision, however defective, of the refulgence of the world to come. Hence only a few decades after the Christian conversion of the ruler of Kiev, that city became distinguished by its magnificence.

It would be an exaggeration to speak of literature in this period: it hardly existed. Like the arts in general, it was an offshoot of a Byzantine development of a Greek transplant. Unlike the other arts, however, which despite their alien origin were sufficiently general in inspiration to achieve an independent identity, literature, with its dependence on intellectual attitudes and linguistic plasticity, found it impossible, in the absence of a cultivated audience, to grow at all. The liturgical requirements of the Russian Church itself were more than satisfied by the generally unintelligible formal complexities of Church Slavonic, which by making Russian society dependent on itself and cutting it off from the

Greek language made literature proper altogether sterile. Literature consisted of sermons, ecclesiastically inspired chronicles, and the lives of saints. There was not even, curiously enough, a complete version of the Bible itself in early Russia; even theology as an art, or science, was totally ignored except in the form of sermonizing of all kinds. The complex and subtle theological heritage of Byzantium, which was, after all, the matrix of Christian dogma itself, was neglected in early Russia in favour of what was at best the rhetoric of celebrated Byzantine preachers.

It was, in fact, the lives of the saints that replaced theology. This was another factor in the popularization of the icon as an art form, since it was in the lives of the saints that veneration could find an object. Since the average man could not, of course, be expected to be or even know a real saint, edification had to be achieved through the contemplation of the visual images produced by the iconographer's handiwork and by listening raptly to the fabrications of the hagiographers. For this reason the icon was the epitome of theological expression in early Russia.

Religion, in fact, was the axis of all the arts in early Russia. For just as the eye was impressed and awed into submission to theology by the overwhelming mass and ornate beauty of the church structures, and charmed into reverence by the icons, so the ear was delighted by the moving chant of the liturgy. The whole of the church service, indeed, was felt to be a unity, designed to bring about the union of the humble worshipper with God through a massive appeal to all his senses. The mosaics, frescoes and icons were objects of beauty to seduce the worshipper, and the vestments of the clergy and the actual orthography in which sermons and chronicles were written down were devices to the same end. The original appeal of religion to the primitive Russians, as perhaps to most people, was not so much in the intellectual tug of its theology, but in the sensual seductiveness of its liturgy and ceremonial. In Russia, even more than elsewhere, church art was in its nature an expression of the religious impulse; it welled up organically as it were from within the inmost fastnesses of the worshipper's soul.

Another simplification of the Byzantine heritage of Christianity, in its turn a development of Judaism, with its great monument in the Hebrew Scriptures, was to be seen in the profound sense of the historical that was planted within the folk-soul of the early Russians; perhaps this echoes the earliest history of the primitive Hebrews, in which religious truth was demonstrated by something concrete like success at arms. The universal claims of Christianity were, of course, ideal for embedding a sense of history deep within indigenous tradition. Christianity, with not only a total explanation of all nature and man, but with an uninterrupted parade of sacrosanct individuals spanning all time from the moment of Creation through the climax of the Incarnation and Resurrection and on to the Day of Judgement, was more than enough to envelop the early Russians in a seamless fabric of meaningfulness imparted to all action and thought.

Unlike the somewhat piecemeal transmission of Latin Christianity to the barbarians of western and northern Europe on the debris of the crumbling Roman Empire, Russia was given a completed and polished edifice of thought and art. To be sure, the thought that had distinguished Byzantium was largely discarded in favour of the art, but the edifice itself, the symmetrical, elegant and profound structure of Byzantine Christianity was felt to be a spiritual unit. Thus all aspects of Byzantine history, including the history of the miracle-charged places of the Holy Land and the glamorous, mysterious empires of the East, brought back by businessmen and pilgrims and embellished by the fantasies of the pious, were all interwoven into the chronicles of early Russia.

No one in Russia could have been expected to know anything about Greek literature in its secular form; the great pre-Christian classics of Greece were utterly unknown, and indeed could not have inspired the smallest interest. The worldly attitude of enquiry and entertainment behind them would have seemed to the simple-minded pietists of Kievan Russia to be the handiwork of the devil. It must be admitted that the chief interest of early Russian literature to ourselves is even more anthropological than is the study of antiquities in general.

The one exception for this early period may be the celebrated prose-poem known as the *Saga of Igor's Host*; assumed by some to date from about the end of the twelfth century, this deals with a campaign against the Qypchak Turks. There is, however, some doubt about its authenticity, and some scholars regard it as a forgery made in the eighteenth century, when it was in fact discovered. If in fact it is authentic, it obviously had no influence whatever on later Russian literature: it is simply an isolated monument. A long silence followed it, and it was not until the seeping into modern Russia of Western European influences that modern Russian literature can be said to have acquired a body of its own.

History was paramount in Old Russia, in both literature and the plastic arts, just because of the absence of rationalism or logic. For this reason the chronicles of early Russia were its sole literary monuments, except for sermons. Chronicles in Church Slavonic antedate French and Italian chronicles; they are no worse than, and are as old as, those composed in Latin. Since no distinction was made between profane and sacred history, the Russian chronicles quite naturally contain all sorts of random information: pagan elements, folk-tales, political and economic comments are all mixed in with straightforward history, which of course was conceived as sacred history. This sense of history – which may be defined as a conviction of the purposefulness of events through their dependence on the will of God – imbued all literary subjects.

It may well be that the sense of history inherited from Christianity, and ultimately of course, from Judaism, was reinforced by the inherent instability of the great steppelands of Central Asia and European Russia. In this sense the assumption of the Judaeo-Christian sense of history marked out the Russians just as the injection of historicism had distinguished primitive Christianity from other pagan religions. Life on the steppelands was organically linked to the procession of the seasons and to the timeless fluctuations of geography; history-mindedness provided the timeless cycles of nature with an axis of meaning, and it was in fact to be the history-mindedness common to the three great monotheisms that in an accentuated form was to continue to mark out Russia among its neighbours and to give it a sense of mission that waxed with the centuries.

It was indeed the spread of the religion that conditioned the spread of the political influence of Kiev; constantly widening concentric circles rolled out in wave after wave, gradually solidifying and establishing the cultural influence of Kiev as well as of the Byzantine heritage Kiev had been assimilating. The uniform use of Church Slavonic as the learned medium implied the steady thrusting back of the languages of the indigenous inhabitants, so that the great group of Finno-Ugrian languages that had seemingly been rooted in the land gradually yielded to the forward surge of the new local idiom that Christianity was expressed in.

The enthusiasm that doubtless accompanied the dynamic thrust of the new religion gave rise to one architectural accomplishment after another. Novgorod, one of the great centres of primitive Russia and the nodal point in relations with the Teutonic peoples surrounding the Baltic Sea, was graced with the majestic Santa Sophia; the opulent Cathedral of the Assumption was erected in Vladimir, which was the northern centre of the Grand Dukes of Kiev and a focal point on the upper Volga.

These remarkable structures were put up in the twelfth century, and were patterned after their namesakes in Kiev itself. But churches and cathedrals were built outside all the cities as well, even in out-of-the-way places like the shores of Lake Ladoga, where the Church of St George was put up around the middle of the twelfth century (1160s) and distinguished by remarkable frescoes. The iconography of this church, named after the same dragon-slayer who became the patron saint of England, was thoroughly Byzantine, with the details of the Last Day of Judgement dominating the frescoes, at least those that have survived. The Old Testament naturally provided an immense amount of the subject matter of these frescoes; the prophets and the heroic kings were presented in a stiff, formal Byzantine style that makes the Virgin Mary stand out because of the relative compassionateness of her depiction. The Orthodox Church showed a marked bent for Mariolatry well before Latin Christendom; the Virgin Mary was the sponsor of Kiev and Novgorod, as she had been of Constantinople.

This architecture was superimposed, as far as we can see, on the wooden churches of the north-east and the brick churches influenced by these. The wooden churches have not, of course, survived, but Kiev and Chernigov had some stone churches of distinction even before the building of the great cathedrals in Kiev, Novgorod and Suzdal. It is in the churches erected in Suzdal and Novgorod after the middle of the twelfth century that some of the most splendid examples of the art of early Russia are to be found; an intriguing note is lent them by the presence of some striking foreign affinities, curiously enough with the Périgueux churches of south-west France. Even at this early date it was necessary to import masons from Germany to work in Suzdal. Italians, too, had to be imported *en masse* for the architectural work in the big cities that sprang up; their work has always been thought perfectly harmonious with the Russian locale.

Sculpture scarcely existed. The great iconoclastic controversy that had shaken Byzantium had ended with the victory of the anti-iconoclastic party, and images were sanctioned by the highest authorities, but *de facto* compromise had also been established, and the Church, while allowing saints to be represented two-dimensionally, forbade their representation in the round.

From its very beginnings the Russian church had shown a spirit of independence, quickly putting itself in the same position of authority, based on historical priority, as had been assumed by the holy cities of earlier societies. A legend sprang up, rather naturally, that just as Peter had carried Christianity directly to Rome, so the apostle Andrew had brought it straight to Kiev from Palestine; the legend was, of course, simply taken over in the baggage-train of Byzantine cultural monuments. Even the caves around Kiev became the subject of legends, like the catacombs in Rome; an idea germinated that Kiev might well turn out to be a 'second Jerusalem'. Kiev and Novgorod were assigned primary roles; the ancient traditional material of the shrines and monasteries of the Middle East and the Mediterranean was simply deposited in the proliferating new ones of eastern Slavdom, firmly embedded within the Greek Orthodox Church.

To the extent that any unity can be ascribed to Kievan Russia, that unity revolved only around the devotion to the Orthodox Church. Internecine strife, combined with a persistent political fragmentation, against the background of a sparse population and the chronic backwardness of the society as a whole, made any notion of a genuine socioeconomic unification chimerical.

Unity was to be found only in the religion which provided this early civilization with its only homogeneity: a fact of cardinal consequence, since worship and belief were the central spiritual content of the community as a whole. When internecine dissension flared up at the end of the twelfth century, and when Constantinople was occupied by the Latin power at the beginning of the thirteenth, any hopes for cohesion on the part of Kievan Russia were shattered beyond recovery.

It may be said that religious painting and church architecture provided early Russia with its sole source of artistic expression; it was only in religious painting, in all its varieties – icons, frescoes, and mosaics – and in church architecture, that anything noteworthy was accomplished in Kievan Russia. In music, too, religion was the sole source of inspiration; the musical remains of the period, meagre as they are, are connected with the Church. In fact, singing in unison was the chief manifestation of the musical ability of the early eastern Slavs, aside from the abundance of folk singing that must have been developing independently of the Church, and hence has left us no records to speak of. Harmony was not to develop until well into the fifteenth and sixteenth centuries.

The cultural isolation characteristic of early Russia, precisely because of its independence in developing a medium of expression of its own, was paid for by its isolation in general. To put it schematically, early Russia was cut off from Latin Christendom and Western Europe by the accident of having been colonized directly from Byzantium; this laid the groundwork for the religious schism that has persisted for so long. At the same time Russia could not compensate for this cultural isolation by the riches of authentic Greek civilization because of the constriction of the Church Slavonic idiom and the parochial religious preoccupations of the tiny *élite*. Accordingly, the aesthetic impulses of early Russia were bound to express themselves in the various excrescences of religion proper – painting and architecture.

But the Kievan period in Russian history was in any case doomed to expire within its spiritual isolation; whatever energies might ultimately have developed from its own inspiration were terminated prematurely by the success of two external foes – the irresistible surging forward of the Mongol hosts of Central Asia and the simultaneous advance of the Teutonic Knights.

These advances themselves did not, of course, develop in a vacuum.

They had been antedated by the general weakening of the position of Kiev; the domestic strife that had always been a feature of early Russia had been consummated in the last third of the twelfth century, when Kiev was reduced to rubble by a Russian prince. Kiev was treated in a manner hitherto reserved for non-Russian cities; it was sacked and burned; its population was butchered, expelled and enslaved. This act of rapine in its turn took place against a background of generally declining economic paramountcy; Kiev had benefited by its strategic location athwart the great waterway from the Baltic to the Black Sea, and by its trading relations with Byzantium, and for this reason became vulnerable when other commercial ties were established between north Russia and western Europe. In addition, its exposed position, so close to the great Russian steppeland, made it peculiarly vulnerable to the attacks of the Asiatic nomads.

The great waterway had thus been made unsafe and the population of the Kiev hinterland began reacting to these various chains of disasters simply by leaving, emptying still further the already sparsely settled countryside. The inhabitants began drifting off, to the west and to the north; and by the middle of the twelfth century the great region that had made such a promising beginning both in the humanities and in the arts was obviously waiting to become a prey to more aggressive and centrally organized forces.

Politically speaking, the decline of Kiev was highlighted by the rise of other political groupings. A state formation was to emerge in Moscow in the north-east, and in the south-west, based on a hitherto obscure power, that of the Lithuanians, began taking shape: the 'Grand Duchy of Lithuania' absorbed the Russian territories of White (West) Russia and the Ukraine, and by the end of the fourteenth century fused with the kingdom of Poland.

Greek Orthodox Slavs, the most northerly branch of the Greek Church, found themselves subjugated in the west by the Lithuanians, at this time still pagan, at the very moment they were being politically obliterated in the east by the Mongol thrust.

For all practical purposes this marked the definitive decline of the social and artistic consciousness of Russian society. The Mongols were to be the major and in fact the all-dominant force in Russia for a couple of centuries; it would be absurd, during this period, to speak of any self-expression of the Russian people. The Mongols, overwhelmingly superior to the still-primitive Russians throughout the area of European Russia, were administrators whose success depended more on their organizational abilities than on their cultural attainments, but their strategic location between the great empire of China in the east, the various state structures of Islam in the south, and Byzantium in the south-west, plus their receptivity to the influences of other cultures, gave them great flexibility.

All Russian centres were subordinated to the Mongol khans. Initially pagans, the Mongols – substantially identical with the various Turkic-speaking peoples of Central Asia – eventually became Muslim. They set up a capital of their own at Sarai, on the Volga, and were ultimately subjected to the same fragmenting forces as their victims. The boundless empire set up by Chingis Khan soon broke up into various autonomous and semi-autonomous states, of which the celebrated 'Golden Horde', the Khanate of the Qypchak Turks, was merely one. Racially mongrel, and quite unfanatical and tolerant, unlike its Eastern Orthodox opponents, the Qypchak state gradually dissolved throughout the fifteenth century. Its various satrapies, such as the cluster of Mongol states in the Crimea, the upper Volga, at Kazan, and along the lower Volga, at Astrakhan, became more powerful than the former Qypchak centre at Sarai, and in fact maintained themselves with varying degrees of success until quite late in the eighteenth century.

The long-drawn-out presence of the Mongols – or Tartars, as they have been called – in the steppelands of eastern Europe served as the axis for the formation of a hitherto novel national consciousness among the Russians; they provided, in fact, a matrix for the genesis of common social aims among the Orthodox eastern Slavs. As the centralized authority of the far-flung Mongol empire was eroded by internal dissension and external rivals, the tenacity of the inhabitants of the central and south-central steppelands gradually manifested itself. The Eastern Slavs, regrouping around a new political centre that slowly emerged from a somewhat amorphous cluster of petty rulers to become the increasingly dynamic state of Moscow, gradually thrust beyond the realm formerly occupied by the Qypchak Turks and across the steppelands of Central Asia, ultimately stopping only at the Pacific.

Russian life ceased being a mere reflection of the political existence of others : it finally shook loose both from its direct dependence on Byzantium and from its political, economic and cultural subjection to the Mongols and Turks. Rooted in the exploitation of the fertility locked up within the soil of the great Russian plains, gradually extending its power into the forest-lands of the north, and nursing the spiritual energies being accumulated in the monasteries, a new power, Moscow, emerged that was to guide the multiplying Russian people to a position of unchallenged strength in its own homeland and beyond.

Chapter 2

# A Central Authority

Without attempting to follow the ramified and far-reaching effects of the great Mongol invasions, we may easily note the cardinal result – Russia shifted northward. The regions lying far to the north of Kiev, largely forest, were now to become the matrix of a new Russian socio-political complex, centring in the area around Moscow, that was to become the focus of Russian national life, as it remains to our own day.

The cultural advances made by Kievan Russia were not entirely lost. The north-east had always had a cluster of cities that were practically as old as Kiev – Vladimir, Suzdal, and Rostov, for instance. Even before the destruction of Kiev itself, Vladimir had been the headquarters of some of the principal Kiev Grand Dukes. The very recollection of the accomplishments of Kiev, the historical reshaping that made Kiev a potent spiritual fact, took place in the north of Russia. It was the north of Russia that in this historical sense actually created Kiev; to our own age, for instance, what is Kiev but our knowledge of it?

Nevertheless the Russian north-east, while remaining indissolubly linked with the Orthodox culture inherited from Byzantium, was to evolve a heightened self-consciousness of its own. This was independent both of Byzantium, now in downright decline and soon to be expelled from the arena of history altogether by the success of another branch of the Turks, the Osmanlis, which obliterated it altogether, and of the slowly resurgent west of Europe, busily engaged in the rediscovery of the classical past of Greece. Kiev had been a relatively familiar subject in early medieval literature, but during the fourteenth century Russia as a concept simply slipped out of men's minds altogether. Even the possibility of the Orthodox Slavs of eastern Europe becoming a unit evaporated, as Russian self-awareness itself made it obvious that the communities scattered over the territory of north-east Russia were a cluster of petty régimes rather than a state.

In the thirteenth and early fourteenth centuries no observer would have thought it likely that the achievements of the Kievan past could be duplicated. The Turco-Mongols were still looming over the whole area of despoiled Kiev and the originally Russian shores of the Dnieper. Not only was the great Volga itself frozen there most of the year, but the Mongol fortifications kept a firm check on any expansion from the Moscow area. The monotonous flatness of the great plain to the south offered no obstacle to any invaders, and the wooden fortifications that were the natural kind of building – stone has always been a rarity in Russia – were not of much help.

From the point of view of nascent Russian nationalism, no help could be sought from the Slavic fellow-believers, while Novgorod, an ancient centre of Russian life, seemed to have embarked on an economic course of its own and was slipping under the influence of the trading complex of the Hanseatic league in northern Germany. The Finns were definitely outside the influence of Orthodox Slavdom; their conversion to Christianity was taking place under the aegis of the Swedes. The same could be said for the other European borders of the germinating Russian statelet of Moscow: the Teutonic Knights continued pressing on the western border, while in the south-west the Roman Catholic Church was extending its influence over the Slav-speaking provinces. The Lithuanians were in West Russia, the Poles in the Ukraine.

Yet in spite of everything, the gradual shifting in culture from the south to the north, from what had come to be called 'Little Russia', (i.e., the Ukraine) to 'Great Russia' took place quite imperceptibly, at least to our eyes; at the same time the term 'Great' gradually came to be invested with a symbolical significance in addition to its purely geographical reference. We occasionally get a concrete glimpse of the process: the glamour of Alexander the Great, a staple favourite in all eastern literatures, was grafted onto the reputation of Alexander Nevsky, a Russian national hero who had beaten back the Swedes and the Teutonic Knights in the middle of the thirteenth century, before becoming Grand Duke of Vladimir. By the end of the fifteenth century it was already possible for a successor, Ivan III, to subordinate most of the big centres in the north of Russia to the direct rule of Moscow and to call himself 'Tsar' (from 'Caesar').

There is a slight cultural problem in connection with the shaping of Russian culture in its new habitat. It cannot be denied that the influence of the Turco-Mongols was highly noteworthy, though this has often been energetically contested by Russian historians. And since the top-most layer of semi-Christianized thought in the formally Orthodox *élite* of the Russian north was superimposed on an altogether barbarian population of worshippers of animistic deities, the formation of the national consciousness must have been powerfully influenced by its pagan substructure.

The influence of the Mongols was indeed overwhelming. They exacted tribute from Russia, after all, for more than two centuries. For the Mongols the Russian conquest was merely a minor episode in a vast campaign that encompassed both China and central Asia; for the Russians, on the other hand, it was the central fact of their national existence for these two centuries and more. The remarkable nature of the Mongol enterprise can be seen from one or two facts: by the end of the thirteenth century the Mongol realm stretched from China to Poland, taking in all Asia except India, Burma and Cambodia. The whole of the Mongol people itself numbered, apparently, not more than a million; yet at its zenith their empire, based on fewer than 150,000 troops, was sitting firmly on the necks of some 100 million people.

Russian national life was practically obliterated during the Mongol period; all decisions affecting Russia were made by the Khan of the Golden Horde, himself subordinate to the Great Khan who ruled China as well as Russia. All Russian rulers were licensed to rule only through the indulgence of the Mongol rulers, who milked Russia steadily and systematically both of money and of manpower. Russian soldiers, in fact, played a substantial role in the campaigns of the Mongols themselves; a Russian division was stationed in Peking, while Russia kept sending drafts of craftsmen and artisans all the way to Mongolia. Alexander Nevsky, the Russian national hero who was canonized by the Russian Church and was to be invested with the aura of Alexander the Great, was in fact a satrap of the Mongols; it was they who installed him as Grand Duke of Vladimir (1252).

There was in fact a very intimate symbiosis between the Mongols and Russians, particularly in the upper classes: in the fifteenth century the Moscow court spoke Turkish, and by the end of the seventeenth century about seventeen per cent of the Moscow aristocracy was Mongol. It was the Mongol tradition that underlay the monolithic Tsarist state that grew up in the sixteenth century and endured for some four hundred years. The cruelty often associated with Russian life may be traced back, perhaps, to the Mongols. There was certainly an enormous zest in the Russian approach to the treatment of criminals: torture, flogging, and mutilation were to become commonplaces of Russian life; it was to become banal for criminals to have noses, ears, and limbs hacked off, and to be impaled, quartered, racked on the wheel or whipped to death; burning alive was routine for religious deviationists and magicians; counterfeiters as a class grew accustomed to having melted lead poured down their throats.

In addition, however, and from the point of view of the arts perhaps most significantly, the Mongols remained a source of fascination for Russians. As a counterpoint to the conventional feeling of detestation of the national oppressor, there was a contrary tradition of admiration for Mongol chivalry; during the nineteenth century a fascination with the glamour of the free nomadic ways of the steppe was to root itself in Russian literature. The fascination was so great that many Russian noblemen, from the fifteenth to the seventeenth century, took on Mongol surnames; even a Russian Tsar – Gudonov – was a Mongol.

But it was not only that the Russians imitated many Mongol institutions, such as the army, or copied features of daily life; the Mongols transmitted to the Russians many words for daily business, clothing, household objects, and diet; they also gave the Russians a census and a postal system. The influence of the Mongol invasions gave a new impetus to the religiosity that already had such deep roots in the Russian people.

From the time between the Kiev period and the middle of the fourteenth century, nothing of interest seems to have survived in Russian painting; most of the few icons which survive seem to be by Greek artists. From the second half of the fourteenth century onwards, however, some unusual painting was done in both Moscow and Novgorod. There was a sort of artistic renaissance that came into being as the Mongol influence, after having been all-powerful, gradually receded. At the end of the fourteenth century Theophanes the Greek, working in Novgorod and Moscow, stimulated the growth of an indigenous Russian tradition in painting, his own contribution apparently being a free brush-stroke technique. His technical achievements were carried on by the Russian Andrew Rublyov (Andrej Rubler), whose name is, in fact, the only one embodied in a continuous indigenous tradition. Rublyov, a contemporary of Fra Angelico, whose work is thought to resemble his, painted the icon of the 'Old Testament Trinity' in the great church of the Trinity Monastery.

Rublyov's execution of the ideas embodied in the Old Testament Trinity was considered so remarkable that the Church Council of 1553 made it a compulsory model for any icon on the subject that was to be done in future. Taking as its starting-point a line in the Orthodox liturgy, it portrays the actual event that was regarded as foreshadowing the revelation of the Trinity. It represents, in this way, the fusion between the spirituality of old Muscovy and the historically minded theology that in many ways paralleled the Protestant reversion to historical themes in the West.

Icons have, of course, a very ancient history. Going all the way back to the death-masks of ancient Egypt and Syria, sacred images had become standard objects of veneration in Byzantium by the sixth and seventh centuries, during the efflorescence of a widespread monasticism. After the abovementioned attempt in the eighth century to extirpate the devotion to images, which was coupled with a movement to eliminate the power of monkdom, the 'iconoclastic' party was defeated and the use of icons was authoritatively sanctioned, towards the end of the century, at the Council of Nicaea (787), the last Council accepted as authoritative by the Orthodox world.

When the eastern Slavs had been converted to Greek Orthodoxy the Byzantine ardour on behalf of religious painting was very naturally transmitted to them. Icons, in fact, became fundamental to the Russian method of expressing religion. Wooden icons became a standard form of worship throughout the evolving Russian state in the north, as they had been in Kievan Russia. As Russian culture shifted further and further away from the Mediterranean, mosaic arts naturally declined, while frescoes lost their predominance as wood came increasingly into use for building, which, because of the great scarcity of stone, it was bound to do.

While carrying on the Byzantine heritage in the stylization of figures, each saint, for instance, appearing motionless in a permanently established pose, details and colours were executed with novel intensity. This was facilitated through the opulent tempera paints that took the place of the encaustic wax paints that had been in use before the conflict about icons. Russian artists developed a technique of their own of using a Byzantine model in order to make the underlying design for a stencil, which they put onto a meticulously prepared panel, and then superimposed on this their own colours and details. In the course of time pinewood took the place of the cypress and lime that had been used for Byzantine icons; new techniques were developed to the intensification and stratification of the colours.

By the late fourteenth century various Russian regions had developed their own styles. In Novgorod, for instance, gold highlighting was used for robes, whereas Yaroslav developed graceful, lengthened figures. The Moscow school made a point of evolving an antithesis to the asceticism of the later Byzantine tradition; the colours were even richer than those used in Novgorod and the figures still suppler than in Yaroslav. Rublyov was celebrated for his use of colour, which he transformed into remarkably luminous creations rather like the originals of nature itself.

Rublyov's celebrated masterpiece, the Old Testament Trinity, is a striking example of the faithfulness of Russian iconography to church theology. The Trinity, an unfathomable mystery, is given only in a symbolic form, with the appearance of the three angels to Sarah and Abraham, the number 'three' being the only connection between the two notions. Since God himself is invisible, he is simply omitted. Nor could the Holy Ghost be depicted in early Russian iconography; when pigeons ultimately came to represent it, on loan from Western iconography, they became taboo in Russia as food; they also came to be venerated for their magical significance.

In continuing the Byzantine tradition, Russian iconography came to be distinguished for a heightened stylization. This was accentuated by the suppression of naturalism, which was carried even further in Russia than in late Byzantium. The hatred of the human figure, which had reached its extreme form with the iconoclasts, was very well marked even in the subsequent compromise based on the general admission of icons, and was retained through the rejection of three-dimensionality. The Russian break with classical art was even more extreme; the hatred of the body was of course represented as a desire to 'spiritualize' the depiction of sacred figures: this led directly to the flatness of a two-dimensional plane, and excluded the possibility of sculpture. It was not merely that no attempt was made, for instance, to develop the technique of perspective painting; a conscious attempt was made, in the so-called 'inverse perspective', to put the sacred composition beyond the physical identification of the spectator. Russian orthodoxy eschewed all forms of physical imagery, such as those that became common in Western Christendom – the stigmata, sacred heart, etc. Physical representation in Russian iconography, in short, was on a symbolic level far removed from everyday life: in its very depiction the human figure was too dematerialized for any affinity to be felt between the viewer and the figure depicted.

The thirteenth and fourteenth centuries in Russia saw an intensified development in the painting and veneration of icons, much like a similar period in the seventh century in Byzantium. The intensified preoccupation with icons accompanied a growth in the monasticism that developed under an enfeebled political régime. It may be that the ubiquitous icons, portraying as they did other-worldly authority, made up for the fragmented power of the worldly princes. The icon came to be venerated not merely in religious contexts, but in secular affairs, as a witness of vows, an arbiter of legal disputes and a banner of battle.

On the other hand, the primitive Slav attitude to religion made it natural to see nothing illogical in the humanization of the divine figure at the very moment that the human figures were formalized beyond all empathy. Thus the fundamental iconic theme for Easter, which in Orthodox Christendom is even more basic a festival than in the West, shows Jesus, looking relatively human, smashing the gates of hell and coming out of the fires he has, presumably, been in since his crucifixion.

In the Western iconography dealing with Easter, of course, the emphasis has always been on a negative – the emptiness of the tomb. Orthodox Christendom has always insisted on the humanity of Christ's nature being violently hostile to the 'Apollinarian' heresy at one time supported within Western Christendom, which tended to deny the human element in Christ.

It is nevertheless true that the victory over the iconoclasts represents the rejection of many attitudes of the Middle East, all rooted, doubtless, in the Jewish interdiction of image-making in the Old Testament; this interdiction, misunderstood, perhaps by the Jews themselves, and further misunderstood, extended and systematized by the Muslims, the heirs of so much Jewish tradition, was carried to the soil of Byzantium and reached its most extreme expression in the struggle of the iconoclasts to abolish images altogether.

Russian iconography showed a humanizing inclination in the portrayal of the Virgin Mary; as early as the twelfth century in Byzantium the conventional depiction of the Virgin began to show elements of maternity, stylized but recognizably human, as well as of divinity. Perhaps the most venerated icon in Russia was that of Our Lady of Kazan, in which Mary's face is held very close to that of Jesus; this most remarkable icon, a product of Byzantium, was taken from Constantinople to Kiev and from there to Vladimir, and eventually transferred to the Cathedral of the Assumption within the great Kremlin complex of Moscow. There, this icon, whose travels may be taken as an illustration of the slow northward shift of Russian culture, inevitably became a symbol of

the spiritual ascendency of Moscow, and thus of its political paramountcy, well in advance of the translation of this symbol into fact.

The symbolic power of this icon is itself an illustration of the dense
*mélange* of worship, warfare, and art in nascent Russia. The icon was
actually transferred to Moscow at the end of the fourteenth century to
serve as inspiration for the defence of the city against Timur-Lenk
(Tamburlaine); the addition of 'Kazan' to its name refers to the conviction that it helped Ivan the Terrible defeat the Mongols at Kazan
later on. The defeat of the Poles in the early seventeenth century, during
the turbulent 'time of troubles', was also ascribed to its magical powers.

The cult of the Virgin was one of the most significant developments
in the religion of the Russian masses. Still basing their work on Byzantine
models, Russian artists nevertheless created an endless variety of new
styles in the depiction of the Virgin, generally linked to the ritual and
hymnal of the churches. Art had always been used as an indispensable
adjunct to the sung liturgy and the hymns of the Church; by the
fourteenth century the murals put on the walls of the churches in the
Russia that was growing up in the north were explicit illustrations of
the music in use.

The classical Christmas icon – 'The Assembly of the Presanctified
Mother of God' – simply transposes into visual terms the content of the
Christmas hymn. There is a series of twenty-four hymns of praise in
honour of Lent (the *akathistoi*) that in Russia served as the source of a
number of backgrounds for scenes featuring the Virgin in a great many
individual icons, such as the 'Virgin of the Indestructible Wall'. This
icon could be found practically everywhere in Russia; it was a Byzantine
depiction of the Virgin fortifying Constantinople against the assaults of
the infidels. Since warfare was bound to be an integral part of religious
preoccupations, and since no distinction was ever made by the religiously
minded between sacred and profane history, these icons and murals
naturally came to include perfectly contemporary scenes, giving us some
insights into the history of Russian society as well as of Russian piety.

Russia's characteristic contribution to the use of icons, in addition
to the fanning out of the subject matter and the technical refinements of
the medium itself, was the evolution of the icon screen (iconostasis). In

both Byzantium and Kievan Russia embroidered cloths as well as icons had been set along the doors connecting the sanctuary with the nave of the church and on top of the screen that divided the two. Images had been painted and carved on the beam set over the screen, and this structural development was extended in early Muscovite Russia by the setting of a whole screen of icons high above the sanctuary. It amounted to a sort of simple-minded encyclopedia in pictures, covering all aspects of the Christian faith. The oldest surviving icon screen is a remarkable work in three tiers designed by Rublyov and two colleagues for the Archangel Cathedral in the Moscow Kremlin at the end of the fourteenth century. From that time onwards, and possibly before then, these complex serialized icon screens have been incorporated as a standard feature in Russian churches. The rows of icons might reach far above the eye level of the worshippers and go as high as the ceilings.

The icon screen may best be understood as the simplest method of making the primitive believers familiar with the intricacies of a religion whose doctrinal complexities might well be expected to be beyond the intellects of all but the subtlest. The remoteness of the One God, humanized and brought nearer by the human component in the nature of his Son, was humanized still further by these pictorial bridges. The icon screen, an intermediate link between heaven and earth, showing the multiplicity of human incarnations assumed by God in his determination to redeem his people on earth, made this complex interplay more tangible and thus more easily assimilable. The icons might be likened to peep-holes into the mysteries of human redemption.

The aesthetic sensibilities of the worshippers were further stimulated by the widespread use of tapers, burning in great candelabra in front of the icon screen. Throughout the divine service and after, the chilly, dark and otherwise forbidding church was turned into a fairyland of charm. The combination of the candles, icons, and icon screens consummated the union in the mind of the Russian worshippers between a sensitivity to beauty and an obsession with history.

An immense amount of talent was lavished on the development of both icons and icon screens; as the icons increased in size and complexity the screens, too, grew larger. The combinations of scenes and motifs grew in complexity until vast historical pageants were assembled, illustrating the totality of all the records of sacred history – that is, all history – portrayed in a vast arch reaching from the concourse of Biblical patriarchs and prophets of the most remote past along the top to the most immediately accessible local saints along the bottom.

Man was reached from God via the Virgin and Jesus Christ, who would be seated in the centre of the chief row of panels – the 'prayer row' – directly above the 'royal' doors between the sanctuary and the nave of the church. The *rapprochement* between the Godhead and the humble worshipper was signalized in Russian iconography by putting a humane, compassionate expression on 'Christ Enthroned', who replaced the Creator of the Universe looming inaccessibly high and lonely on the central dome of Byzantine cathedrals.

The holy figures that traditionally had surrounded Jesus were given a more homely emplacement on both sides of the traditional portrayals of the Virgin Mary and John the Baptist. The human element in the relationships between all these figures came to be stressed: as the saints, brought down to an accessible level, inclined their heads in human homage to Christ. Christ himself came into a far more intimate relationship to the congregation. The Gospel text he would be stretching out towards them would generally be the celebrated remark calling on 'all ye that travail and are heavy laden' to 'come unto' Jesus. This made the congregation's response both natural and moving: worshippers would throng up to kiss the saints standing nearest them on the screen, accompanying this act of veneration by a public confession of the faith – a large-scale two-fingered sign of the cross.

The amplification in the use of the icon screen and the increase in the veneration of icons performed a special function in the actual theological attitude of the worshippers. This in itself made the icon radically different from the art of Western Christendom, where the sacred representations were often external adornments devoid of religious meaning. Russian art remained wedded to a conviction that the splendours of belief were to be illustrated in a moving way; no attempt was made, or for that matter could be made, to give any analytical insight into the philosophical posture behind the art. Sacred images and representations remained the magnet for the soul of the believer; neither the rationalism of classical antiquity nor its arts could seize hold of the early Russian imagination. The Italian and Netherlandish art of the Renaissance seems to have struck no sparks in Muscovite Russia, even though both countries were quite familiar to some Russians. The Orthodox Church's adamantly negative attitude toward the rationalist notions that began seeping into medieval Russia through Novgorod, always westward-oriented, doubtless had the support of the pious masses.

It has been thought that this emphasis on the deep intellectual-cum-emotional content of pictures, on the *importance* of images, that is as distinct from their charm as decoration, may reflect the intellectual structure of the State. Early Russian political ideology has been described as a belief that the Tsar was the icon on earth of God just as the whole of the Orthodox realm was the icon of heaven. Moreover, the icon screen was a rather natural way of representing the hierarchy prescribed for Russian society, since each figure's relationship to every other figure was fixed and changeless, and all were equally dependent on the central section depicting Christ enthroned.

As Russian history developed, the fixed relationships and hierarchical forms of society were clung to, while the idealism originally needed to explain and justify them slipped away into the bloody maelstrom of events. Then, in the seventeenth century, the iconographic tradition native to Russia began being eroded, with the somewhat haphazard and clumsy introduction of Western naturalistic figures. The sacred tradition of painting icons in the original primitive religious spirit became subordinated, together with so much else, to the demands of large-scale production. The painting of icons became a State concession; ultimately the whole tradition became part of the new forces stirring Russian society in the nineteenth century.

Yet it would be foolish to deny that what the iconic attitude represented went on living in the minds and attitudes of countless Russians. The feeling that some ideal projection could be embodied in a fixed artistic form, almost independently of the mere artistic talent implied by the actual creation of the work of art itself, went on in Russia and has, indeed, come down to our own day. The ideal has always been in some way more real to Russians than mere technique. It may well be that the 'corny' quality of Soviet art under the Soviet dictatorship, the embodiment of ideals in a simplified, streamlined and static form, may be in some sense a continuation of the veneration of icons, even though the large-scale restoration of the ancient icons that took place in the early twentieth century did not bring about a revival of artistic values but simply the extension of the iconic method to propaganda.

The Russian Church imbued the artists who illustrated the great church themes with a spirit of anonymous piety, and in this respect as in others must be given credit for the bridging of the gap between the cultivation of Byzantium and the barbarism of Russia itself. For even though Russian painters remained unknown, with an odd exception or two, there can be no denying their talent, unquestionably the equal of that of the finest Byzantine painters, whose traditions they were upholding. It is true that the Byzantines had been emotionally more picturesque and at the same time more realistic, but within the limits of the stylization that was to become their hallmark, Russian artists conserved the grace and fluidity of the best Byzantine painting.

At the same time, Russian painting seems to have reflected the same sort of motionless, static quality that was characterized by the liturgical formality of the church *per se*. Just as Russian theology took over the fixed formulations of the Byzantine thinkers, while disregarding their complex trains of thought, so the Russian painters, while developing great technical talent in the realization of their gifts, were content with fixed and motionless stylizations. It might even be thought that the autocracy evolving on the monolithic model of the Mongol state, reinforced by the divine sanction of the Church, was reflected in the ideal of fixed adoration so admirably illustrated by the motionless rows of saints turned toward Christ in a sort of congealed transcendence.

The revival of religious painting had its other side, to be sure, since the vast Mongol claims drained away all sorts of artisans who might otherwise have gone on developing a native tradition. The ablest jewellers and craftsmen were drafted off to work for the Great Khan or allocated to various Mongol hordes; even the most evolved artisans were subjected to the same fate. With the total destruction of Kiev in 1240 the artisans were all either slaughtered or kidnapped, and the Russian art of making *cloisonné* enamels, which had been developed to such heights in Kievan Russia, simply disappeared. It was not until the late fourteenth century that enamels were made once again in Moscow, of the champlevé type; it was not until the sixteenth century that *cloisonné*, though of an inferior kind, was again made by Russian craftsmen. Filigree-making also came to a stop, to be resumed again under the direct influence of Asiatic models. The niello technique was also smothered by the Mongol overlordship, and was not used again until the sixteenth century. A number of other arts and crafts, such as the making of glazed, polychrome pottery and decorative tiles, as well as masonry and fretwork, and for that matter all the construction crafts in general, were crippled by the Mongol invasion. The last masterpiece of stone-cutting seems to have been the reliefs in the Cathedral of St George in Yuriev-Polsky, in Suzdalia, which were finished just before the Mongol torrent burst over the land.

The artistic depression, except for painting, lasted in eastern Russia for a whole century; it was not until the Mongol power began weakening in the middle of the fourteenth century that the industrial arts, especially in the working of metals, began to grow again.

The working of metals was of immense consequence for the Russia that began to develop with hesitant, though giant strides, in the north. The first large metal objects that were manufactured in this north Russian world were of course the basic adjuncts of Russian life. The ubiquitous axe was an object of day-to-day utility, just as the icon was an object serving an everyday spiritual purpose. In the larger sphere of national life the cannon acquired a primary position in warfare, and the bell became a cornerstone of the public demonstration of devotion. The fact that both bell and cannon were made of metal meant a basic interdependence; the same foundry that made the first cannon also made the first bells, and in wartime bells were always in danger of being melted down to be used as cannon.

The bell, inherited from Byzantium to give a properly aesthetic sounding board for the worship of God, was developed and elaborated in Russia. The bell-tower became an immensely elaborate device, with many tiers and a copious abundance of bells and gables in the shape of onions. This seems to be parallel to the evolution of the icon screen; the clamour of the bell-ringing was, like the icons themselves, the constant companion and unvarying accompaniment of church processions.

As early as the fifteenth century, the Russians developed a completely distinctive system of bell models, quite different from the bells of Byzantium, Western Europe or the Far East. The styles of bell became as remarkably varied as the styles of icons; great Russian bells, mobile and monumental, were rung by metal clappers that enabled them to resound with greater effect and complexity than bells in the west, generally smaller and often with the clappers made of wood.

The bells were only one component in the general musical accompaniment of devotion. The church services depended for their effect on being chanted; the life of the people was enriched by the remarkably complex development of hymns as well as of ballads, while on the purely secular level the streets and highways would be the scene of roving folk singers equipped with an unusual array of stringed instruments. Just as the eye of the Russian believer was intrigued and seduced by the immense array of visual effects such as the icon, the fresco, the illuminations of the sacred texts, and the chronicles themselves, so his ear was enchanted by the flood of sound. Eye and ear alike propped up the devotional stance; this is very different from the Western predilection for hairsplitting philosophical subtleties or literary flourishes.

Though early Russia lacked polyphony, or even a systematic scale, the complex system of bells could be manipulated to provide a great range of harmony. A novel method of musical notation evolved in early Russia, after the decline of the classical Byzantine chant in the fourteenth century; it was known as the 'signed chant', and served as a background of solid melody on which the words could, so to speak, be set out in relief. In many respects the emphasis on music as an independent medium, a sort of abstraction of a spiritual attitude, paralleled the contemporary Russian distaste for perspective and naturalism in religious painting and the clinging to an abstract stylization of images

# A Central Authority

'The Virgin and Child of
Georgia': the traditional cult
of the Virgin is illustrated
in this magnificent fifteenth-
century icon attributed
to the Moscow School.

One of the masters of
fourteenth-century painting
in Russia was Theophanes
the Greek. This fresco,
painted in 1378, is from the
Church of the Saviour of the
Transfiguration in Novgorod.

Another important painter of
frescoes was Andrej Rubler.
'The Old Testament Trinity'
(*above*) was completed in 1417,
'The Ascension' (*left*) in 1408.

A fifteenth-century painted overdoor depicting the Eucharist; it is attributed to D. Chyorny, who died in 1430.

'St George and the Dragon': a late fifteenth-century icon of the Novgorod School. This icon shows clearly the curiously elongated figures which are typical of this period.

'Boris and Gleb': a fourteenth-century icon of the Moscow School.

Two icon screens of the seventeenth century: (*below*) In this screen by S. S. Kolmogretz of the Yaroslav School the prophet Elijah is surrounded by paintings of episodes from his life. (*lower illustration*) 'The Virgin of Vladimir with Feasts and Saints', by P. Chirin of the Stroganov School.

КНАЗА ВЛАДИМИРА АНДР̃ЕКИЧА ПЕ̃ІКЪ СТОІТЬ ВЛѢ̃ЗЂ КРЫЛА
ПРИДВⷦѢЪРАКⷮ КАІТЬ О̃ІМАТЮ ЧАСА.

Manuscripts of this
period were boldly
illuminated: these
Russian warriors appear
in an early fifteenth-
century manuscript:
*The Tale of the Bloody
Encounter with Mamai.*

Three pages from the
so-called *Radziwill
Chronicle*, a fifteenth-
century manuscript of
the earliest Russian
chronicle, which was
originally compiled in
about 1113 and called
*The Tale of Bygone
Years.* The manuscript
is in the Library of the
Academy of Sciences of
the USSR but a facsimile
can be seen in the
British Museum. The
illumination on the left
illustrates the cult of
icons; the centre one
depicts the town of
Vladimir, and the lively
scene on the right
shows peasants dancing
and playing musical
instruments.

MOSCOU.
Capitale de la Moscovie
suivant Olearius.

NOVOGOROD
Ville de la Moscovie, Capitale
de la Principauté de même nom.

Metalwork was particularly
fine at this time: this
engraving shows the largest
bell in the world, hanging in
the Kremlin, and is taken
from J. G. Korb's *Diarium
Itineris in Moscoviam,*
published in Vienna in 1700.

(*opposite*) Two engravings
from Peter Van der Aa's
*Agreeable Gallery of the
World* (1719). (*above*) Map
of Moscow with key in
French to the principal
places of interest. (*below*) The
engraving of the town of
Novgorod appeared in the
same volume as the map.

Views of three cathedrals
in Moscow, showing the
onion domes surmounted by
a cross which are typical of
ecclesiastical architecture in
Russia. (*left*) Cathedral of
the Assumption, 1475–9;
(*top picture*) Archangel
Cathedral, 1505–9; (*above*)
The Annunciation Cathedral,
1482–90; this cathedral was
enlarged by Ivan IV in 1564.

The Church of the Transfiguration on the Island of Kizhi was built in
1714. Behind it can be seen the Church of the Intercession of the Holy
Virgin, built in 1764; the bell-tower was added much later, in 1874.

and poses which kept the worshipper's heart at a proper distance from the medium and thus in the right mood for devotion.

In the field of the plastic arts, moreover, Russian identity began taking shape relatively quickly after the coagulation of new forms of life in the north and north-east. Two novel shapes were to come to distinguish the silhouette of the Russian north – the tent roof and the onion dome – and by the early part of the sixteenth century these had already set their stamp on the flat skyline.

By the late twelfth century, Russian architecture was already showing characteristic features of its own; it had departed from its Byzantine models and was following what gradually came to be an indigenous course. In the great Cathedral of St Dmitri in Vladimir, for instance, the 'white stone' (limestone and mortar) had replaced the brick and cement still in use both in Kiev and Novgorod: this made possible the use of sculptured relief on the surfaces provided by the simple, massive structure: thus the relief that had been confined beforehand to perishable wood could be preserved more lastingly. The cosmopolitanism of pre-Mongol Russian culture, heavily impregnated though it was with Byzantine influences, is shown by the traces of Armenian and Romanesque influences, as well as by the abundance of exotic flora and fauna in the reliefs.

The Russia of the north had always been limited to the use of wood, which antedated Christianity. In the sixteenth century, however, the Russian tent roof was translated out of its flat log-construction and expanded into new forms of stone and brick. The dome, arches and gables in the shape of pointed onions were anticipated in other societies, primarily the Islamic Empire, itself enthralled by eclecticism, but the new form with its elongation, which replaced the spherical Byzantine and early Russian dome, was an indigenous Russian development, as was its ornamental use.

It was with the rapid evolution of ecclesiasticism and monasticism that lavish attention came to be paid to architecture for its own sake. The increasingly hierarchical and ritualistic aspects of society were reflected in the sculptural forms of its architecture; this went with a growing inventiveness in technique. The Church of the Annunciation

4

in Suzdal, for instance, shows in its three asymmetrical cupolas the ingenious use of stone for the reproduction of the ornamental onion-shapes previously executed in wood.

By the end of the Muscovite period, the classical Byzantine circular dome had been replaced completely by the pointed flying forms known as the tent roof and the onion dome. These were developed first in the wooden buildings of the Russia that was taking shape in the forests of the north, as in the Church of the Epiphany (1605), Chelmuzhi, Karelia. The large bell-tower, characteristically attached directly to the building, grew inevitably with the development of bell-ringing. The steep slope, essential for the protection of the buildings from snow, also protected the heavy flat logs beneath, which were raised in their turn in order to allow entry over the snowdrifts. Naturally, very few of these wooden churches have survived, though recent expeditions have found a number, some of them going back as far as the fourteenth century.

By the eighteenth century the onion-gables and domes multiplied with great extravagance, perhaps because the obsession with silhouettes was growing very strong. In addition, the proliferation of these onion-shapes may be ascribed to a sort of indigenous Muscovite reaction against two forces felt to be threatening it: an archaistic harking back to purely Byzantine origins in the name of religious orthodoxy, and the contrary influence coming in from the West through Peter the Great's introduction of Western ideas. During the very period, for instance, in which Peter was constructing the thoroughly artificial, misplaced city of St Petersburg at the junction of the Neva River and the Baltic Sea, the extraordinary wooden Church of the Transfiguration, for instance, was being set up at Kizhi, on Lake Onega; it may be the best surviving example of this 'Muscovite' style. The new vertical thrust of the steeply slanted pyramidal roof surmounted by twenty-two onion domes reflected the practical need for a roof to shed snow as quickly as possible, but also expressed the spiritual exaltation of a new generation of craftsmen in a Russia that had already begun its quest for original symbols. These novel shapes, gilded to boot, that could now be seen looming out of the northern snows and forests constituted a striking departure from the spirit of both Byzantium and Western Europe.

New centres of civilization gradually expanded and began draining the countryside of its people; perhaps Moscow, with its new church-fortress of the Kremlin, was the most majestic of these new centres. By the beginning of the seventeenth century the Kremlin had come to encompass the greatest bells, the most glorious icons, such as the Vladimir Mother of God and Rublyov's, and a great many grand new churches; Ivan the Great's bell-tower overtopped them all.

It was Moscow, of course, that was to become the core of Russian life, far more enduringly than either Kiev or St Petersburg: these three cities may be said to have constituted the framework of Russian society through the ages. Moscow was an organic outgrowth of local conditions, of the slow, molecular growth of Russian life in its new habitat; unlike St Petersburg it did not represent the imposition on nature of the arbitrary will of one man. Numbering 100,000 inhabitants at the beginning of the seventeenth century, Moscow was to remain the biggest city in Russia and the axis of the Russian national imagination.

As a new society gradually began to take form, at first under the crust of the Mongol dominion and then openly piecing itself together while the Mongols, very slowly, receded into history, the word 'Muscovy' came to be applied to the new state long before the name 'Russia' became general. By the sixteenth century the role of the Third Rome was transferred to Moscow, at least in the minds of monks bemused by phantasies of the apocalypse; there was enough of an aesthetic element in the look of the city, especially in the Kremlin – which contained a substantial Italian component – for the city to be more than a mere cluster of dwelling-places.

There is something mysterious in the rise of Moscow to a position of centrality in Russian life. The name does not even occur until the middle of the twelfth century; it had no Grand Duke until the early fourteenth century; and its original buildings, built of cheap wood along a small tributary of the great Volga river, did not survive beyond the sixteenth century at most.

Since there is practically no history of the period between the destruction of Kiev by the Mongols in 1240 and the date, 1380, conveniently taken by Russian historians as indicating the beginning of a fundamental

Mongol recession, the emergence of Moscow remains something of a conundrum. Perhaps the answer is best sought, is perhaps found, in the religious background against which the city made its appearance. The Church gave the early eastern Slavs their sole sense of community, and its role was heightened during the period of Mongol bondage precisely because the political and socio-economic reasons for union among the eastern Slavs had become attenuated to the point of non-existence. The enslavement by the Mongols, through strengthening the relative importance of the religious bond, gave the Russian Church a pre-eminent position among all the factors that ultimately came into play in the shaping of the nation.

It was in the cultural field, perhaps, that the Orthodox Church made its inspiration most manifest, and within the Church as a whole it was doubtless the monasteries that played a seminal role in the re-creation of national life. Within Russia at large it was this monastic revival, during the Mongol oppression and afterwards, that secured the primacy of Moscow. It was doubtless the spiritual exaltation associated with the religious impulse, linked with the territorial expansion of an actual centre that was to explain the gradual thrusting forward of the Muscovite state and its rallying of the gradually solidifying forces of the nascent Russian people.

By the end of the first third of the fourteenth century there was a monastic revival in the north; a great many churches were erected within the Kremlin, providing centres for some new monastic congregations. Monastic communities in Russia have never had much structure, perhaps just because they played so fundamental a role in Russian life that there was simply no need for them to be centralized. The early Russian monasteries had generally been built inside the central princely cities; leaders carrying on perfectly normal worldly lives might very well take monastic vows, whereas church leaders very often played a decisive role in the affairs of society as a whole.

In Russian society the monasteries' specific weight was added to by a mystical movement, originating in the Byzantium of the late thirteenth and fourteenth centuries, that sought contact with the divine through personal purification, which it was held would prepare the individual for the divine illumination. This was, of course, a form of proto-Protestant-ism, since it bypassed the focal role played by the Church in Western Christendom. The essence of Protestantism is, after all, the assumption that the path to God can be direct, that is, can transcend agencies; this naturally eliminated the magical indispensability of a church, and served, accordingly, to estrange orthodox Slavdom still more from the imposing edifice of the Roman Catholic Church. This mysticism contradicted the point of the Russian Orthodox Church too, yet it was somehow encompassed by it with no discomfort.

The monastic movement in early Muscovy, while revolving around notions of personal purification, nevertheless played a seminal role in the expansion of Russian culture in the fourteenth and fifteenth centuries. The establishment of scores of monasteries was instrumental in the colonization of the country and in the spreading of the Russian Orthodox faith. By the fifteenth century monasteries had spread more than six hundred miles north of Moscow; one monk carried the Orthodox version of Christianity to the foot of the Ural Mountains some 750 miles east of Moscow.

The monastic revival stimulated both arts and letters, making innova-tions in the decoration of manuscripts and the style of writing, known as belt weaving and word weaving respectively. The literature of the period, unusually copious considering the total lack of a cultivated audience, intensified the hagiographic and history-obsessed strains already present in Russian writing. Both a pronounced anti-Roman Catholic spirit and a thoroughgoing identification of Orthodoxy with the Muscovite state became embedded in the nascent literary-cum-ecclesiastical tradition: the war against the Mongols also formed part of the sacred struggle against evil, and Dmitri Donskoy, who led the Russians to victory against the Mongols at Kulikovo in 1380, was canonized. A whole hagiography was composed about him in the exalted religious atmos-phere following the monastic revival. Dmitri is made an out-and-out saint: 'The Tale from Beyond the Don', a saga dealing with his exploits, makes the Russian cause unquestionably the cause of the Church against Satan.

Pure fanaticism, utterly inimical to any form of naturalistic and pagan detail, such as had found expression in the primitive epics of Kievan Russia, came to infuse all literary expression. Indeed, the attribution of such a pivotal role to Kulikovo itself represents the triumph of the crusading motif being developed by the Muscovite historians and hagiographers: Kulikovo had no particular significance, in fact, with respect to repulsing the Mongols, who continued holding Russia in thrall for generations after it; but since it was the first Russian victory over the Mongols it was a natural choice for hagiographical exploitation. Kulikovo was turned into a sort of Orthodox copy of the Latin Christian rallying cry in the first crusade against the infidels, who had made their first major impact on Christendom as a whole with the Muslim successes of the seventh and eighth centuries.

The basic concept of a Christian crusade against the infidels of the east was thus reincarnated in the growing self-consciousness of Orthodox Slavdom; it proved to be the spiritual or ideological counterpoint to the gradual emergence of the absolutist Moscow state during the fifteenth century. The role assigned to the Moscow Grand Dukes was clear: to unite the Russian people – 'the Russian land' – by means of a crusade against the Mongols.

This political-religious background to the monastic literature of the fourteenth and fifteenth centuries explains the emergence of some cardinal themes in the Muscovite view of life, such as the proclamation of Orthodoxy as the natural climax to the uninterruptedly ascending series of sacramental events in the course of all preceding sacred history. This was another form of the fanaticism that has been characteristic of Christianity throughout so much of its history; the claim of exclusivity put forth for Russian Orthodoxy was a mere repetition of similarly exclusive claims put forth by Latin Christianity, and for that matter by the bulk of Protestant sects. The tight intermeshing of religion and politics in the Russian mind was reflected in this instance, too, by the parallel assumption systematized during this period of monastic revival: that the inevitable and sole bearer of this transcendental destiny was, naturally, the expanding Moscow state.

The claim of Russian Orthodoxy was itself simply an aspect of its heritage from Byzantium; Byzantium, after all, had been the New Rome, and for that matter the New Jerusalem: it was most natural for the Messianism inherent in some form or other in Christianity to be transmuted into the new organism evolving so rapidly in the wilderness of the Russian north. The claims made by Byzantium and the Eastern Christian Church had always been total: just as the Byzantine Church was the one true Apostolic Church, so the Byzantine Empire naturally claimed paramountcy in history as the one true heir of everything inherited by Rome. A slight difference in emphasis – between that laid on personal salvation and that laid on the redemption of the world – made it natural for Russian Orthodoxy to lean wholeheartedly in the direction of the chiliasm that in the West was expressed in merely sporadic outbreaks.

There had always been a split in the minds of Christian believers because of the vacuum that had sprung up in the disappointment over the failure of Jesus' mission: if the Kingdom of Heaven as proclaimed by Jesus did not arrive, what was to take its place?

In Western Christendom it quickly became a settled belief that no one could tell when the end of the world was near, in other words, when the Second Coming of Christ was to be expected; hence the Church was a stable institution shepherding mankind into personal and individual salvation pending an ultimate resolution of the Divine Mystery through the Second Coming.

In the east, however, Russian Orthodoxy developed an extension of the Byzantine view that the Kingdom of God could be achieved through the agency of Orthodox Christendom. The spiritual purification of individuals, as recommended in the personal mysticism of the above-mentioned monastic revival, was understood as an intensification of personal virtues thought of as a paradigm in miniature of the whole world, that is, the whole Christian world. Thus the way was cleared for the Church's arrogation to itself of a paramount role in becoming the sacred spearhead of the heavenly hosts of faithful believers. With the stunning success of the Ottoman Turks in overrunning the Balkans, smashing the Orthodox Serb power at Kossovo in 1389 and soon taking over the whole of the Balkan Peninsula, it was obviously the role of Moscow to take up the shattered hopes of Orthodox Slavdom.

The upshot of the Balkan collapse under the impact of the Ottoman Turks, combined with the Mongol overlordship in Russia itself, was simply to obliterate the Byzantine Empire from the Russian conscious-ness as a source of authority: it remained a mere historical recollection, fraught with emotion but no longer a moving force. The union between the Byzantine Church and the Roman Catholic Church at the Council of Florence (1437–9), came to be viewed as a betrayal by the Byzantine Church of its own mission, punished by God through the Turkish seizure of Constantinople a half-generation later.

Such was the background for the assumption by Russia of the paramount role in Christendom. The imperial centre, having left Constantinople, simply landed in Moscow. This transfer was signalized by the lavishly arranged marriage of the ruler of Moscow to the niece of the last Byzantine emperor, followed a little later by the taking over of the two-headed eagle as an imperial seal.

There was an immense amount of apocalyptic turbulence in the fifteenth century, revolving around God's plan for the world: the fact that the ancient Orthodox calendar was supposed to come to an end in 1492 – on the curious assumption that the world was due to last seven thousand years, no more no less, beginning with its creation in 5508 BC – led to an abrupt upsurge in prophetic travail. Since it was difficult to figure out what was in God's mind, of course, people were divided between optimism and pessimism: either the Second Coming was around the corner, followed by Christ's millennial reign on earth, or else the Antichrist was on his way.

This apocalyptic agony led to all sorts of Russian experiments in self-torment, such as 'columnar motionlessness' and the constant roaming about of the 'fools in Christ', plus mass self-burnings, etc. Perhaps the most famous of the ascetic hermits that Russia was teeming with in the fourteenth and fifteenth centuries was Nil Sorsky, who, after travelling to Palestine and to the holy Mount Athos, returned to Russia and laid down a model monastic community, to consist of only a dozen brethren living in poverty, close to nature, disregarding all institutions and accepting only the direct authority of God as revealed in the Scriptures.

From a social point of view, the dangers involved in this notion of a direct channel between God and man bypassing the Church itself are obvious. They were to contribute to the general confusion of political thought in Muscovy, since the confusion already inherent in the Byzantine failure to distinguish theoretically between the two sources of authority – civil and religious – lumping them both together as simply two types of equally holy authority, was compounded in Russia by a hazy formation even of this division of authority. Muscovy was palpitating with religiosity on the eve of its political ascent; the confusion about political authority was actually one more reflection of a sort of general shapelessness. The monolithic type of régime that was to emerge may be attributed to a singular confluence of circumstances, which included the Mongol hierarchical authority, with all power devolving from the paramount Khan, and the religiously inspired quest for a divinely charismatic figure, like the traditional saints.

It may be said that the early Tsardom laid down in the beginning of the sixteenth century was created by the intense life of the Russian monasteries. Its spiritual father is often assumed to have been Joseph Sanin, the contemporary rival of Nil Sorsky, mentioned above; on two crucial points, which placed him in systematic opposition to Sorsky. Sanin held a position that underlay the principle of the centralized spiritual and civic authority. Sanin too had established a monastic institution in the forest, foreshadowing an ideal Christian community, but whereas Sorsky had been an exponent of the inner light as a method of illumination, Sanin believed in the symbolically and spiritually purifying effects of external behaviour, with the corollary that a total regulation by external authority of every detail in the life of the worshipper changed his inner life for the better and gave him hopes of illumination. This had a further corollary in the sacred value of property; in contrast to Sorsky's ideal of monastic poverty, Sanin defended the vast wealth that had been accumulated in the numerous monastic establishments through the bequests of various rich and princely sponsors. Sanin did not, of course, take the view that wealth was for private pleasure, but maintained it to be a sort of mechanism for the radiation throughout society of the goodness of the monks.

Thus Muscovy took shape under the aegis of a monkish conflict. The opposing sides, perfectly united on the central notion of the religious nature of the Muscovite realm under the unquestionable authority of its prince, were at odds only concerning the conflict between the centralized, disciplined external structure of society and the individualistic, unorganized expressions of personal piety. In the event, of course, the Moscow that grew up under the sign of Sanin was a monolithic structure of constraint buttressed by the spiritual authority of a monastic patriarch.

Perhaps the clearest exemplification of this densely intertwined *mélange* of religious and secular motifs can be found in the career of the notorious Ivan the Terrible, who ascended the Muscovite throne in 1533, when he was three years old, and ruled for more than half a century, the longest reign in Russian history. He was the first Tsar, a formidable ideologist and a fanatically pious psychopath and sadist; in spite of his ferocious traditional piety he was a potent innovator and the first ruler to fling Russia headlong into the millstream of modernization it has followed more or less consistently ever since.

# Chapter 3

# The Aristocratic Prism

Russia was to become totally immersed in a headlong scramble to modernize, or Europeanize, itself, but even though Western influences were ultimately to swamp it completely, in the very beginning of the modern interplay of Russia with the West – say, from the fifteenth to the seventeenth century – the West that was to affect most thinking Russians was the West not of technology or techniques, but of broad all-embracing ideas.

At first, for instance, the Russians found panaceas in the West – keys to the secret workings of the universe. The first diplomats sent abroad by nascent Muscovy were fascinated not so much by what was even then the beginning of the Western conquest of nature, both technically and scientifically, but by its astrology and alchemy, by the heritage from antiquity and the Middle Ages.

Then this interest in generalities was suspended, for a while, and in the eighteenth and nineteenth centuries the obsession with all-embracing metaphysical structures was supplemented and overshadowed by an industrious, though piecemeal application to the economics, politics, and technology that in Western Europe were growing by such leaps and bounds. It was these empirical pursuits of the Russian thinkers of that time that were to transform the country completely; when the fascination with general systems of ideas resumed its vigour, towards the middle of the nineteenth century and later, the material base through which it could be effective was far more substantial.

But even the interest in empirical techniques was to be a long time in the realization. Russia was so devastated and churned up by the confusions that followed the reign of Ivan the Terrible and of his feeble-minded son and heir, at the end of the sixteenth century, that the resulting chaos can scarcely be summed up. The social oppression of the masses of the people increased enormously, accentuated by the centralizing effects of several of Ivan the Terrible's structural reforms; the half-generation called the 'time of troubles' at the beginning of the seventeenth century saw an immense swirling about of the population, with an intensification of the mass exodus of peasants and, for that matter, tax-payers in general that had become a constant feature of the Russian scene.

By the time a Romanov, selected by fellow-nobles perhaps because of his very insignificance, ascended the throne in the early seventeenth century, to launch a ruling house that was to last more than three centuries, the country was in a state of almost total devastation. It was a vast charnel-house; and through the exodus of taxpayers, which depopulated the country very substantially, the gradual development of Russia in the direction of a police-state was strengthened still more.

The Church itself was seriously affected; its unity was broken far more than during the so-called 'Judaizing' and 'rationalist' heresies that had agitated it a couple of hundred years before. Russia's afflictions, the wholesale impoverishments and the calamities of warfare, the incompetence and absence of solidarity in the ruling class, torn by internecine strife, and the political control being exercised in the very heart of Russia by outright heretics, enfeebled the Church both politically and morally. Dogmatically, too, the Church authorities found it difficult to conceive any new formulations that could satisfy the discontent of the times. Echoes of the Protestant Reformation had come even as far as Moscow, partly because of Kiev's re-entry into the orbit of Russian culture as the result of a peace treaty made toward the end of the seventeenth century.

A reform of the Church was finally embarked on, under the Patriarch Nikon; it consisted of minute changes in some texts re-translated from the Greek, a change in the spelling of Jesus' name, and so on, but though remarkably trivial the 'reform' gave rise to a tempestuous movement of resistance. Even though Nikon's reforms involved no change in dogma they met with violent opposition, which may indicate the magical conception of the rites and of the Church itself. The Russian clergy, which fell into a fury of passion around the details of Nikon's reforms, regarded any deviation *at all* from custom as blasphemy.

Nikon himself was also singularly fanatical; the collision between his reforms and their opponents was total. The dissidents rejected them all, called themselves the 'Old Believers', and by the last quarter of the seventeenth century were anathematized: Avakkum, the most famous – a talented fanatic priest – was burned at the stake.

Avakkum and his followers regarded the tiny changes in spelling suggested by Nikon as a cardinal criterion of Christianity as such, and a portent of the coming of the Antichrist. The dissident movement turned to mass suicide by burning, a death considered preferable to eternal hell-fire. This was facilitated by the conviction that the end of the world was once again at hand, scheduled for 1666 or 1669: when it failed to materialize another date was established – 1698. During the two decades between 1672 and 1691 some twenty thousand people burned themselves to death. Whole groups, sometimes as many as 2,500 at once, would stuff themselves into huts and set fire to themselves.

Though the dissident movement of the 'Old Believers' proved indestructible, and has in fact survived to our own day, the insensate violence that characterized this Russian religious struggle was quite unable to bring any principles to the fore. The Russian Church was not opened up to new ideas, as was the Roman Catholic Church in Western Europe after the Protestant Reformation.

Perhaps the explanation of the singular intellectual penury that characterized Muscovy on the eve of its ascension into the ranks of the major powers was the backwardness that was still its hallmark. The educated classes, after all, were scarcely educated at all; those who read would read only devotional literature, or perhaps an occasional translated romance. The upper classes were quite indifferent to the wealth of the folk-culture; contrariwise, the folk-culture could not expand in any intellectual way. The intellectual short-sightedness of the upper classes was reflected in the postures adopted over Nikon's reforms. Both parties to the schism displayed the same dumb devotion to fixed attitudes, and were equally incapable of generalizing their respective positions intellectually by contriving any new concepts. Doctrine as such, distinct from ritual and formulae, remained essentially unintelligible. Perhaps partly because of this, the fervour endemic in Russian religiosity was capable of generating one heresy or sect after another. Since the dissidents lacked any intellectual guide-posts there was nothing to check the proliferation of phantasies.

The religious schism was intimately associated with various aspects of social protest at the conditions of society at large; the schism may even be regarded as a concomitant of the persistent upheavals, sometimes actual rebellions, of the peasant masses.

Russia for centuries gave the impression of a brutish dreariness enlivened only by cruelty. Both depravity and illiteracy seem to have been ubiquitous. Women were universally secluded; the Kremlin had the look of a monastery, a night-club and a bazaar all at once. Since reading was virtually unknown, especially for secular purposes, there was no standard of education that meant anything at all. There was no question of any knowledge of Latin or Greek even in the highest clergy. A great many noblemen could not read at all. The only interest that could excite the Muscovite gentry was huckstering. The cultural level was so low that no social differentiation could be based on it. Boorishness was the keynote of all milieux, from peasant to nobleman to priest. Aristocrats and plebeians were much the same in manner, while moral standards, such as they were, indicated few gradations in behaviour from one end of the social spectrum to the other.

There was some slight progress against this general background of primitivism, but it was painfully slow. The only school textbook in use during the seventeenth century was an adaptation of something that in its turn was more than a century old; since mathematics had to be carried on with the old-fashioned Slavonic characters – it was not until the eighteenth century that Arabic numerals came into use – it was practically impossible to get beyond addition and subtraction. Euclid did not arrive in Russia until the eighteenth century; the first textbooks in algebra and trigonometry did not appear until the century was well advanced. Newton, to say nothing of Copernicus and Galileo, was quite unknown.

Partly because of the savagery of the pious emotions released by the church schism, obscurantism set its stamp on all intellectual life. The slightest doubt concerning anything at all in Greek Orthodoxy entailed a risk of Siberian exile; the stake lay in wait for converts to any other religion, and for any who made a pejorative reference to icons or sacred relics.

Nevertheless this singular self-centredness or parochialism could not seal off outside influences altogether; by the end of the seventeenth century, despite all repressive efforts, Russia was being infected by a trickle of notions from the West. This was to make something systematic out of the mere physical contacts with foreigners, who had been drifting into Russia since the end of the fifteenth century. Ever since then, indeed, foreigners had been necessary to make use of the natural resources of the country. The few thoughtful members of the upper class had been compelled to recognize the need for some reform. During the two generations between the first Romanov and the accession of Peter the Great, the Muscovite autocracy had been more or less at war for almost half the time; by the time Peter the Great appeared, there was no denying the plain fact that Russian society had fallen so far behind even its backward neighbours that an effort was needed if only to go on fighting them efficiently.

Peter the Great, who reigned from 1682 to 1725, is celebrated as the paramount innovator in Russia's history, second, perhaps, only to Lenin in the twentieth century. Peter's general stance in life was completely materialistic and secular. Physically a giant, with remarkable energy, he was quite alien to the pious sleepiness of traditional Russian life. Self-made intellectually, with scarcely any education, he was to be completely mesmerized by the technological accomplishments of European civilization, which dominated him throughout his life and led him to embark on a series of radical, though quite haphazard experiments aimed at the comprehensive overhauling of all Russian life.

It is true that his intentions could scarcely be called 'serious'; he never formed a well-thought-out plan. Peter's chief energies went into debauchery and clownishness. While still in his adolescence he organized his cronies, all disreputable libertines and drunkards, into a sort of satirical organization ("The Most Drunken Assembly of Fools and Jesters') that concentrated on both tippling and lechery. It had an intricate system of rites making fun of both the Roman Catholic and the Greek Orthodox Churches. Peter would spend most of his time organizing preposterous jokes along these ritualistic lines for mock-marriages and mock-ceremonies of all kinds.

Yet in spite of his essential frivolity, Peter found himself led by the logic of his career into a course of action that was to have the most far-reaching effects on Russian society. One of his amusements, after all, was warfare, and it was on the field of battle that the Russia of his time was so outclassed by the states lying to the west that he found himself, with no plan or ultimate aim, involved in a full-scale attack on the Russian society of his time. This entailed the liquidation of the inevitable opposition, which Peter accomplished with a maximum of bloodshed and savagery, in a mass slaughter he led personally, chopping off heads and torturing people with his own hands.

Warfare was in fact the background of all Peter's reforms; during his thirty-five years of rule Russia was at peace only in the last one. The need to modernize his army, in a situation of total primitivism, involved him at once in a clash with all forms of traditional behaviour, including the way people dressed and wore their hair. His snipping off of beards, for instance, was in reality an onslaught on the Church, which taught that a beard was inevitably implied by the notion of man as a reflection of God. This shaving of beards, originally thought to be an obscene joke, was in fact the harbinger of a revolutionary onslaught on all Russian life. His cultural reforms, including the reform of the calendar, of orthography, and of social amenities, were accompanied by a widespread overhauling of education and by the introduction of new technical disciplines such as the teaching of geometry.

Peter was so determined to change things from top to bottom that

The Aristocratic Prism I

Frontispiece of the first dated
book printed in Russia:
*The Acts of the Apostles*, 1564.

The first Russian edition of Aesop's *Fables,* printed in St Petersburg in 1700, showing the frontispiece and the first page.

The engraved title-page from a Bible printed in Moscow in 1663. The text, which is in Ecclesiastical Slavonic, was revised under the supervision of the Patriarch Nikon, whose minor reforms had caused a split in the Russian Orthodox Church. The title-page has Biblical scenes and, in the centre under the two-headed eagle, a plan of Moscow, 'the city of the great Tsar'.

PETRO PRIMO
CATHARINA SECUNDA
MDCCLXXXII

In 1782 Catherine II erected
a monument to Peter the
Great in St Petersburg. The
memorial was by Falcoret
and was set on a granite base
formed by a huge single
block which is being moved
by workmen in the engraving
on the left.

Russian paintings from the
second half of the eighteenth
century:

*Opposite*
*(above left)* D. G. Levitsky:
Portrait of Count Y. E.
Sievers (1779).
*(above right)* I. P. Argunov:
Portrait of a Peasant Woman
in Russian costume.
*(below left)* V. L.
Borovikovsky: Portrait of
V. I. Arseneyeva (*c.* 1790–
1800).
*(below right)* D. G. Levitsky:
Portrait of H. N. Novikov.

*This page*
*(above)* F. A. Alexeyev:
View of the Palace Quay
from the Peter and Paul
Fortress, St Petersburg
(1794).
*(centre)* D. G. Levitsky:
Portrait of Catherine II.
*(bottom)* D. G. Levitsky:
Portrait of two Smolny
pupils (1773).

Mantelpiece and chair of cut steel, both made at the Tula foundry towards the end of the eighteenth century.

Wooden gingerbread form, 1776,
showing traditional peasant motifs.

КОМЕДИА ПРИТЧИ
ПРИЛОГЪ

Блгородніи Благочестивіи
Гдрие премилостивыи .

Нетапо слово вꙑимати держитса
Аиоже аще что дѣломъ явитса .

Woodcut from the Prologue of the first
edition of Simeon of Polotsk's comedy *The
Parable of the Prodigal Son*, 1685, one of the
first Russian plays.

(*left*) Two scenes of Russian village life at
the end of the eighteenth century, showing a
man hanging from a gibbet and a girl
carrying water.

he very naturally overreached himself. He insisted on importing a troupe of German actors, for instance, at a time when no conceivable audience for them could even have understood the social backgrounds of the German and French plays they put on; there was not even an understandable polite idiom to translate them into. He launched a comprehensive educational programme when there were practically no schools at all in the country. It was in order to implement his radical reforms, indeed, that the country had to be straitjacketed: Peter was so different, in his cosmopolitan, technological and materialistic obsessions – quite apart from his personal extravagances – that the chasm between his aims and the parochialism of the milieu he was part of could be bridged only by fiat. His social ideal was thus bound to be the police-state, and it was precisely as a result of his global reformism that the police came to be the paramount institution in Russian life.

Peter's unique combination of energy and blindness, or of peremptoriness and obtuseness, led to reforms that, while devastating in their own way, fell short of his actual purpose. On the other hand, his reforms, while fragmentary, churned up the countryside and did, perhaps, launch the upper classes on a course of Europeanization that eventually bore fruit. He thus had a certain effect on the cultivation of the upper classes, yet his reforms touched only the surface; the very fact that the upper classes were slightly changed while the Russian masses remained the dumb objects of State regimentation and general dragooning meant that a social division came to replace the homogeneity spread throughout the nation as a whole by general brutishness.

After Peter's death the State summit was rocked back and forth almost completely haphazardly for more than a generation, until the ascension of Catherine the Great.

Peter had disregarded the monarchical principle of succession by torturing his son and heir to death and dying before nominating another heir. His annihilation of the principle of succession, compounded by the extraordinary importance that was assumed by the Guards regiments saw to it that the régime remained wildly unstable.

Perhaps Peter's most enduring achievement was the city that until the Russian Revolution bore his name – St Petersburg. This was the third of the trio of cities that were the matrix of Russian culture and nationhood. The city may be thought to symbolize the westward turning of the Russian spirit, or, in the cliché launched by an Italian observer (Francesco Algarotti) in 1739, it opened a 'window onto Europe'.

St Petersburg was a remarkably artificial construction; more than anything else in Peter's reign it represents the arbitrariness of his will. There was not the smallest natural reason for the city to have been placed where it was; it seems to have been an irresponsible whim. Since the site was quite unnatural as an emplacement for a city, it cost the lives of untold tens of thousands of workmen, who died in the marshes and the bogs picked out by Peter's caprice. Though intended to constitute a realization in stone of Peter's determination to Westernize Russia, against the background of enduring Russian backwardness it remained merely one more eccentricity. Indeed, Peter's sustained attempts at Europeanization were largely abortive; from a cultural point of view his actual reign was one of relative decline, compared even with the reigns of his predecessors. Yet in spite of everything St Petersburg was eventually to acquire a look of great elegance (though outsiders' reactions have varied).

The foundations laid by Peter were to serve for the systematic entry into Russia of European forms and institutions, which soon flooded the country.

The Academy of Sciences, the first institute of scientific studies, a purely secular institution, came into being shortly after Peter's death on a model he had authorized; a German mathematician (Christian Wolff) was put in charge of its organization and personnel; it was to become the hub of a new system of education.

It is true that the Academy did not make a substantial impact on the Russian *élite* until the 1750s, under Elizabeth, by which time the trickle of influences channelled by Peter's reforms had matured. In the middle 1750s, within the space of only a few years, the Academy's technical publications, concerning other peoples and places, produced a slight effervescence within the aristocracy and familiarized it to a certain extent with other cultures outside Russia; it was perhaps the most important first step in making the Russian aristocracy as cosmopolitan as it was to become.

Around this same time came Russia's first university and first permanent theatre, to be followed by a variety of other institutions, such as an academy of arts, a factory for the manufacture of ornamental china and so on.

Russia came into the maelstrom of the secular enlightenment that had already made deep inroads on the old order in Western Europe, but it was a process that was late in starting and was, moreover, a response to stimuli derived from abroad and from on high. Westernization came to the country not only through monks and foreign technicians, but also from the ancient headwaters of Russian culture in the Westernized regions of the Tsarist empire. Speculative philosophy and, for that matter, classical artistic modes that came to dominate the culture of the *élite* were centred at first in Kiev, which during its period of Polish dominion had become an outpost of education and of baroque architecture. It is odd to recall that, during the hundred years that followed its restoration to the control of Moscow, Kiev was by far the most cultivated city in the empire.

The foreign technicians who were to do so much in importing modern concepts and gimmicks into Russia were generally sealed off from the rest of the country in the ports and administrative centres. The foreign ideas that Peter the Great was responsible for importing were of primary importance in serving as the underpinnings of a new system of education organized by the State. In retrospect, Peter's principal service was perhaps the introduction of an official civil script and the reform of the alphabet; this, together with the assimilation of countless Western ideas and words by the language, made a transition to a more secular style of life natural.

It took a number of decades for the Academy of Sciences founded after Peter's death to play a major role in intellectual life, but once it had emerged as a fully fledged spiritual centre it was to have a permanent effect on the formation of the *élite*. Perhaps the beginning of the Academy as a seedbed for the education of native Russians in the sciences may be said to have begun with the group research launched by the Russian students of the biologist, mineralogist, and linguist Peter Simon Pallas, and of the mathematician Leonhard Euler. By the end of the eighteenth century a substantial number of native Russians were quite capable of introducing their own developments of advanced mathematics into the programmes of institutions of learning throughout the country.

An indigenous scientific tradition did finally develop in Russia, but even before then the career of one of the most remarkable figures in the evolution of Russian culture had crystallized the self-confidence of scientifically-minded Russians. Michael Lomonosov, who arrived in St Petersburg at the beginning of 1736, was one of the few modern embodiments of the concept of a universal man; his personal evolution may mark the beginning of the Russian scientific community as an autonomous body, no longer an appendage of the scientific culture of the West. Under Christian Wolff, Lomonosov not only acquired the training that made him an outstanding trail-blazer in physical chemistry, but he became a primordial force in the establishment of educational institutions. Lomonosov was in addition a poet, writer, speaker, and historian. Perhaps it was his activities as a grammarian and his endorsement of colloquial Russian as a means of expression that stimulated the vernacular's growth as a national language that could become the channel for the new secular enlightenment.

Lomonosov was by no means a radical in social affairs; indeed, he was an ardent supporter of monarchy on principle and so an admirer of royalty; he was also pious. Yet even though his technical innovations were put to old-fashioned purposes – his new chemical techniques for the composition of glass were used for church mosaics, and his rhetorical innovations were put to ceremonial use for coronations and religious holidays – his practicality, his breadth of interests, and his questing intellect had an effect on the establishment of an indigenous pragmatic tradition in Russia.

It must be admitted, on the other hand, that he was so far ahead of his times that he has survived largely as a unique phenomenon in Russia: though he is universally looked back to by Russian historians and thinkers as one of the authentic fathers of his country he was so little understood by his contemporaries that it was not, in fact, until the early twentieth century that many of his technical achievements were discovered and implemented by his fellow Russians.

Artistic life began to change, with growing momentum. It is true that even under Peter the Great's father some changes had already taken place; the baroque had made a successful invasion of Russia in music, with polyphonic music dislodging to some extent traditional Russian chants, while original secular dramas were written for the first time. An attempt at secularization had even been made in architecture, when Peter's father put up a palace outside Moscow (in 1666–8) with light streaming in through thousands of mica windows, disclosing a fresco representing the universe, and a quite unfamiliar interior of mirrors, luxurious furniture and odd mechanical gimmicks. Classical antiquity had made its first reappearance in Russia, with portraits of Caesar, Alexander the Great and even Darius taking the place of icons. The palace might be considered the first obeisance to the Russian taste for technology that was to thrive with such vigour during the eighteenth century and afterwards. It was, in fact, the first of the palaces built for fun, like those that came to be commonplace under the later Romanovs.

By the eighteenth century these tentative innovations had become commonplace. St Petersburg in the natural course of events became the embodiment in miniature of the various innovations initiated by Peter the Great and carried on by later sovereigns. Socially the Europeanization of Russian life, symbolized by the new and highly artificial capital, also broadened the chasm between the Russian *élite* and the masses of the population; artistically the capital established standards for the rest of the country to strive after.

By the second decade of the eighteenth century Peter had already begun importing all sorts of Western European artists, architects and engineers. Since he was in a great hurry and had no general plan, they would often be set to work indiscriminately on buildings very close to each other, and without being enabled to carry anything through. A general background was common to these European architects; it was the international vogue of baroque, though it was of course quite usual for each architect to impose his own taste on the general fashions. The homogenizing effect of the vogue was accentuated by the fact that one architect might very well complete the work of another on the same building. Thus under the reign of Peter himself the capital became a curious *mélange* of French, Dutch and Italian; no Russian influence had yet made a national style of the modish baroque.

For the first generation after the city's founding, St Petersburg was characterized by the lack of a general plan. A new Winter Palace was built by Bartolomeo Rastrelli, son of a sculptor imported by Peter. This was the first permanent imperial seat of the newly created capital whose foundations had been laid at the beginning of the century.

It was perhaps under Rastrelli's influence, during the reign of one of Peter's daughters, that Russian utilitarian architecture developed a new style, the so-called 'Elizabethan rococo'. In this style the European baroque, with its great façades, pompous interiors and majestic staircases, served as the foundation for ornamental effects borrowed from the ecclesiastical architecture of Muscovy. It became natural to imitate both Western Europe and the Western rediscovery of classical models. Secular portraiture, perhaps stimulated by the new revelation of men's faces through the shaving of beards, went together with more personally styled dress.

The court ballet was launched; the new styles made fashionable at the great imperial balls marked a further break with the coarse rigidity of form and movement typical of old Muscovy. An ornate heightening of individual elegance became a characteristic of style. This was accompanied by a new attitude toward classical antiquity, whose forms now began to be appropriated first from Poland, as the most Westernized of Slav countries, and then from Italy and France directly, through the increasing numbers of visitors.

For the first time Christian conformity was felt to have become somewhat irrelevant to the satisfaction derived from classical models. In the eighteenth century Aesop's *Fables* were translated into Russian for the first time; characters from the fables were used as the subjects for statues by the older Rastrelli, whose sculpture was a novelty in the St Petersburg of the time.

By the 1740s a new school of literature made a humble appearance:

for the first time classical forms were used. New operas, plays and ballets were based on classical subjects, rather than on Scripture; Latin became a scholarly language, despite the Orthodox tradition.

Of course there was something artificial about this harking back to remote antiquity in a country whose educated classes were still so exiguous. The city in which these classically inspired entertainments became so common, in court circles, was itself an artificial construction; the defiance of the natural order which the emplacement of St Petersburg suggested was to grip the fancy of later writers. By the middle of the eighteenth century the new capital was nevertheless a solidly rooted fact, in culture much like many European capitals and with a population about the same size as Moscow's.

The Winter Palace designed by Rastrelli saw the end of the utilitarian building of the preceding era. The frivolity of Peter's daughter Elizabeth was perhaps the cause of the second phase in the artistic consolidation of Petersburg life; under Catherine the Great the city gradually achieved its final position as an imperial centre, in this way integrating and extending its previous utilitarian uses as a harbour, military bastion, or purely imperial seat. The centre of the city itself was given over to government bureaux, whereas the suburbs were devoted to the new palaces that began springing up.

A peculiarly Russian style of monumentality was finally achieved in the coalescence between the talents of the various foreign architects and the environment that was the background of their work. This came about partly because of the fusion that was gradually taking place throughout Europe between the various national styles, and partly because more and more Russians were familiarizing themselves with other countries. This was the beginning of a sort of homogenizing process, furthered by the growing importance of the European academies, and the growing number of architectural publications, which came to influence all European architects in a quite non-national way.

The principal background for this general fusion was perhaps the above-mentioned study of antiquity, which, because its general attractiveness exceeded any prescribed ideological content, could serve as a touchstone for the most various socio-political tendencies in Europe. It

came to be a cliché that classical art was somehow inherently superior;
this was reinforced by the revelations of the actual life of antiquity that
became familiar through archaeological excavations, notably those of
Herculaneum and Pompeii. This general recognition, or general
mythologizing of the charms of antiquity, made it easier to bypass
national chauvinisms, and ultimately established a general European
attitude that had been quite unknown since the medieval period.

It became commonplace for public buildings to look the same everywhere, from Russia to America. Classical symbolism could be injected
into any philosophical or political concept whatever: Tsarist absolutism
and American egalitarianism could easily find philosophical 'roots' in
any wished-for interpretation of the classical world.

Rastrelli remained Elizabeth's favourite architect; he had been sent
abroad to study as soon as he had shown his talent, when a very young
man, and had studied first in Paris, under Robert de Cotte, and later in
Austria and Italy. Elizabeth's predecessor, Empress Anne, had already
acknowledged his gifts by commissioning him to build the Winter
Palace designed by Trezzini and Michetti; under Elizabeth, Rastrelli
designed all major government buildings during two decades and
served as general supervisor of all architecture throughout the country.
It was in fact Rastrelli's influence that became paramount in the
fashioning of the Russian style of the mid-eighteenth century.

Rastrelli may be thought of as an exponent of a superior type of
eclecticism. He managed to fuse the best elements of both European
styles and Russian traditionalism into something that looked both
Russian and international. He built innumerable town houses for the
nobility, and a great many other palaces and churches; perhaps his best,
known works were the Summer Palace, which was torn down at the end
of the eighteenth century, and the Anichkov Palace, which has been
extensively rebuilt. In his churches Rastrelli's inclinations led him to
turn from Peter the Great's taste for innovation, and to favour an evoca-
tion of the far older Orthodox style: in his celebrated Cathedral of St
Andrew of Kiev, and in the Smolny Convent in St Petersburg itself –
which by an historical irony was to become the seat of the revolutionary
Soviet in 1917 – he managed to achieve an unusual mingling of elements

of balance and spontaneous improvization. Both buildings are acknowledged as displaying a purely mundane lightness of touch combined with a rather personal stylization of the baroque.

The chief imperial palaces built by Rastrelli were the Catherine Palace in Tsarskoe Selo and the Winter Palace reconstructed by him in St Petersburg. If his work is to be summed up at all, it may be said to be the invention of a quite Russian-coloured baroque. It was distinguished by his gift for combining a magnificent scale with striking colours and an unusual proliferation of detail both ornamental and functional. Rastrelli's public buildings had a singularly histrionic effect; in a way they embodied a sort of spiritual transition between the celebrated merry-making of Elizabeth's frivolous court and the imposing quality generally associated with institutional construction.

Rastrelli's career came to an end with Catherine the Great's accession to the throne. During the 1760s, Catherine, largely because of her contempt for her predecessor, did her best to obliterate the rococo associated with Elizabeth's reign. In this as in many other ways she inaugurated a new era.

Catherine the Great reaped the benefit of the initial groping and tentative advances made by Peter the Great and his immediate successors, especially by his frivolous daughter Elizabeth. It was Catherine who removed all obstacles in the path of the Europeanization that had been fitfully embarked on. It was she who generalized the Russian approach to the culture of the West: thoroughly German herself, she was quite free from Peter's technological obsession with the Protestant countries of northern Europe: she was full of enthusiasm for the Latin Catholic countries, primarily of course France and Italy, although she did become absorbed in the political philosophy of England.

From a purely cultural point of view, Catherine's career is very instructive as an illustration of the chasm between talk and action. A thoroughgoing blue-stocking, immensely garrulous, and an enthusiastic partisan of French intellectual fashions, she naturally became enthralled by sweeping plans for reform, even while the social background she was operating against made it quite out of the question for her to effect her plans, or even for her to become aware of the social contradictions that

made the gap between the idea and the realization altogether unbridge-
able. What she succeeded in doing, primarily, was to impress various
intellectuals, largely French, with her articulateness. She had had, it is
true, a rather frivolous upbringing as a provincial German princess,
but when forced into seclusion under the reign of her husband's aunt,
Elizabeth, she had begun to read an inordinate amount of literature of
all kinds: she became, in fact, one of the most outstanding intellectuals
in Russia. Her energies were so abundant, moreover, that she also
became a fount of literary productivity: endless numbers of tragedies,
comedies, essays, polemical works, musical comedies, treatises on various
subjects, allegories, and historical studies, to say nothing of her memoirs,
poured from her pen – all of them remarkably second-rate. She managed
to fill a dozen heavy tomes; her only serious writing was, of course,
done in French: her Russian was scarcely good enough to be a literary
idiom. What she wrote in French seems to have been gone over and, in
fact, processed for release, in the manner of celebrities in our own
day.

The addiction to French culture of Catherine and her court had none
of the element of criticism that characterized the culture itself. The love
of France was really a sort of Francomania that implied a global acceptance of Frenchism as such; even more than in the case of Byzantium,
when Byzantine culture was imported *en bloc* at the very beginning of
Russian nationhood, French culture was viewed quite externally, as an
indivisible whole, to be accepted or rejected as such. It also played a
decisive role in the formation of the Russian *élite*, since the assimilation
of culture via the French language became an indispensable hallmark
in singling out the Russian aristocracy from the other elements of the
nation as a whole. Russian aristocrats could simultaneously set themselves apart from the broad masses of the peasantry, which went on
speaking Russian or Ukrainian, and from the other, non-Russian
nationalities of the Empire.

In the eighteenth century, under Catherine's reign (1762–96),
Francomania very quickly became incarnate in the adoration of Voltaire.
Though Catherine herself had shown an avid interest in some of the
English political theorists, like Jeremy Bentham, it was really with

France that, after being given an excellent grounding in French culture while still a girl in Germany, Catherine came to identify herself. She began a correspondence with Voltaire, then almost seventy, the very first year she was on the throne, at the age of thirty-four. To Russia at the time Voltaire was simply a synonym for sceptical rationalism and a general taste for at least the idea of reform. Practically all of Voltaire's writings, amounting to some sixty volumes, were translated into Russian, nearly all of them appearing while Catherine was on the throne. Some one hundred and forty translations of Voltaire were printed in the eighteenth century; no aristocrat could regard himself as the owner of a library if it did not include a major portion of Voltaire's writings, of course in the original. The very chairs that came into vogue in aristocratic salons were modelled on the one in which Voltaire sat for a number of paintings of himself; his name became a Russian word for a certain type of easy-chair.

On the basic questions of government another Frenchman, Montesquieu, joined Voltaire in influencing Catherine's approach to the central problem of her régime and indeed of all succeeding régimes – how to govern vast masses of people from above, or, put another way: How could the ruler retain absolute power, perched on top of a fixed social hierarchy, while at the same time spreading education and launching reforms? Montesquieu's celebrated *Spirit of the Laws* became Catherine's Bible in her struggle against the obscurantism and chaos of the Russia she was intent on ruling philosophically. Her attempt to organize philosophical principles into a system of government, published in 1766–7 and based on a philosophical defence of monarchy as a principle, was called the *Instruction* (*Nakaz*). Almost half of it was founded on Montesquieu. The rationalism Catherine thought she was aspiring to in politics was soon paralleled by a sort of rationalism in the ordering of information about the world; when the *Encyclopaedia* of Diderot and d'Alembert began appearing in 1751 she instantly became a fanatic about it.

It must be said that Catherine's approach to the many-faceted French Enlightenment was essentially frivolous; her failure to perceive the practical problems involved in the application of French philosophy to the conditions of Russian society, in fact, made the chasm between the *élite* and the masses still broader. Because of this overemphasis on principles in contradistinction to practice, what happened was the exact opposite of what Catherine would have maintained she was seeking in her devotion to principles: the social problems afflicting Russia were exacerbated and the aristocracy, prevented from participating more fully in the actual process of government precisely by Catherine's blanket defence of the principle of monarchical absolutism in her *Instruction*, remained sequestered more and more on their grand estates. While benefiting materially from the growing enserfment of the peasant population, the aristocracy was nevertheless stifling in a kind of social encapsulation that made it impossible for it to play a real role in the life of the country.

Thus Catherine's flirtation with the ideas flowing out of Western Europe, primarily France, and her transmission of these influences to her surrounding milieu in a purely literary form, left the Russian *élite* churned up intellectually, but with no conceivable vent for their newly acquired intellectual interests. By confirming the right of aristocrats to travel abroad she ensured that a substantial number of youthful aristocrats saw life in Paris and assimilated the new ideas more organically, as it were. Her example, perhaps just because it was so theoretical, served as a model for their gradually evolving ambition to copy the institutions and customs of Western Europe in the effort to modernize Russia; at the same time the practical reforms accomplished under her reign were so exiguous that they led nowhere. Perhaps, too, the very generality of French philosophical thought, which was what made it so attractive to someone with a theoretical view of society, also made it natural to conceive of reform on the broadest possible ground of abstract principle, rather than in the mere empirical and piecemeal groping toward a general improvement by specific and concrete change on a small scale.

A curious aspect of Catherine's love for the abstract was the passion she conceived for territorial aggrandizement, at a time when Russia was incapable of digesting its already vast lands. She had an inflated idea that the new areas her armies conquered to the south could provide a matrix for a new civilization; it became her major territorial ambition to wrest Constantinople from the Turks and divide the Balkans with the Hapsburgs.

Perhaps most importantly, Catherine originated points of view that had far-reaching effects on the arts of her time. She was the first Russian sovereign to make a clear distinction between public and private buildings. In this way the general European revival of classical architecture, already well rooted in Russia and with a slight national tinge, developed along two quite different lines. As a 'modernist' Catherine thought it quite normal to have a highly personal private life, while at the same time, in her capacity as sovereign, she equally naturally, by means of public symbolism, laid the foundations for an imperial governmental apparatus.

Thus she institutionalized the classical approach to construction in two different kinds of building: great public constructions of a scope to suit the immensities of Russia, and great private houses for the top-heavy *élite* that now, through the consolidation of serfdom, was looming very high above the masses of the country. The two types of monumentality were expressed in different styles, with perhaps an intermediate stage between the two represented by the buildings Catherine commissioned for her countless lovers. Catherine's own tastes for privacy could be satisfied because of her position as sovereign; the nobility were somewhat swamped by the conspicuous splendour they were inspired to by her example, without, after all, being able to afford quite so much seclusion.

Catherine's reign, from an architectural point of view, is generally linked to the transition between the European baroque and the later classical style she was inspired by. The main architects who worked for her during the first two decades of her reign were a German, Velten; an Italian, Rinaldi; and a Russian, Bazhenov. Each architect created at least one major building that, while baroque in design or elevation, indicated an unmistakable shift toward the classical in its use of detail.

Catherine also hired a gifted Frenchman, Jean-Baptist de la Mothe, whom she invited to Russia in 1759 and to whom she gave a chair in the

newly established Academy of Fine Arts in Moscow. He was com-
missioned to build the first Hermitage, as a private dwelling for
Catherine, attached to the somewhat draughty magnificence of the
Winter Palace reconstructed by Rastrelli. De la Mothe also created the
great market-place of the capital (Gostinny Dvor) on the Nevsky
Prospect.

Catherine completed the new and integrated character of St Petersburg
in what may be called the third and last stage of her interest in architecture, which was, in fact, the consummation of eighteenth-century
Russian architecture. It took a form that quickly established itself as
classical, in the form of a coalescence of ancient Roman styles with the
revival of the celebrated sixteenth-century architect Palladio. This fusion
of influences came to be characteristic under Catherine, who was
addicted to frenetic construction for its own sake, as well as to the life of
ancient Rome. The fusion was carried on by another trio of architects
whose names were to become embedded in the history of Russian
architecture: Cameron, a Scot, Quarenghi, an Italian, and Starov, a
Russian.

Starov's principal distinction was doubtless achieved in the construction of the great Tauride Palace, which Catherine gave to one of her
chief loves, the remarkable Russian statesman Potyomkin. After a
remodelling, it was to become the seat of the government during the
1917 revolution. Starov gave it a magnificent colonnade that was to be
much copied in private dwellings as well as in public places. The
Tauride Palace, itself an imitation synthesized by Starov from patrician
Roman buildings, began being imitated throughout aristocratic Russia:
it dotted the Russian landscape and in the imagination of generations of
both Russians and foreigners became a characteristic addition to the
undulating outlines of the Russian woodlands and meadowlands dotted
with birch-copses.

The Scot Cameron came to Russia in 1779; he was to remain
Catherine's favourite architect until she died, in 1796. He was well
known for his love of classical art and of Palladio; for some unknown
reason he also had a particular interest in eastern Europe.

Cameron's Russian career enabled him to become a rival of the well-known Adam brothers; his own style was based on an adaption of Palladio, somewhat filtered through the work of another Frenchman popular with Catherine, Charles Louis Clérisseau; it represented a personal adaptation of Roman styles as generalized by the Adams. It was a deft combination of classicism and comfort; he developed a rather supple use of scale to combine intimacy and the majestic austerity that was called for. Also, since Catherine was a sybarite, Cameron went in a good deal for opulent materials, by contrast with the more primitive brick and plasterwork of traditional St Petersburg. Cameron's love of the exotic fitted Catherine's tastes; he also developed very involved decorative effects, and a highly discriminating use of colours which contrasted very noticeably with the stark primary colours used in Tsarskoe Selo under the influence of Elizabeth.

Cameron was a vital link in the establishment of the style, ultimately rooted in the work of the Adam brothers, that was to come into prominence under Catherine the Great's grandson, Alexander I. This style is most obvious in the Tauride Palace, especially in its 'Pantheon', a characteristic manifestation of it. The style of Alexander I was also displayed in Tsarskoe Selo and Pavlovsk, which have examples of fundamental importance, and in the Russian provinces as well.

Yet it was Giacomo Quarenghi who may have been the most outstanding architect of Catherine's reign, as well as of the Russian eighteenth century as a whole; his arrival in Russia shortly after Cameron was the result of Catherine's displeasure with most of her other architects. Quarenghi made an enormous reputation for himself as a master of a classical mode that never descended to the point of mere archaeological pedantry; he also achieved an atmosphere of the majestic on a scale that remained within the confines of the human. Perhaps it was his ability in combining these disparate qualities that made Catherine constantly use the cliché 'charming' about his work. His very first building, the 'English Palace', was to remain a typical mixture of classicism, Palladian design and Russian proportions. Quarenghi's authority made him a direct influence on the development of the last part of the eighteenth century, though after Catherine's death he was reduced to designing mere utility buildings.

The so-called 'classical' style was soon completely adapted to its Russian background; by the early nineteenth century it had given rise to a distinctive variation of it, the celebrated 'Empire' style.

The last part of Catherine's reign was obsessed by her ambition for earthly and external magnificence. The celebrated legend of the 'Potyomkin villages', contrived by her former lover to shield her from the perception of the national misery on a number of triumphal tours, was a splendid adumbration of the situation of Russia as a whole.

During her last years her love of external splendour led to the construction of some of the most famous buildings her name is associated with: Tauride in St Petersburg, and Gatchina and Tsarkoe Selo nearby. Her architectural innovations were of cardinal importance in creating a whole new environment for the interplay of ideas. By replacing the monastery with the city as the focus of Russian intellectual life she provided a new sounding-board for the spirit of secularism that was to dissolve all emotional ties with the pietistic traditions of Old Muscovy. She went much further along the road marked out by Peter the Great: she shut down numerous monasteries and destroyed the wooden symbols of old Moscow, and in some of the monasteries that she left unmolested she installed pseudo-classical bell-towers that were a material contradiction of everything in their surroundings.

Catherine's interest in city planning made her launch a whole series of basic changes in the appearance and lay-out of many cities, especially, of course, Moscow and St Petersburg; the latter was quickly turned into a splendid stone capital from its beginnings as a copy of a Dutch naval base. At the beginning of her reign Catherine not only had plans made for the reconstruction of the two capitals, but for hundreds of other cities as well. New cities were actually laid down, and the general urban population, only slightly larger than it was in Peter's day, almost doubled in the decade beginning with 1770. Some of the rebuilt cities represented a realization of her rationalist ideals of harmonious uniformity. The technical accomplishment of manufacturing on a large scale bricks of the same size made it possible to rebuild almost in their entirety many provincial cities that were still built of wood in the old Russian style. Throughout Russia a new conception of architecture began to

*The Aristocratic Prism II*

Stage design for a masquerade
at the court of Anna Ivanovna.

Views of Moscow:
*(above)* Podnovinsky Square,
by H. Guttenberg after G. de
la Barthe.
*(right, top to bottom)*
Along the River Neva from
the Admiralty to the
Academy of Sciences towards
the East, by Makhaev.
Looking towards the Peter
and Paul Fortress, by
Makhaev.
View of the old Winter
Palace and the canal joining
the Moika and the Neva, by
Makhaev.
The Summer Palace, by
Makhaev.
View of the magazine court
provisions on the Fontacka
River, anon.

The Ekaterinsky (Catherine) Palace at Tsarskoe Selo (now Pushkin) near Leningrad, built by Rastrelli from 1749 to 1756; the engraving by Makhaev shows the Maison de Plaisance and the photograph shows the palace after restoration.

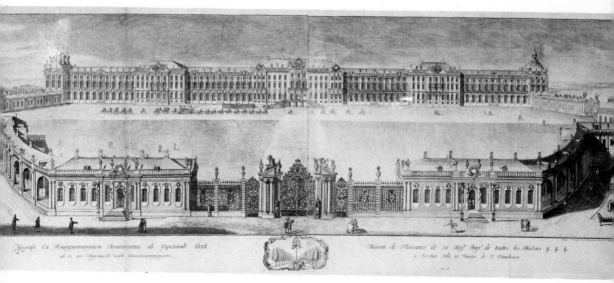

The Peterhof Palace and the cascades; the palace was designed by
Leblond and completed by Rastrelli.

Contemporary engraving of the Peterhof Palace.

(*opposite*) The park and pond of the Catherine Palace.

The Smolny Convent,
designed by Rastrelli
(1748–64).

The Winter Palace, St
Petersburg, begun by
Rastrelli (1754–62).

The Hermitage, which is part
of the Winter Palace.

*(opposite)*
The interior of the Peter and
Paul Fortress, where Peter I
is buried; built by Trezzini
from 1712 to 1733.

The Old University of Moscow, showing the exterior and Great Hall.

oust both the elaborate ornamentation of the Old Muscovite style and the floridity of the rococo favoured by Elizabeth. The new architecture of the cities came to be dominated by the simplicity of neo-classical outlines, such as semi-circular arches, domes and Doric columns. A further development was the subordination of individual buildings to a general design.

It is true that in this enterprise, too, Catherine's impact was somewhat superficial; most of her projects were abortive, and while the urban population increased at a great rate it nevertheless remained a tiny fraction of the total population. Cities were rebuilt only in respect of the over-all highways and squares; design was limited to important emplacements; all the smaller streets and the interiors of the blocks remained untouched.

Nevertheless, the new secular ideals imported from France were furthered by the new approach to architecture; Russian culture was given a new material framework that had a seminal effect on thought, in many ways just as important as the medium of the written word. Catherine's new cities were essentially aristocratic both in origin and function; they were not the traditional commercial centres that had served as the background for the emergence of bourgeois culture, but were natural display points for the elegance and the political power of the aristocracy scattered throughout the country. In the nature of things the town planners were preoccupied with providing squares and boulevards for army parades, rather than mere market places or arenas for the development of industry. It was only natural for them to devise ingenious theatrical ballrooms doubling as theatres, rather than utilitarian structures.

Aesthetically this meant that the core of the city was completely subordinated to political rather than to religious buildings. As the narrow alleys, the tent roofs, and the onion domes of the old wooden cities were partially pulled down, the vertical lines that had characterized the old cities were replaced by horizontal lines: an elegantly sprawling effect was achieved, with a reassuring sense of the spaciousness the aristocracy was naturally addicted to, when the ratio of two to one between the breadth of major streets and the height of the buildings facing on them was often expanded to four to one.

6

The conquest of the southern steppe during the latter part of Catherine's reign finally justified the Russian sense of the vastness of the land: moreover, the last great peasant insurrection had been crushed, with the execution of its leader Pugachov, and the Mongol headquarters still remaining in the south were finally seized for good. In the new cities there was also far less danger of fire, since the wooden buildings and narrow alleys had been significantly reduced. This changing townscape, with the expansive promenades and the immense squares that gradually came to be seen from the pseudo-classical porches, changed the physical environment of the aristocracy in harmony with its expanding intellectual horizons.

It may of course be thought that the essential artificiality of the Russian aristocracy's position, perched precariously as it was on the backs of a vast, oppressed, and explosive peasantry on endless stretches of land, might have increased the insecurity many aristocrats were bound to feel. The reassuring, cocoon-like quality of the ancient Muscovite wooden cities, with their encircling walls and inner fortresses organized in domes and spires, had been replaced by the newer cities, hubs of a horizontal highway gridwork that stretched from a flat city centre to the immense expanses beyond.

It was the very beginning of Catherine's seminal reign that had the most important effect on the formation of a new kind of public opinion. Regardless of the content of Catherine's own mind, her intellectual bent, or conceit, made it natural for her to impose a new gamut of ideas and interests on the *élite* public, small as it was. A whole new series of problems was presented to the upper classes, from sociology to architecture, and for that matter agriculture.

A single statistic is revealing: the year after Peter the Great's death in 1725, only seven books were printed in the whole of the Empire; by the end of the 1750s there were twenty-three printed a year, and in the 1760s the average soared to one hundred and five a year. From then on the rate of growth in the production of books was ever-increasing; even more important, the kind of book changed in nature very substantially. In the first half of the eighteenth century practically all the books printed were religious in character; but, during the second half of the century, of the eight thousand books printed, nearly all under Catherine the Great, forty per cent were entirely secular. In the two decades after 1760 there were seven times as many books published as in the two decades after 1740.

There was a corresponding increase in the number of books imported from abroad, and perhaps most significantly there was a steadily growing flow of secular learning to the provinces, greatly fortified by an abrupt influx of foreign tutors for private families, initiating another form of seepage throughout the provinces. The Academy of Sciences also backed a great many scientific expeditions to the north and east during the 1760s, which automatically entailed the involvement of many provincials in these large-scale attempts to collect, organize and interpret the scientific data.

Catherine was in a position only sovereigns can exploit. Her authority led to her being imitated by her favourites and by richer aristocrats; vast fortunes were spent on luxurious palaces, private and public, churches and other public buildings. It was Catherine's open-handedness that laid the foundations for the gigantic collections of art that Russia soon became celebrated for. The Hermitage, designed by De la Mothe as an annex to the Winter Palace, came to contain a huge collection of the work of many masters: Raphael, Murillo, Poussin, Van Dyke, Rembrandt and others. The collection in the Hermitage, started by the fusion of a number of small collections, was to become world-famous. Indeed, St Petersburg, begun so inauspiciously and with so much bloodshed and toil in the first decade of the eighteenth century, grew so rapidly that by the end of the century it was not only a great capital but a premier art centre of Europe.

Catherine, though for all practical purposes tone-deaf, regarded it as her duty to make a show of liking music. She made a point of patronizing the opera as well as the theatre; Paisiello conducted his own works at the Hermitage. Western secular music flooded the public life of the tiny *élite* in the capital cities, and Western music, both instrumental and vocal, became commonplace at public performances of all kinds. The fashion of the court naturally seeped down throughout the country, to be taken up by rich landowners who would use their armies of serfs to organize orchestras and choirs. By 1835 Italian opera arrived in St Petersburg; some Russian operas, rather mediocre, were written in an imitation of Italian models.

In literature, on the other hand, there was practically a complete drought: there are hardly any names worth recording. Those of the upper classes who bothered to read would satisfy their cultural cravings by reading French or occasionally English and German writings. Russian literature was to wait until the nineteenth century was well advanced before bursting out in a cascade of talents that irresistibly attracted worldwide attention.

In painting, the somewhat abstract stylization characteristic of Rublyov and his immediate successors had naturally evolved, ultimately becoming something to foreshadow a purely secular approach to subjects. In a seventeenth-century icon by the court painter Simon Ushakov, for instance, the treatment of the theme of the Trinity illustrates the transition to semi-naturalistic, relatively personalized figures, with realistically opulent *décor*; it seems to adumbrate the transition to the secular portraiture that in the eighteenth century was to replace the painting of icons. A portrait painted in 1773 by Catherine the Great's court painter, D. Levitsky, of an aristocratic businessman (F. Demidov) gives a realistic full-figure treatment of the subject in the style of the 'parade portraits', with pseudo-classical surroundings. The switch to the importance of history-making individuals demonstrates the transition from a religious view of life, in which the subjects might be conceived to be the mysterious workings of God in the world, to the concrete performances of real people. This particular portrait of Levitsky's has, to be sure, a slight note of satire in its ostentatious failure to idealize the subject in any sense: it gives a slightly comic effect.

From a socio-political point of view, Catherine's principal achievement was no more than the consummation of the peasants' enserfment and the consequent worsening of the aristocracy's social quandary. Her own point of view was so alien to the actual problems of the country that while paying lip-service to the ideas she was familiar with through her knowledge of French she merely intensified the contradictions of society.

Even a bird's eye view of Russian cultural development would be incomplete without a reference to the basic social institution in Russian history – the slavery of the overwhelming bulk of the population.

Russia is, oddly enough, the only major country in which the population gradually came to be enslaved by itself; historically slavery had always been the result of foreign wars or the purchase of foreigners; in Russia, over a period of centuries, the peasant population came to be enslaved by its own rulers. By the eighteenth century serfdom was full-fledged; it had been completely entrenched by Catherine. Landowners had full disposition of the lives and persons of their slaves: there was no rule to prevent their having torture-chambers, and some did. Even fully formed penal codes could be applied on private estates; in individual cases the cruelty, endemic, as it seems, throughout Russia, assumed demented forms. One landowner had thirty professional torturers, with their assistants. The law did not even forbid landlords to kill their slaves.

It was against this sinister background that Catherine's other achievements are doubtless to be assessed. Her chief aim was to Europeanize Russia so as to make it live up to the esteem of her French friends, but since she could do this only by demonstrating her own articulateness, she unwittingly prepared the way for the evolution of an intelligentsia that was ultimately to be provoked into a radical solution of the whole complex of socio-theoretical problems that have been plaguing Russia since Peter the Great's attempt to turn it into a modern European country. Under Catherine, European influence was consolidated in the flesh, so to speak, by an exodus of Russian aristocrats to all the capitals of Western Europe. Peter had begun to give Russians permission to travel abroad, and under his reign they began to do so, complementing the influx into the country of all sorts of foreign influences. Under Catherine's reign the movement abroad became a stampede. It was perhaps the immediacy of this contact, initiated during the eighteenth century, between Russian aristocrats and Western Europe, that was to agitate Russian life with increasing insistence for the next four generations.

It is instructive to recall what may be called the evolutionary arc between the middle of the eighteenth and the middle of the nineteenth century. The first Russian opera performed by Russians was, for instance put on in the 1750s, which also saw the establishment of the first permanent Russian theatre and of the first Russian university, while only a hundred years later the social order was to be churned up by the annihilation of serfdom.

The creation of a new social category, consisting of intellectuals who had been secularized by the spread of the French Enlightenment to such a degree that they could stand outside society and exercise their critical faculties on it, may constitute Catherine's most enduring historical link with the succeeding generations, whose activity during the nineteenth century was to produce such turbulence for Russia and the world. Though her practical reforms never amounted to much, even in education, nevertheless some individuals were shaped by the new influences. While retaining an abstract approach inherited from France, their incessant churning up of the torrent of ideas under Catherine's reign made them the harbingers of the intelligentsia that was to evolve in the course of the nineteenth century. The notion of a third category of citizens, alongside the aristocracy and the peasantry, had come into prominence during her reign; in fact, intellectuals as a class grew up in a manner quite unforeseen by Peter the Great in his attempt to congeal the hierarchical Russian system. These intellectuals did not become mere servants of the State machine, which had been the aim of educational reformers under Catherine, but perhaps because of the power of the ideas in which they were trained were altogether estranged from the State and became the chief architect of its destruction.

It was precisely during Catherine's reign that the influx of ideas from the West transformed the source of disaffection in Russia. The first half of her reign was characterized by the unbridled and perhaps inherently hopeless upsurge of rebelliousness on the part of a peasantry tormented beyond endurance by the rigours of its condition; its climax was the above-mentioned peasant insurrection headed by Pugachov. The latter half of her reign, however, was already beginning to witness the more and more systematically expressed discontent of the educated individuals produced by some of the academies. The opposition to the existing order was localized in the educated aristocracy. Nor was the progressive alienation of cultivated noblemen motivated by growing disagreement with Catherine as she herself gradually turned her back on the principles expressed by the French Revolution: it was simply the ferment of ideas working on themselves, expressed by an inner dynamic of logic and generalization, that alienated the bulk of the thinking community from the existing order and planted the roots of something that came to fruition in the nineteenth century.

It is illuminating to reflect on the sources of this progressive alienation of the nascent intelligentsia. In a way it represented a total contradiction between the reality of Russian history and a 'class' explanation of it. The conflict between the classes as such was actually muted during the latter half of Catherine's reign; the peasantry was simply defeated. The flood of ideas hit essentially the topmost fragment of the cultivated aristocracy, and even before the *élite* was joined, around the middle of the following century, by a growing trickle of plebeians, the conflict revolving around social and philosophical questions took place within the same privileged group, sometimes, indeed, even within the minds of individuals.

The fundamental conflict that shook and divided the aristocratic *élite* was essentially ethical: as the aristocracy grew more and more remote from the masses, as it succumbed more and more to the tug of French thought, and as it grew more and more repelled by the pleasure-seeking of the profligate upper classes, a moral attitude toward the world at large came to envelop the minds of sensitive upper-class thinkers who were tormented by the contrast between the life of the upper classes and that of the rest of the country. Towards the end of Catherine's reign, the French ideas of the upper classes came to be turned against France itself, not so much on a political basis as on the basis of a reassertion of native Russian values against foreign corruption.

There was thus an indigenous moral reaction away from the superficial Voltaireanism characteristic of the first half of Catherine's reign. This was reflected, oddly enough, in the theatre she did so much to encourage. The Russian theatre that began emerging in Catherine's epoch turned into a first-class, though veiled ideological confrontation between attitudes. An enormous number of plays, ballets, operas and so on were produced, including Catherine's own work, and against the background of the somewhat stilted life of the hothouse aristocracy the stage turned out to be the only medium in which any public discussion could take place, however transposed, of the concerns that were becoming commonplace for an aristocracy gradually learning to think.

It was precisely in the theatre that many serious minds began expressing their distaste for the frivolity of Catherine's theatre and its preaching of the coarsest hedonism; there was a reversion to the moral values of the non-Voltairean thinkers and dramatists – Fénelon, Racine, and classical Stoicism. Alexander Sumarkov, especially, the director of the St Petersburg theatre, who was the principal support of its repertory during the eighteenth century, led a quest for moral values by harking back to the world of antiquity, especially in its Stoic form, as a counterweight to the hedonism and cynical self-seeking associated with Voltaire's name.

The aristocratic turning away from what was thought to be the incurable frivolity of the Voltairean attitude towards life also, very naturally, took the form of satire; this was perhaps what expressed most dramatically the growing alienation of the aristocracy. Catherine herself, curiously enough, wrote a few plays making fun of the Russian aristocracy; even though here too her pretensions outstripped her abilities, she nevertheless stimulated the growth of a new genre of Russian literature, consisting of a purely secular attitude toward society, in the form of social satire.

Perhaps one of the earliest precursors of the immense flood of social comment, criticism and satire that was to fill the second half of the nineteenth century was a play by Denis Fonvizin, *The Adolescent*, which ran directly counter to the fashion current under Catherine of pseudo-classicism in literature and in some ways anticipated the later style, associated with Gogol and Chekhov, of melancholy jesting. *The Adolescent* is a complete contrast to the heavy, rhymed mythological tragedies currently in vogue; it is a short prose comedy satirizing the

conventional education of the aristocracy; it is curious to recall that
Fonvizin was the secretary of an aristocratic opponent of Catherine's
who had lost the struggle to curb her absolutist power. His returning
to satire in order to carry on a campaign against the régime was an
attitude that became typical of the growing movement of disaffection
in Russia throughout the nineteenth century, a movement that began
in the upper classes and only very slowly and gradually took in the
masses.

Fonvizin's satire is not wholly negative; while holding up to scorn
the conventional virtues of the aristocracy in contrast to the surrounding
sea of loutishness, he does not seem to preach nihilism by denying the
virtues themselves; it is simply that they are inappropriate in their
present environment. The implication is that what is needed is simply
secular reform. Fonvizin himself had not turned away at all from the
interests and goals of the Russian Enlightenment; it was rather as
though he were reminding his audience that a great deal had to be done
for such virtues to be realized. In its implications, in short, the play was
a summons to the realities of life rather than a priggish sermon on the
charms of abstractions.

There are some other noteworthy precursors of the Russian intelligentsia that during the nineteenth and twentieth centuries was to
make such an impact on the world.

A political note was struck by Alexander Radishchev (1749–1802),
who launched a major onslaught on serfdom in a bitter attack entitled
*A Journey from St Petersburg to Moscow*. Patterned very closely on
Laurence Sterne's *Sentimental Journey*, Radishchev's attack slashed to
bits the slipshod working of the primitive bureaucracy that had already
become rooted in Russian life, and even went so far as to flail away at
the principle of absolutism itself. Radishchev himself, after having
studied French philosophy in Germany, had become a modest bureau-
crat; for some reason his book went by the censorship unnoticed.
Catherine was livid with rage when she saw it and had him sentenced
to death, though he merely suffered Siberian exile for ten years.

There was a curious element of philosophic abstraction even in his
criticism of serfdom, doubtless the boldest and most original aspect of

his book; his criticism of the institution was made not on grounds of compassion, or for that matter even of practicality, but for the odd shortcoming he complained of that serfs were prevented by serfdom from using their minds fruitfully in the search for a way out of their debasing plight. The book actually had a great deal in common with Catherine's own generalized, abstract views of society, but it seems to have cut too close to the bone, perhaps because it appeared during the first year of the French Revolution, which just because of Catherine's adoration of French ideas disturbed her profoundly.

Radishchev's book was actually the first in a long series of literary onslaughts on conditions that the aristocracy, long before the advent of mass movements in the nineteenth century, was privileged to launch. With a rather pretentious style, and in the usual moralizing tone of the epoch, his social criticism was put in the conventional language of the Enlightenment. It was highly rationalistic, and was based on the theory that the source of evil lay in the very nature of man, though that nature was perfectly rectifiable as soon as the right notions were apprehended.

Radishchev has a chiefly historical importance; his book would scarcely deserve attention in and for itself now, but since it made much of the principles underlying the French Revolution against the material background of a functioning social institution, it had the effect of shaping the future intelligentsia.

Another figure, representing this time a total disaffection with the existing order, was Gregory Skovoroda, who together with Alexander Radishchev and Nicholas Novikov constituted the most talented group of minds in Russia towards the end of the eighteenth century. Unlike in most respects, they represented, taken together, the break between the autocracy and the aristocratic *élite*; the latter came to reject root and branch what it regarded as the lifeless purposelessness of the culture of the court, and was in turn rejected by the autocracy.

Oddly enough, Skovoroda was of Cossack origins; he had studied at Kiev Academy and in the 1740s had acquired a reputation as a vocalist. After becoming a seminary teacher he took up a roving life devoted to reading and thinking. As a teacher he had been in all the chief theological centres, and was forced to the conclusion that the secret of life lay in thoroughgoing introspection, itself dependent on a mystical communion with God. He thought the conflict between the two worlds – spirit and matter – was primordial, that sexuality and ambition were the handiwork of Satan. Skovoroda (d. 1794) had a rather high opinion of himself, as the 'Russian Socrates'; his mystical and highly personal attitude gave him many affinities with the various religious sects outside the official Russian Church, though in his isolation he never joined any particular sect. The cause of Skovoroda's malaise extended far beyond Russia, indeed, as far as the whole world; his mystical discontent could scarcely be satisfied with mere knowledge of any kind, and of course he could never accept an actual position in the Church. His ideal was the inculcation of religion through poetry; he carried a copy of the Hebrew Scriptures with him, and thought a symbolical interpretation of them would lead to some spiritual insight. Though his works were largely unpublished, and the autocratic régime forbade any collected edition, he became a sort of legend; his 'conversations' on metaphysics stimulated the endless lucubrations of later Russian thinkers on the most abstruse 'cosmic' questions.

Skovoroda and Radishchev may be taken, by those who like prototypes, as forerunners of two categories of alienated intellectuals in Russia. Skovoroda represented the inward turning, romantic and socially alienated mystics, all lone wolves, who at various times in Russian intellectual life have been common, and have also inspired a great many purely literary constructions. Many passionate believers in Russia have found themselves estranged from any actual system of belief organized with roots in society, and have developed their personal longings into a private spiritual edifice or at least attitude that may be called, according to taste, either sainthood or egocentricity. Yearning for the spiritual lushness of an ideal world, they side-step the workaday world they live in, and because of their indifference to that world they also remain indifferent to its socio-material and spiritual afflictions. Radishchev, of course, represented the opposing category: his spiritual depression led him to the contemplation of this world, even though his starting-point was bound to be that of a privileged aristocrat, cultivated in the Western European style in a manner that had become characteristic by the end of the eighteenth century. His own personal malaise thus received a social expression – his conscience was afflicted not only by his own torments but by the torments of others. In this respect he was the precursor of the 'conscience-stricken nobility' of the nineteenth century, with many echoes in literature as it became more and more entangled with the insoluble problems of Russian society.

Radishchev's rationalism too was to be echoed in the social optimism, in the inherent belief in the reformability and even perfectibility of man through the light of reason, that was the mainspring of all movements for social reform. Though he was not distinguished enough for any direct influence to be extricated from the entanglements of his own era, all Russian revolutionary reformers have regarded him as an obvious prototype, at the very least as a trail-blazer. But Skovoroda, too, though a purely religious thinker and mystic, is illustrative of one of the great underlying traditions of Russian life, perhaps the more profound for being less obvious. His cast of mind shaped the actual temperaments of countless individual Russians, even though its concentration on the purely personal and egotistic element of a transcendental mystical yearning for some absolute naturally eliminated it as a motivation for a collective social force.

A seminal influence may be ascribed to Nicholas Novikov (1744–1818), regarded as the leader of Russian Freemasonry, which had come to Russia at the end of the third decade of the eighteenth century. In Tolstoy's *War and Peace* there is a perceptive description of the effect Freemasonry had on Russian aristocratic intellectuals. Freemasonry was in fact a movement of considerable consequence, though the secrecy peculiar to it naturally makes it difficult to determine its actual numbers or the identity of its participants. A weekly satirical journal launched by Novikov in the 1760s, and a couple of successors in the 1770s, were the first organized expressions of social criticism in Russian history. They were all closed down by Catherine, but Novikov, who was both an able thinker and a remarkably energetic organizer, poured his zeal into two institutions that were to have the most profound effects – the Moscow University and the idea of the restricted 'circle' devoted to talk.

Novikov's energies made Moscow University the centre of an unusually intense intellectual life: he took charge of the Moscow University Press at the end of the 1770s, and also started a public library linked to the university. The university, which had been more or less in a state of collapse, with about a hundred students attending lectures in German and Latin, was gingered up by Novikov to such a degree that in the first few years of the 1780s he printed more books on the university presses than had appeared in the whole quarter-century it had been in existence.

Novikov was instrumental in restoring Moscow to the intellectual prominence it had surrendered to St Petersburg during the eighteenth century. Moscow's return to authority may have had something to do with an outburst of Russian national feeling, even chauvinism, that had followed the first partition of Poland, the first war with the Turks, and the crushing of the peasant uprising of Pugachov. As part of the chauvinistic revival of purely Great Russian culture, distinct from the foreign elements of the Enlightenment, this helped make the ancient Russian capital a headquarters for the emphasis on the Russian past and a sort of cultural haven for all those who had begun expressing their distaste for the Frenchified upper crust of St Petersburg. In architecture, too, Moscow successfully withstood the artificial innovations of Catherine, who even tried to force a European style inside the Kremlin; this, however, retained its somewhat exotic and old-fashioned character, with wooden buildings still clinging to the old onion-domed style. Moscow, though with its more than four hundred thousand inhabitants it was twice the size of St Petersburg, was always considered very provincial by the intelligentsia, yet precisely because of this homegrown loutishness, as well as its size, it could be made to seem a more indigenous capital to the great stretches of Russia than St Petersburg. It was perhaps a natural hub of the resistance to the cosmopolitanism of St Petersburg and more generally to the very ideals of the rationalistic Enlightenment; it is true, of course, that Moscow itself contained forward-looking elements of the nascent intelligentsia that believed in the ideals of the Enlightenment as fervently as any in St Petersburg, but in its narrowness of outlook, self-contained quarters, and closeness to the great

Russian hinterland, Moscow remained as it were the symbol of arch-Russian rejection of the European cosmopolitanism of St Petersburg.

Novikov's career may be regarded as an illustration of a more general split in the intelligentsia that in the first phase originated within the aristocracy. The break in his career signalized by his removal to Moscow paralleled the general split between the St Petersburg phase and a Moscow phase in Russian Freemasonry. This in its turn illustrates the ambivalence of the Russian aristocracy as a whole with respect to the great tendencies of rationalism and mysticism.

There were two characteristics of Freemasonry that made it profoundly symptomatic of the European aristocracy in the eighteenth century. One of them was the warmth of the fraternal aspect of the order, in which the landholding officerdom of the continent could feel itself amalgamated in one vast club. At the same time, quite apart from the clublike atmosphere, which enabled members to infiltrate aristocratic society with relative ease, Freemasonry also was a sort of religious order organized outside all churches. The mystery and the emotionalism that many upper-class people could no longer find in the traditional churches were transmitted to them encased in a sense of a higher mission; it provided the ancient, and, indeed, the fundamental eighteenth-century conviction that the universe rested on a natural order that was inherently moral, with a new symbolism embodied in an effective executive structure. For those who were receptive to this simple truth the secrecy of Masonic initiation rites was very tempting; on the other hand, the pervasive belief in the perfectibility of the human race was reinforced and encouraged by the various philanthropic functions performed by the order.

As early as the 1730s Freemason lodges were established in Russia, characteristically by foreigners, this time by Englishmen and especially by a Scottish nobleman, James Keith, who brought Freemasonry from Britain to Russia. Keith's career was most unusual; exiled for his support of the Stuart Pretender, he had served in the Spanish army before becoming a general in Russia and, for that matter, the military governor of the Ukraine; he also became the 'Provincial Grand Master' of Russian Freemasonry.

In its initial phase Russian Freemasonry, modelled on English attitudes, found it natural to adapt itself to the dilettantism of Catherine's court. The Order tended to be a mere entertainment, especially under the influence of a rich courtier, Ivan Elagin, the Provincial Grand Master in the Russian Empire. He elaborated initiation rites to replace the rites of the Church, mainly out of his general boredom. When Novikov became a Mason in the St Petersburg lodge he stayed only a year; he was instantly dissatisfied with what he regarded as the play-acting of the bored aristocrats in St Petersburg, and was to be instrumental in deflecting the movement away from its somewhat childish rituals towards a higher system of values, based on a sort of German-oriented mysticism that was to flower in Moscow after Novikov moved there.

Russian Freemasonry participated in this intensification of feeling together with European Freemasonry as a whole; it was part of a general turning away from English to 'Scottish' Freemasonry: this more elevated Masonry not only added to the 'levels' of membership, but made the secrecy more systematic and intense, introduced special training-texts and various new costumes and rites, sometimes with a vague resemblance to imported notions from the East, or the imagined East. The Scottish lodges created a legend of immense antiquity, all the way back to the Essenes, in fact, and Gnosticism. The Russian movement referred to these higher orders as 'Orders of Andrew', an apostle who, some apocryphal legends maintained, brought Christianity to Russia even as Peter was said to have brought it to Rome.

This form of Freemasonry was naturally called 'true Masonry'; it was so intense in its ritual and atmosphere that for many aristocrats it had all the effect of a religious conversion to the true faith. In the last third of the eighteenth century numerous Russian aristocrats, in their quest for meaningfulness in lives characterized by a certain spiritual aridity, a *tedium vitae* in fact, began turning to this exalted form of Freemasonry, away from the profligacy and spiritual rootlessness of life at court. Divorced from the simple ardour of the peasants' faith, and at the same time thoroughly dissatisfied with Voltairean rationalist superficiality, they found a spiritual haven in the Freemasonry movement as broadened and deepened in its new, Scottish turn.

This exalted, mysterious and intense form of Masonry embodied, in fact, a large part of the general revulsion of feeling away from the somewhat disembodied and abstract form of French secularist rationalism that had become prevalent during the half-generation preceding the French Revolution.

In Eastern Europe generally the model taken for the new 'Scottish' preoccupation with the occult side of life modelled itself on the 'Swedish' pattern: this had nine grades, plus a tenth, secret group, also numbering nine, who carried on special prayers and fasts, as well as other kinds of self-mortification. It was, of course, a new kind of order, based on a sort of militarization of mysticism; it was quite popular in Germany. The intensity of the new brotherhoods organized along these lines was illustrated by the adoption of new names in a sort of spiritual rebirth designed to recover the true inwardness of primitive Christianity, a return to 'first principles', like so many movements of religious reform. The mystical speculations and the theosophic treatises of Jakob Boehme, long an inspirer of such attitudes, were complemented by those of the celebrated Swedish mystic, Emanuel Swedenborg, who in the course of the three decades preceding his death, in 1772, had written an interminable series of works on occult truth. By the 1770s there were about a dozen such special Masonic lodges in eastern Germany and the Baltic areas; the following decade saw them multiplying like rabbits in Russia as well as Prussia.

This mystical Freemasonry had a special appeal for the aristocratic rulers of eastern Europe as a tool for squelching the insidious reformism inherent even in the abstractions of the French Enlightenment.

Russian Freemasonry came very largely under the influence of Johann Georg Schwarz, a young Transylvanian educated in Germany, who together with Novikov and others helped shape the beginnings of the movement in Russia. Schwarz lectured at Moscow University on philosophy and mystical philosophy, as well as on the philosophy of history, and made use of his immense popularity to attempt to convert higher Russian education into a channel for the diffusion of Masonic ideas. Very pious, Schwarz held that science and religion were merely two aspects of the same truth. Schwarz became a Prussian Rosicrucian, which he regarded as a purer expression of the truths embodied in Masonry; basically his position was that reason, feeling and revelation were the three factors leading man to the attainment of a progressively higher stage of knowledge. Schwarz agreed with Boehme that the whole of the universe was marching toward ultimate perfection: the march was taking place, he thought, in triads: the Trinity itself, plus man, who was also a trinity (body, mind, spirit), was proceeding toward the 'ultimate trinity' – the 'Good, the True, and the Beautiful'.

Schwarz and Novikov founded the first secret student society in Russian history, in 1781; Schwarz also seems to have been the coiner of the word 'intelligentsia', taken from the Latin word for intelligence, to express a concept of man as a totally unalloyed spiritual essence, acting eternally. In this sense, of course, the word seems to denote a sort of magical force; however, it very quickly became the designation of an actual quasi-social class. In fact Russian Masonry has been given the credit for being the first force that imbued the aristocracy with a sense of mission; during the nineteenth century this missionary zeal was continued by a class that, while retaining some aristocratic links, split itself off from society as a whole by opening itself up to plebeian and purely intellectual influences. The intelligentsia, in this historically more comprehensive sense, was to become the moving agent of Russian change, upheaval and convulsion during the nineteenth century and later; ultimately it may be said to have given rise to the Russian Revolution itself.

Catherine had always been systematically hostile to Masonry as such, even before she ascended the throne. When Novikov began criticizing the Jesuits rather savagely in 1784, Catherine rebuked him severely and intensified her persecution of Masons: she finally closed down all the Masonic printing-presses, and arrested Novikov himself in 1792. It is true that her persecution of both Radishchev and Novikov is generally ascribed to her disillusionment with the French Enlightenment because of her autocratic revulsion against the social and political results of the French Revolution. In reality, however, her treatment of Novikov, as well as her attitude toward Masonry in general, stemmed from a profound mistrust of any form of secretiveness or philosophical

7

obscurity. She combined a general suspiciousness of anything mystical, as a distraction from the world, with a certain political apprehensiveness concerning the political influence exercised by Sweden and Prussia over the higher mystical orders of Masonry and Rosicrucianism.

In all likelihood there was some foundation for her fears, since it was only natural for the mystical idealism of the occult orders in the Empire to seek links with the general disaffection of large portions of the population. Catherine had had a great deal of trouble with the movements of sectarian discontent in the countryside, in the form of the various claimants to the title of True Old Believers; it was inevitable for her to sense the perils inherent in a union between the disaffection of the countryside and the disaffection of the intellectual classes, regardless of the high philosophical or occult plane on which that disaffection was expressed.

It was simply an oddity that religiosity, having been politically defeated – though never suppressed – in the countryside, should now be having a resurgence in the mansions of the aristocracy. In their revulsion of feeling against the aridity of the Enlightenment, many aristocrats naturally looked back to the fancied charms of old Muscovy. In any case Catherine's repression of Novikov, as well as of all the people she called 'Martinists' – followers of the mystical protagonist of the anti-Enlightenment in France, Henri de Saint-Martin – marked the liquidation of her own movement of enlightenment. Novikov himself, by shifting from St Petersburg to Moscow, seemed to symbolize the development of the Russian Enlightenment in a way that was inimical to Catherine's own tendencies and to the abstract philosophy of the Voltairean type of enlightenment. By developing an intense religious interest and moving away from his early predilection for satire, moralism, and the philosophical abstractions coming from France, and to some extent from England, Novikov marked out a path that in the nineteenth century was to broaden and ramify itself in various movements of social protest.

The alienated, intellectual aristocrats of the end of the eighteenth and the beginning of the nineteenth centuries were characterized by an ardent desire for *earnestness*. Whatever form their yearnings took, a preoccupation with abstract principle, a mystic exaltation, or a concern about mundane matters like politics and economics, they were united by a deep sense of commitment. In their own persons, in fact, these alienated aristocrats constituted a synthesis between two aspects of the personality – the mind, considered as an instrument of thought, and a passionate desire for justice. The very word for truth in Russian means both ordinary mundane truth and the higher Truth as an embodiment of justice.

The last years of Catherine's reign, and the last decade of the eighteenth century, were a wilderness in Russian culture. Catherine herself ended her days in total disillusionment over the disheartening divergence between her youthful ideals and the political realities virulently let loose by the revolution in France. The social contradictions that Catherine herself had done so much to exacerbate were sharpened still further during the reign of her son and successor, Paul, though it lasted only a few years.

The aristocracy suffered from the increasing harshness of the autocracy, propped up by a comprehensive censorship mitigated only by the incompetence of the officials, and from the Prussian-inspired atmosphere of political purge; these sufferings drove the alienated aristocratic intellectuals back to France once again. The indignation and repugnance aroused in the Russian aristocracy during the first few years of the French Revolution were forgotten; Paul's arbitrariness aroused so much spleen that the old humanitarian ideals of the French Revolution were resurrected. Concomitantly, political discussion revived during the first half of his successor Alexander's reign, and reform was once again the order of the day.

On the other hand, Paul's religious obscurantism, and his determination to mobilize religious mysticism against politics, by which, to be sure, he meant revolutionary politics, created a sort of socio-political model that was much leaned on by Alexander I during the second half of his reign, when his own emotional ardour on behalf of political reform had been chilled into its opposite by the actual contact with the intractabilities of political affairs.

Politics, which towards the end of the eighteenth century had locked hands with philosophy, was from then on to play an increasingly executive role in the affairs of society.

Chapter 4

# The Modern Age Takes Root

By the beginning of the nineteenth century, reform of one kind or another seemed imminent. When Alexander I mounted the throne in 1801 all the hopes cherished by many different groups in the aristocracy – there was no question at this time of any other articulate group in Russia! – could coagulate, so to speak, in the optimism diffused by his personality.

As a pupil of the Swiss liberal La Harpe, Alexander was undoubtedly sincere in his determination to 'modernize' Russia – a handy catch-word, of course, to soothe everyone; at the same time the very vagueness of his promises of reform made his personal qualities of good looks, charm and energy an ideal prism for the optimism animating various aristocratic coteries. That optimism ran through an entire gamut of shadings, and by explicitly placing political reform on the order of the day Alexander flung open the gates to a torrent of discussion.

Two main currents can be singled out in the maelstrom of ideas that agitated the *élite*. During Alexander's initial phase, in which his own youthful optimism was predominant, the idea of constitutional monarchy was a favourite. During the second half of his reign, as Alexander himself grew embittered or disillusioned, the régime reverted to an hereditary panacea – autocracy was reinforced.

In a manner that may be thought a hangover from the rationalism of the Enlightenment, these currents of opinion received purely theoretical and abstract formulations. The notion of providing any particular argument with a base in economics or the social structure seems to have been alien to the aristocratic theoreticians, who also took it for granted that the whole discussion was taking place in a club that only an aristocrat could belong to. Even the discussion – to say nothing of the execution – of ideas was considered a prerogative of the aristocracy.

Perhaps the most characteristic spokesmen in the disputes generated by the accelerating acuteness of Russian social afflictions were the two contrapuntal figures of Michael Speransky and Nicholas Karamzin.

Speransky, socially something of an outsider as the son of a priest, perhaps a precursor of the non-aristocratic influences that were to come to the fore during the nineteenth century, was divided, in the conventional manner of his age, between advanced abstract political theories and religious preoccupations. He was very influential during the first decade of Alexander's reign, when hopes for rapid, though gradual social reform were still fresh. He put forward a series of comprehensive suggestions designed to transform Russia into a Western European constitutional monarchy, with the topflight executive roles being played by State servants, recognized as such, rather than by aristocrats in the traditional manner.

Though in his nature a practical administrator, and far from an abstract theorizer, Speransky was nevertheless so far ahead of the possibilities at hand that his scheme of reform never came to anything. Since he was naturally, because of his lower-class origins, identifiable with the French alliance that had been formed during Alexander's honeymoon with Napoleon, he plummeted into active disfavour when the French invaded Russia. He took with him into exile the only serious attempt to overhaul Russian administration that was to be made for almost a hundred years.

His opposite number was a cultivated aristocrat, Nicholas Karamzin, who was intelligent, philosophical and literary enough to provide the conservative resurgence of the second half of Alexander's reign with an effective spokesman. Disappointed in his feelings about reform in the abstract by what he regarded, together with most of his class, as the excesses of the French Revolution, he swung all the way round from a pious endorsement of the rule of reason to a resumption of faith in the mystical inwardness of historical laws. The mere abstractions of human reason were contrasted, unfavourably, with the charms of traditions and the spirit of the people. In an epoch churned up by the proliferation of new ideas and the collapse of traditional social structures, for all of which the French Revolution was of course the absolute paradigm, it was easy for renewed conservatism to glorify the Russian nation when it was attacked by Napoleon, reformer-in-chief of Europe and thus the arch-fiend simultaneously in the world at large and as an enemy of the fatherland.

Probably the head-on collision between rational reform and mystical conservatism was best personified in the person of Alexander himself; one of the commonest clichés about his character was his 'enigmatic', 'sphinx-like' charm. Alexander, brought up on French abstractions in a backward and despotic state, and striving to reconcile the two contradictory situations in his own mind, was bound to have an essentially declamatory approach to socio-political affairs. Perhaps the hallmark of his duplicity is to be found in his being the sponsor, during Speransky's ascension, of the latter's precise opposite, Arakcheyev, a synonym in the Russian language for extravagant administrative ferocity and highhandedness.

It was under Alexander that Russia became a paramount European power; the aristocracy that had been shaped by the leaven of French thinking during the Enlightenment dominated a country whose role in the undoing of Napoleon gave it a pivotal position in the aftermath of his defeat. The primacy of the Russian position was heightened by the acquisition of vast territories, including Finland and Bessarabia, as well as great areas in Poland and the Caucasus. The whole of this period of political and social history has come down to posterity in a totally unbalanced form, curiously enough, due to the fantastic success of Leo Tolstoy's *War and Peace*. The fact is that the Napoleonic invasion lasted no more than half a year; the Grand Army retreated in less than seven weeks. The Russian invasions of foreign territory that followed Napoleon's retreat were far more calamitous than anything the French had ever been able to accomplish.

Throughout Alexander's reign the social imbalance characteristic of

Russia continued. The growth of the cities was slow; no new grouping came to fill the immeasurable gap between the aristocratic *élite* and the peasant masses. The school system was laughably exiguous; at the beginning of Alexander's reign the only schools were the private schools of the nobility, which taught the skills regarded at the time as 'accomplishments' – French and dancing!

This social imbalance was made more precarious precisely because of the dislocation of so many Russian officers and noblemen during the Napoleonic upheavals. This had shaken up even the landowning class; even those squires who were fearful of rocking the institution of serfdom that their welfare depended on were diluted by the young officers who during the upheaval had been steeped in the turbulent ideas churned up by the French Revolution. They were disturbed, moreover, by the manifest superiority of the Western European peasantry in comparison with their own: the mere fact that European peasants, despite their endless afflictions, were not subject to corporal punishment had an eye-opening effect. On top of all this the contrast between the backwardness of the Russian peasantry as peasants and their valour as soldiers was bound to have an inflammatory effect on the youthful officers, still under the influence of the ideas of the European revival, the moment they returned to Russia to suffer again from the obscurantism of Arakcheyev and Alexander.

The liberal aristocrats were affected by two factors, one domestic and the other foreign. The first was the intensification of the repressive apparatus of the régime, enveloped by the pervasively religious atmosphere of the Tsar's entourage; the other was the increasingly obvious reactionary role in foreign politics of the 'Holy Alliance' brought about by Alexander. This was counterposed by the stimulating effect, on the more radical of the dissident aristocrats, of the bubbling over of social conflict in southern Europe, as well as in Latin America.

A proliferation of secret societies was a natural outgrowth of this combination of strongly felt ideas and the repressiveness of the State structure. The malaise, encouraged to some extent by a misunderstanding of Alexander's own style of liberalism, boiled over in an aristocratic attempt at a military uprising in December 1825. This was instantly suppressed, largely because of the remarkable slovenliness of the preparations and the divergent attitudes of the conspirators, yet it became famous as the first insurrection in Russian history powered by an attitude rooted in principle, as distinct from the pursuit of selfish aims.

The futility of this 'Decembrist' revolt was due largely to its falling between two stools: on the one hand the masses of the people were bound to be excluded from a purely aristocratic enterprise, on the other, the aristocrats thought of themselves as theoreticians, and so were incapable of behaving like makers of a mere palace revolution. They were in the grip of general ideas, but the ideas were just general enough to make them behave as though they represented larger forces, while not general enough for them to see just why their own milieu made the generalization of their insurrection, in accordance with their ideas, quite impossible.

In spite of the extremist means selected by the conspirators they were curiously conventional in their approach to the central problem of reform. The principal theoretician of the conspiracy, for instance, Paul Pestel, was rather like both Speransky and Karamzin. As a trio of diverse though related theorists, they illustrate the gamut of intellectual possibilities created by the very vagueness of the Enlightenment, with its purely abstract formulation of principles. All three were, for instance, patriots and former Masons; they all based their arguments on rationalism. They all believed that State authority was indivisible, and that order was to flow from the State down instead of being determined by the outcome of factional byplay. Pestel was a republican, but also a Great Russian expansionist who wanted to deport the Jews from Russia wholesale, for instance, and to conquer some areas still held by Mongols. Karamzin and Speransky simply thought a republic was unsuited for Russia because of its size. They all represented, in fact, the reactions of the same aristocratic coterie to the increasingly complex problems of Russian society.

Despite the sloppiness and ineptitude of the uprising the Decembrist enterprise too was symbolized in a characteristically mythologizing manner: it became the beacon for succeeding generations of disaffected Russians, even though the thoroughly effective and ruthless crushing of the enterprise was to stifle liberal thought for quite some time. This was easy to do just because the aristocratic mutineers had never thought of actually annihilating the social system; once the régime declared its intransigent opposition to all forms of dissidence a revolutionary attitude, however attenuated, became quite unfashionable.

Nevertheless, since the conditions that had engendered the aristocratic opposition continued, and Russian society remained in a state of explosive imbalance, the ideals of change remained even though the régime, under Alexander's successor Nicholas I, became utterly repressive, and indeed was turned into an early version of a modern police-state. It was not so much that Nicholas was blind to the afflictions of Russian society: on the contrary, he was thoroughly aware of the necessity for a sweeping reform of some kind, but he was still more aware of the difficulties and angers inherent in its implementation.

Russian absolutism may be said to have reached its zenith during the two decades of Nicholas's reign. Nicholas, energetic though limited – he thought things like politics, economics, government, etc. were mere 'abstractions' – gave Russian autocracy a colouring all his own by emphasizing a mixture of dynastic, religious, ethical and nationalistic elements. He gave the Russian life during the middle of the nineteenth century, during what may be thought of, in fact, as the incubational phase of the modern era, its characteristics of explosiveness and repression, an interaction that was to reach its height under the reigns of his successors.

Nicholas's outlook was summed up in a formula that became celebrated: 'Orthodoxy, autocracy, and nationality'. The last word, sometimes thought to be a mere euphemism for 'serfdom', is generally considered in Russian literature to convey the meaning of 'official patriotism'; in effect it meant a systematic attempt to keep all 'subversive', i.e., liberal, influences out of the educational system. Nicholas's régime had plumped for one horn of the dilemma universally confronting all authority in a situation of social disaffection: repression as the alternative to mollification.

It was the natural goal of the authorities to stifle all thought, but the notion of concentrating complete control of all intellectual life in the hands of the government was bound to be frustrated: in the event, Nicholas's régime coincided with an immense burst of literary as well as intellectual activity. Not merely were the seeds of the most influential Russian literary masterpieces sown during his reign, but almost the whole of the later cultural development was hatched in the outburst of creativity that began fermenting in the intellectual *élite*, tiny as it was.

During Nicholas's reign Russia, after having – at least through its *élite* – aped other European countries, now turned its face once again to Germany. In the past, advanced Russians had been enthralled by gimmicks: economic and industrial techniques as demonstrated in Holland, Germany and Sweden had been admired by Peter the Great; the elegant Russians of the eighteenth century had then turned to the French Enlightenment; and for a short period after the defeat of Napoleon England had moved into the fore as an example to forward-looking Russians, with the English utilitarians, the Byronic romanticists, and the economists. During the reign of Nicholas, with his Germanic interests and his Hohenzollern connections, Germany once again became a magnet for the official classes because of its efficient bureaucratic organization and rigid conservatism, and, for the growing class of intellectuals, because of its general systems of thought, its various 'Weltanschauungen'. German blood was absorbed wholesale by the upper classes and by the dynasty itself. Indeed, every Russian ruler since Catherine the Great had married a German, so that even if her son Paul was a bastard by some Russian lover, the amount of Russian blood in any Romanov after Catherine was minute.

Throughout the history of Russia, especially after the Europeanization of the *élite*, social differences were even more fundamental than in other societies. By the time the *élite* was elevated above the lower classes, with the rise of Muscovy and the progressive enslavement of the bulk of the population, the differences had acquired the impenetrability of hermetically sealed partitions. European influences had poured into Russia during the eighteenth century, and by its end were concentrated within the nobility; it was these influences, pervading and humanizing the society of the *élite*, that differentiated it fundamentally from the rest of the country and split it into two fundamental classes – the aristocracy and the plebeians. The chasm between these two did not even begin to be bridged until the end of the eighteenth century.

The various social classes in Russia, in fact, lived in quite different universes. With the exception of St Petersburg and Moscow, Russian cities and towns were no more than big hamlets. The small merchant class could scarcely be distinguished, either in dress or manners, from the peasantry it had sprung from. It was only on the eve of the twentieth century that it turned into a *bourgeoisie*, when the process of industrialization was sweeping everything before it. Russia was like a vast expanse of meadow and forestland; the scattering of hamlets made up of squalid huts had vistas, perhaps, of splendid mansions and parks, giving a Grecian effect, where elegant people could be found prattling away of culture and enjoying works of art, books, and French tutors.

The endless ranks of the enserfed peasantry had become quite unlike the aristocracy in appearance, manners and even in language, since even if the aristocrats spoke Russian it was likely to be a fairly 'literary' Russian that itself was modelled on French or German. The peasants seemed to everyone to be pious and deferential; their lives were wholly taken up by toil, religion, and festivals. They remained quite untouched by the Westernizing movements that had made their masters almost a different race.

Education remained restricted to a tiny *élite*, despite the merits of individual Russian scholars, who had been sent abroad by Nicholas during the first part of his reign. Some of the professors who had been trained abroad in this way were personally distinguished and had able pupils, yet the actual number of students remained very small. Nicholas had been still further reinforced in his aversion to what he interpreted as subversion by the French Revolution of 1848 and its consequences all over Europe. The number of independent students was rigorously restricted. There were very few lower schools, and the standards of these were exceptionally low. As for literacy among the peasants, it scarcely existed.

Such roughly was the background against which the Decembrist conspiracy erupted; its effects scarcely reached the masses of the people at all, but were confined within the summits of society.

Yet the ferment begun by the repression of the Decembrist insurrection bore fruit nevertheless, appropriately enough in the universities. A naive attempt to suppress the chair of philosophy at the Moscow University, for instance, had the effect of shifting the interest of the inflamed student body to physics. Young people started effervescing; ideas began sloshing around the supercharged atmosphere of the university, and a number of discussion groups were formed. The themes of these discussions proliferated and, inevitably, came to include social and political questions, and the participants shared a general and sometimes quite individual personal alienation whose target became 'official' Russia. It was just this element of alienation that was to be the hallmark of the intelligentsia as long as it remained in existence, perhaps, indeed, down to the present day.

The informality of the fragmented, diffuse, but passionate discussions among the students spread very quickly, to become part of the atmosphere of the period for all those who were not spiritually identified with the régime and what it stood for. Without any programme as yet, still less with any organization, the talkative groups flowed freely from one subject or cluster of subjects to another. Yet from outside one can detect a sort of general movement.

Under the reign of the police-Tsar Nicholas I, the French Enlightenment, with its wide range of ideas and its abstract rationalism, still retained great authority, if only because of the permanent foothold the French language had acquired in the *élite*. Yet the return of the autocracy proper to Nicholas's German ideas of discipline was paralleled, among the minds newly awakened by the above-mentioned ferment of ideas, in the gradual swing to an obsession with German ideas. A class contrast may be detected here: the tormented social misfits who managed to trickle into the universities without, of course, becoming members of polite society, in fact were revenging themselves on the hedonistic, detached, urbane and ironical *élite* by putting flesh and blood into their determination to *believe* as well as to *know*. The elegance of the French-speaking salon, characteristic of the reigns of Catherine and Alexander, came to be replaced by the gradual upsurge of a small but intense group of educated commoners who swerved away from the scepticism, atheism and liberalism of aristocratic Russia to be swept into the current of systematizing German philosophy. In some ways this can be considered a triumph of the romantic spirit over the classical; for the Germany that attracted the early Russian intellectuals was the romantic Germany that had also had an influence over the imagination of French romantics like Victor Hugo. Just as the State summit itself, imbued with Nicholas's drillmaster spirit, turned to Prussian discipline, so the intellectuals, of many hues, turned to the romantically passionate German universities.

The sudden plunge into the headwaters of German romantic philosophy and intellectual systematizing served both as a rejection of classical French rationalism and as a method of circumventing the craggy realities of contemporary Russian society. The new intellectual universe being born in Russia came under the mighty influence of a whole group of German philosophers: Schelling, Kant, Fichte and Hegel. Hegelianism, perhaps because of its immensely dynamic structure, powered by a sort of semantic ambiguity that enables it to be pivoted in any desired philosophic direction, came to have the most enduring influence not only in Russia, but also – if one accepts Marxism as a direct heir of the Hegelian dialectic – on the world of today.

German metaphysics was ingested with remarkable dedication; the fascination with philosophy in the abstract that had characterized the Russian mind even at the height of the Enlightenment, acquired such dynamism with the advent of German philosophic idealism that it became a motor for implementing the dreams for world-reform. When the autocracy, perfectly aware of the perils to society inherent in any generalizing of the yearning for knowledge, forbade the study of philosophy altogether – a ban that lasted for fifteen years after the European revolutionary upheavals of 1848 – what happened was that the study of philosophy, freed from the restraints of classroom discipline, became a channel for unbridled passion.

To be sure, the obsession with what was thought of as philosophy also implied a certain fascination by the occult; to many Russian thinkers philosophy implied the search for a mystically attainable key to the secrets of the universe, rather than a system of rational, analytical, and ultimately empirical inquiry in the manner of rationalist philosophers like Descartes and Hume.

Perhaps the cardinal single influence on the formation of the early Russian interest in philosophy remained Jacob Boehme, the inspirer of the mystical orders of higher Freemasonry referred to above. Boehme's work was one vast metaphor, in which the whole of the universe, including, for instance, evil, reflected the 'wisdom of God'; for Boehme, the ideal was theosophy rather than the 'love of wisdom' or philosophy proper. The deists of the eighteenth century had thought of God as a sort of super-mechanic contriving the complexities of the universe out of nothing, but still contriving them. In the mystic view of God represented by Boehme and recreated by the Russian mystical philosophers of the early nineteenth century, God's essence was the source of everything; all man's intellectual and emotional yearnings, to say nothing of his political impulses, were themselves reflections of the longing for the lost unity between God and man.

What was attractive to many Russian thinkers about Schelling, for instance, was his pantheism: he preached the organic unity of all nature, its encompassing of a creative 'world soul'. This was considered by Russians to be an admirable counterweight to the shallow mechanistic philosophy of the eighteenth century, since there was a place in it for both the beauty and the variety of the organic world, to say nothing of incontestable phenomena like mesmerism, telepathy, occult apparitions and so on.

Schelling had a dual effect on Russian thought, doubtless because of his all-inclusive and somewhat emotional moral purposiveness. On the one hand, many of those disaffected from religion felt the vacuum in their psyches replaced by Schelling's reassurance that both life and history had an ultimate harmonizing goal: from this point of view Schelling's views might be taken to be a consolidation for the ills of the status quo, hence a warrant for social conservatism. On the other hand, Schelling's implication that cosmic redemption was both desirable and possible led to an upsurge of interest, ultimately, in ways and means for making it come about. Schelling's philosophy led to the view that the process of becoming, the very essence of the life force, implied radical changes, which though unpredictable were indispensable for the achievement of cosmic redemption. This in and for itself led to a revolutionary attitude towards the possibility of contributing to the changes imposed on society and history by the nature of things. It was only natural for the conviction to be formed that the search for a key to the universe was not in and for itself absurd, but that the previous generation's search had simply been unthought through, an inadequate attempt that must now be looked into again.

In other words, the determination to find answers that would take in everything was merely stimulated and encouraged by the study, very often at third hand and in vulgarized digests, of Schelling's mystical and all-embracing philosophy. Schelling may thus be regarded as a sort of half-way house between the occultism of Jacob Boehme and the rounded, all-encompassing philosophical systems of Hegel and Marx.

The purely philosophical approach to nature led directly, in the minds of many Russian thinkers, to a study of history itself, with all the implications that that study was to disclose in the course of time. A cluster of questions, the 'accursed questions', associated with the meaning of history, life and the structure of society, began to preoccupy intellectuals under the reign of Nicholas I. Perhaps as a result of the Russian involvement in the Napoleonic upheavals and the comprehensive immersion of Russia in the affairs of Europe, many intellectuals were determined to clarify their views of the Russian status in history. The rationalism of the Enlightenment had been replaced by the insistence of the anti-Enlightenment that irregularity and traditionalism in history had a legitimate place and indeed a deep significance of their own. Russian romantics, like romantics elsewhere, were bent on divining the irrational workings of the historical process, and just as Russian theology had had an historical colouring, so the Russian concentration on philosophy implied a study of history.

It was inevitable that a study of history, embarked on from practically any point of view at all, was bound to lead, concomitantly, to a study of social questions. The very fact that an historical background for all problems came to be taken for granted, even if it was 'History' understood in some mystical teleological sense, implied that social studies were both relevant and indeed indispensable. And in this variety of Russian intellectualism the timelessness of non-historical philosophy began being replaced by investigations of concrete social situations. In the case of Russia, of course, this was actuated by a growing preoccupation with the above mentioned 'accursed questions' springing up out of the tormented Russian terrain.

The increasingly intense discussion of both philosophical and social issues gradually began to crystallize, towards the 1840s, in a controversy that remained at fever pitch for a large part of the nineteenth century – the dispute between the 'Slavophils' and the 'Westernizers'.

It was perhaps the work of Peter Chaadayev that triggered this vast, shapeless, unofficial but intense debate on the destiny of Russia. Chaadayev was an aristocrat and Guards officer who, after fighting Napoleon as an adolescent, had been immersed in the intellectual disturbance of the second half of Alexander's reign. He went abroad, travelling about and devoting himself to philosophical meditation, until after the Decembrist uprising of 1825; he came into contact with Schelling, and after his return for the coronation of Nicholas I in 1826 he set about the composition of 'philosophical letters' – eight in number – that after being discussed privately during the early 1830s were published in 1836.

These letters served to crystallize in a philosophical form one of the attitudes that for centuries of Russian history had been a recurrent motif: the need for Russia to divest itself of its own tradition in order to realize, on a higher plane, all the values of European civilization that Europe was too corrupt to realize itself. In brief, it laid it down that Russian tradition and independent thought did not amount to a row of pins. Chaadeyev was totally immersed in European ideas, and especially influenced by Roman Catholicism, under whose aegis he looked forward to the unification of all Christian sects as a necessary stage in the re-establishment of the Kingdom of God.

When his first 'philosophical letter' appeared, after several abortive attempts at publication, it was like an electric shock to official Tsarist chauvinism. When Chaadeyev got through with Russian history, nothing whatever seemed to be left. As he said, 'Not one useful thought

8

has been born on our soil'. As a partisan of the Roman Catholic Church, he blamed the Byzantine source of Russian Christianity for its pernicious isolation from Europe, and took the darkest possible view of Russia's condition both past and present.

However, the sombreness of his exposition of Russian history pointed up the brightness that was to be expected from the future. The very fact that Russia had never made a proper appearance of its own on the stage of world history implied that its future development, unencumbered by the dead past, might be all the more refulgent. In a way, of course, this also justified an extreme form of Russian chauvinism: since Russia had failed to participate in the afflictions and shortcomings, as well as in the contributions, of European civilization it could still act as world saviour.

Chaadayev was repeating what various foreigners had said to Russian sovereigns ever since Peter the Great, but it was the first time a Russian, and an aristocrat at that, was speaking inside the Russian milieu and moreover not addressing himself to an actual sovereign but to the beginning of 'public opinion', at least aristocratic public opinion. His open contempt for the aridity of the Russian cultural tradition and of the Orthodox Church naturally brought him into disfavour with the régime, but nothing serious was done to him. He was declared insane, but never incarcerated; the restriction on his movements was kept to a minimum and he remained a venerated figure in the aristocratic life of Moscow. The likeliest explanation of this, of course, is that even the 'official patriotism' insisted on by the Tsar was confined, in fact, to a rather small circle; even then the régime was beginning to alienate the topmost milieu of the aristocracy.

From the point of view of the Russian idealists who had come under the influence of Schelling, an influence characteristically in Chaadayev's view that Russia must undertake and leap over the crassly materialistic West in the interest of Christian civilization as a whole, a belief in the special destiny of Russia by no means implied a turning away from Western Europe. On the contrary, it was part of Russia's special destiny to implement just those great values implied by, but not realized by Europe itself.

Contrariwise, simply because of this, a pro-Western view never implied a sympathy for either secularism or rationalism, also products of Europe, if only because of the strong religious and romantic tinge of the Russian idealists. Chaadayev, for instance, in spite of his sympathy for Roman Catholicism, disliked scholastic philosophy and Aristotle above all.

These basic motifs illustrate the contrast, as well as the resemblance between the 'Slavophil' and the 'Westernizing' movements that began to constitute a framework for discussion from the 1840s on. In the very beginning, to be sure, the factors that ultimately brought about a schism were far from apparent. Both sides were religiously minded, both were against revolution as such and in general against any 'excesses' in the direction of social levelling. Both groups tended to idealize the village commune and the 'spirit of the people' as a sort of principle inherent in the voiceless masses of Russia. The adoration of this mute and amorphous notion of 'the people' was, in fact, part of the baggage of ideas held by all sorts of thinkers in Eastern Europe generally, to say nothing of their counterparts elsewhere. It was shared by radical 'Westernizers' and by Polish insurgents.

At bottom the Westernizers were, as indicated, romantic humanitarians. Their belief in the universal implications of Western European culture was linked to a concomitant belief in Russia's special ability to transcend its unfortunate parochialism, caused by the shortcomings of its national past, and achieve the world significance its potentialities enabled it to. Of course, the basic notion that became a sort of watchword – 'Europe' – itself meant practically nothing from any concrete point of view, since without clearly marked principles of selection there was no way of knowing just which aspect of 'Europe' was to be held up as a desideratum.

Since the Westernizers as a group had altogether different premises as their starting-points, almost any aspect of European life could be and was taken as a criterion. A wide range of institutions and ideas, from science to constitutionality of government, liberalism, abolition of censorship, and so on, gave ample opportunity to inveigh against Russian institutions from a selected vantage-point. Theoretically the Westernizers were generally against serfdom on principle; in practice they were very discreet in expressing themselves on this prickly and dangerous subject. It was also fashionable for Westernizers to regard the abyss between the cultivated *élite* and the masses of the peasantry as deplorable. As socialism came to the fore, the Westernizers never committed themselves to it in any sense.

The Slavophils, contrariwise, generally took a more obviously patriotic tack. They held up for glorification the legendary qualities of the Russian past *per se*. Needless to say, the past they looked back to was itself largely a creation of their own philosophical *parti pris*. They generally regarded the West as utterly decadent from a moral point of view, despite or perhaps because of its technological ascendency. They regarded the role of materialistic rationalism as pernicious, and in any case as quite unsuited to the expression of the Russian national spirit. As a corollary of this cluster of attitudes, they tended to consider the Orthodox Church the hub of the Russian people as a collectivity, hence the principal warrant of its success in the future.

Socially, the Slavophils were generally affiliated with the landowning class, yet though conservative in terms of Russian tradition were by no means wholly identified with official policy. Actually, as romantic partisans of the Orthodox Church they were often opposed to the State's historically consistent exploitation of the Church in its own interests. Nor did their Great Russian nationalism imply solidarity with other Slavic nations, since those that were Catholic were opposed by the Westernizers as traitors to the Orthodox Church, the natural expression of Slavdom. It was, indeed, because they considered the Great Russian State the embodiment of authentic Slavdom that they were also rather opposed to the national self-expression of the Ukraine. From this point of view, of Great Russia as the true incarnation of Slavdom, any splitting off from Russia could be considered a form of separatism or treachery. Even the Balkan Slavs, so many of them Greek Orthodox in faith, were not of much interest to the Russian Slavophils until the Crimean War (1853–6).

The initial independent period of Slavophilism, in which it was not in the least identified with the purely secular interests of the Russian

State, allowed the Slavophils to be critical very often of any particular policy of the government; it even allowed for a certain mood of alienation from the government as such. Yet there was a sort of logic inherent in its evolution that ultimately made the Slavophil movement converge with official policy. In the minds of its opponents, at least, it came to be willy-nilly identified with the régime. This naturally implied a substantial loss of influence as the movement came to be regarded as a mere appendage of a concrete social institution, one that, moreover, became the target of all alienated social opinion, among the intellectuals at large and to an increasing extent among the liberally minded gentry and even aristocracy.

The split between the Slavophils and the Westernizers was ultimately sharpened through the influence of still another German thinker, Georg Hegel, who swayed the imaginations of Russian intellectuals during what was perhaps the most pregnant decade in the Russian nineteenth century, the decade that began at the end of the 1830s. The all-embracing scope of Hegelian philosophy, plus its fusion of rational and emotional factors, and the rigours of its logic, combined with a flexibility perhaps partly derived from an inherent ambiguity rooted in its play on words, made it an ideal vehicle for the longings of generations of Russian intellectuals.

It was Hegel more than anyone else who hardened the divisions between views, and for the first time the Westernizers began taking a turn of thought that could and did lead straight into politics, with the positive contemplation of the possibility of revolution as an ultimate corollary.

What underlay Hegel's view of history was quite simple: his infectious conviction that it made 'sense', and sense that his method of analysis enabled to come to the surface. This notion enabled those oppressed by history to find consolation in the most disastrous and depressing aspects of contemporary life. If the 'rational' is actually 'real', in accordance with Hegel's celebrated remark, then solace could be found everywhere, and it became possible for depressed and alienated young idealists to turn back to the swamp of daily events, away from the self-seclusion of secret societies and lodges, and find truth in action.

Just as a study of anthropology can become a tool in the hands of a young man groping for self-assertion, since it enables him to put his fellows into categories that they, as his objects, remain unconscious of, so Hegelianism enabled young men to condescend to everyone; it was they, after all, who had been given the key to the universe through Hegel's understanding of history. Anyone who thought he was talking as an individual would be listened to by a Hegelian with amused or interested condescension: the individual would in fact become a category or species, without even knowing it. This was balm to the Hegelian's soul. It enabled him to disregard the misery of his own existence, link himself to Hegel's 'objective' necessity, and achieve salvation through the identification of himself with something outside himself that was both 'real' and 'rational'. Hegelianism in this sense was interpreted as a perception of the irrelevance of merely personal, 'subjective' feelings: what counted was only the self-evolution of the objective World Spirit.

It was only natural for the preceding generation of Russian thinkers, both Slavophils and Westernizers, to be somewhat alienated by this disregard of both personal feelings and aesthetic and moral judgements. In contrast with Schelling, Hegel seemed to be projecting the discussion beyond morality, into a non-aesthetic sphere of impersonal compulsion.

Hegelian thought was institutionalized in Russia in accordance with a pattern that ever since the eighteenth century had become classic. A 'circle' was formed around a local disciple of the Master; a new foreign centre came into being, for the purpose of pilgrimage and close-hand acquaintance with the wellspring of the new ideas; the Master became a new source of light, and a whole generation identified itself with him. The Hegelian circle that came about in the generation after the Napoleonic wars no longer thought about the sentimental, declamatory hopes of the Alexandrian epoch, but was more preoccupied by the afflictions of Nicholas's police-state..

The Hegelian dialectic, with its symmetrical progression of both thoughts and things from a 'thesis', through an 'antithesis' to a 'synthesis' – a very attractive notion, both emotionally and intellectually, if only because of its combination of simplicity, profundity and momentum – enabled endless combinations to be made in any desired direction. If history proceeded from one 'contradiction' to another, after all, a perfectly natural case could be made out for anything, and in the hands of many Russian Hegelians Hegel became a weapon against the régime. Some of his Russian followers turned into exponents of the idea that the State was the paramount expression of the World Spirit, as did many Germans, but far more took a different twist of the Hegelian dialectic as their take-off point and dedicated themselves to the thought that what the dialectic demanded of the rational man was not the deification of the State but its annihilation.

The alienation of the Russian upper classes, of which Hegelian extremism was a radical development, came to be summed up in the Russian coinage, the 'conscience-stricken gentry', for whom the notorious 'accursed questions' afflicting Russia provided an axis around which views of life, as well as views of politics, came increasingly to revolve. It was, of course, the sharpening of the social question in particular, the paramount 'accursed question', that was to have the most explosive consequences.

For even though Russian upper-class radicals had come under the general influence of German philosophy, and of Hegel most of all, some of them at the same time began turning back to France – this time to a different, non-rationalist France, itself enthralled by the preoccupation of 'accursed questions' of its own. Socialism, in a French version, began sweeping into the intellectual milieux of the country, in the writings of Saint-Simon, Fourier, Proudhon and Louis Blanc. A potent synthesis between German and French thought was, in fact, to be formed on Russian soil.

Saint-Simon's theory of history had become an article of faith with many of the youthful Westernizers; both he and his disciple, Auguste Comte, put forth a complex of theories that while religious in inspiration had no attachment to the organized forms of Christianity. Saint-Simon called for a new version of Christianity based not on theological doctrine but on ethics, and also for a new social hierarchy that was to be based not on social privilege, but on managerial function. Saint-Simon's influence in Western Europe was due to his theories of organization of industrial society and the relations between social classes, but what attracted Russians was the majestic scope of his philosophical and historical views.

One of the principal channels for the propagation within Russia of the lively, though diffuse, fanciful and seductive theories of Saint-Simon, and the most influential forerunner, indeed perhaps the paramount progenitor of the intelligentsia as it took shape around the middle of the nineteenth century, was Alexander Herzen (1812–70), one of the first of the 'conscience-stricken gentry'.

An aristocrat by birth, though on the wrong side of the blanket, Herzen received an aristocratic, conventionally Gallic education; initially he was attracted by the romantic pathos of Slavophilism. Although Slavophils and Westernizers have roots in the same social milieu, they represent, perhaps, different temperaments; ultimately, towards the middle of the 1840s, they fell into a more or less formal split. When this happened, Herzen adopted a socio-political posture of his own, a synthesis of elements drawn from both camps equally that evolved into a system characteristically his own known as 'Populism'.

The synthesis itself seems to have been based on a perhaps obvious compromise, in which the adoration of the Russian spirit was incarnated in the idolization of the common people, i.e., the peasantry. The village commune was revered by the Slavophils as the quintessence of Russian congregationalism, which as a paramount strain in Orthodoxy had always been the very hub of their doctrine: it was a convenient vehicle for the expression of all forms of social mysticism, since it was linked to a concrete, ancient institution rooted in Russian life yet at the same time could be poeticized as the arch-symbol of nationalist pathos.

Herzen took the basic idea of the village commune and cast the general romantic adoration of it into an altogether different form. He simply adapted some general socialist theories to it, and claimed it as the fountainhead of virtue by emphasizing its socio-economic and organizational side, while disregarding the Slavophils' emphasis on the ethical and religious motifs.

The influence of Herzen on the formation of the Russian intelligentsia can hardly be overemphasized. Both his personality and his interests enabled him to become a unique inspiration for this singular and influential social caste.

The object of Herzen's chief revulsion was the State in its contemporary form. His ideal became a Russia made up of free communes: all the elements of the Russia of his own time – such as the condition of serfdom, the nobility and the bureaucracy, which he blamed on the Romanovs – were at bottom simply alien to the 'people', whose Russianness could include only the figure of the Tsar himself, the peasants, of course, and the clergy. These were what was native, with roots in the Russian folk-psyche; everything else was a foreign product and pernicious to boot. All Russia had to do to live up to its destiny as a nation was to eject serfdom, aristocracy, bureaucracy and the Byzantine element in the Orthodox church – that is to say, all the dominant factors in Russian society – and then create a wholly new society whose foundations would be a spontaneous alliance between the village commune and the nascent working-class: a great new emancipatory revolution would then take place. To Herzen the contemporary Russian State was no more than 'Chingis Khan plus the telegraph'. In addition, he also detested the liberal West, and was on principle opposed to every form of dry legalism as an infringement of the individual's freedom of self-expression.

One of the touchstones in his view of the world was the role he ascribed to Peter the Great. The figure of Peter is, indeed, one of the criteria by which the attitude of a Russian historiographer can be judged at once. Herzen thought Peter's role admirable in one respect; he had brought the Tsardom down to earth by mingling with the people, whom he had turned into a nation of democratic workers; he had also damaged the topheavy and exotic element in the national church, and eliminated the seeds of women's harem-life.

At the same time, he elevated the nobility above the masses and Europeanized it; this created a chasm between master and slave. The German bureaucracy that followed in Peter's wake and kept growing was necessary in order to bridge that chasm. Ever since Peter, accordingly, the history of Russia was no more than the actions of the Tsar and the nobility, with the bridge to the masses being provided only by the army of office-holders and bloodsuckers. The Russian people itself had simply slipped out of history, except, possibly, for a short space of time during the foreign invasion of Napoleon. The only thing that had managed to survive in Russian life was the commune and the workers.

Herzen felt that the split in the nation, between people and rulers, was the source of the profound imbalance of Russian society and its consequent malaise. His views on the inward nature of the Russian 'people' were to find their finished expression, in a dynamic and tempestuous form, in the generation that followed.

Herzen was doubtless the prime inspiration of the intelligentsia, but its technical formation may be ascribed to an energetic literary critic, Vissarion Belinsky (1810–48) who not only exercised a remarkable influence on the dissemination of new ideas but played a formative role in the shaping of Russian literature; and in Russia, perhaps more than in any other country, literature was the medium for the changing of society.

At the height of Belinsky's short career, every youthful thinker in Russia could quote him by the bucketful. A penniless plebeian by origin, he represented a sort of crystallization of the activities of the intelligentsia considered as a collectivity: since he was socially rootless, and neither a creative writer nor an original thinker, his journalism was his only mode of expression; as the zealous exponent of other people's ideas he played a genetic role in the shaping of the intelligentsia.

Belinsky was a sort of bubble in the rising yeast of Russian intellectualism. An ardent dilettante and chatterbox, his chief function was talk. With no knowledge of foreign languages – a calamity for any Russian thinker of the time – and not much of a reader even in Russian, he propagated his ideas almost exclusively in conversation, letters and reviews. His activities were so abstract that in this alone he may be regarded as the very incarnation of the intelligentsia. Belinsky was a worshipper of both Peter the Great and Hegel; at first, as a Hegelian, he had taken up Hegel's famous championing of the Prussian monarchy: whatever exists is right, i.e., what is 'real' is 'rational'. But he did not stay a Hegelian long; after breaking with Hegel he became a revolutionary, and also the proponent of the idea of utility in literature, a position that made him the progenitor of the endless series of moralists and propagandists that Russian literature was to become celebrated for.

Hegel's idiom was so capacious, to be sure, that even after Belinsky rejected Hegel he remained a Hegelian as it were structurally. Anticipating a total transformation of Russian society as part of Europe, he turned to the French socialists, but nevertheless expected the actual change in social relations to take place in a Hegelian progression. History remained a march, in which the embodiments of various ideas moved forward necessarily toward the realization of the World Spirit: the steadily progressing dialectical series of theses, antitheses, and syntheses would ultimately be dissolved in one vast unaccountable 'final' synthesis, in which the realm of freedom would supplant the realm of constraint. Hegel's theory, in short, as a chiliastic view of history, was imbued with a sort of Messianism it never lost in any of its derivations; in spite of the variety of people who have been influenced by Hegel it was this Messianic teleology that was its permanent element, and doubtless the chief source of its attraction for intellectuals.

Belinsky's personal interests were characteristic of the Russian intelligentsia as a whole. Summed up, these interests revolved around the service of mankind in certain ways, primarily through the devotion to Western ideals and socialist doctrine, however vague its expression. This complex of ideals doubtless rested on the mysticality of religion, transformed into the longing to atone for the wrongs inflicted on suffering mankind. The service of mankind was in fact substituted for the traditional emotionality of religion, as felt by those who were sincerely pious, not mere lip-servers. At the same time this emotional attitude was so strong that it caused all discussion to be fundamentally moral discussion: philosophizing could be carried on endlessly with no special knowledge of philosophy as long as the emotion behind the discussion was sufficiently ardent.

From the point of view of this underlying emotionality, all the arts and all the sciences were merely media for the ethical emotion. It is, indeed, only the ethical criterion, implanted in the soul of mankind, that makes it possible to exercise any judgement at all. On the personal level this mystical attitude requires self-sacrifice – asceticism and dedication to duty. In other words the individual is called upon to subordinate himself, for moral reasons, to the ideal of the collective welfare.

Perhaps the most uncompromising of all Hegelians, the most dynamic and extravagant, was Michael Bakunin, who was wholly obsessed by the idea that total freedom had to be preceded by total destruction. This extremist form of anarchism, coupled with Bakunin's personal magnetism and energy, exercised great influence on European thought in the middle of the nineteenth century, especially in the south of Europe. Though thoroughly Russian in disposition, Bakunin spent most of the turbulent decade from the end of the 1830s in Western Europe, where he had an extraordinarily crystallizing effect in the turmoil of 1848.

It would be hard to overestimate the impact of Hegel's ideas, or rather their vulgarization, on the Russian intelligentsia of the mid-nineteenth century. Russian thinkers had always had a weakness for the all-embracing philosophical systems; with Hegelianism, and its structural technique as a pivot for lunges in all directions, the fascination by systems of thought turned into a sort of obsession: Hegel's thought was so all-inclusive, primarily because of this technique of the 'dialectical' confusion of words, ideas, and events, that even those who abandoned it could never be satisfied with anything less. Whatever the source of their emotional need for all-embracing formulae, the need remained even after Hegelianism was discarded: moderation, tentativeness and groping, in fact, the whole paraphernalia of inductive science, empirical inquiry and piecemeal solutions was felt to be somehow tiresome and vexatious. A permanent motif in Russian philosophical and political discussion was to be a hatred of the ordinary, the obvious, the mediocre – all summed up, perhaps, in the detestation of 'philistinism' common to all varieties of intellectuals.

Hegelianism added, moreover, a new note to the general discussion revolving around Russia's place in history. This debate, with the two general camps of Slavophils and Westernizers, was envenomed by the Hegelian approach to history as a procession through a series of progressively necessary contradictions. The celebrated Hegelian principle of the 'negation of the negation', leading ultimately to the 'final synthesis' that was to usher in the millennium, led most Russian dissidents,

Hegelians and ex-Hegelians, into a position of extreme opposition to anything that was already in existence. In Hegel's countless progeny this notion of a 'final synthesis' was held by all those on the Left, all those, that is, whose interpretation of Hegel's ideas made them reject rather than affirm the established order. After 1848, the most influential Western revolutionaries were Marx and Proudhon: the latter's insistence that history was the accomplishment of an *élite* group, not the outcome of blind economic forces, was taken up by the two chief Russian dissident thinkers of the period, Herzen and Bakunin, who thus opposed the early Marx.

Hegel's splendidly supple rhetoric, the majestic progression of his abstract structures, created a framework of relations but gave no clue as to the relationship of specific social factors. This gave a maximum of latitude to his numerous interpreters; in Russia they were free to cast about for various social elements to play the roles allotted them in the great cosmic drama outlined so abstractly by Hegel. Bakunin's fabulous energies were consumed in his progressive quest for different agents of the World Spirit in its contemporary phase: peasants, sovereigns, political movements, and finally small groups of plotters. Herzen switched back and forth between Paris, the Russian peasantry and Tsar Alexander II before losing heart altogether, in the 1860s.

It can be seen that the interaction between social disaffection and literary activity was singularly dense; perhaps one of the most striking things about it was its matter-of-factness. For the Russian thinkers who had become emancipated during the 1840s the role played by artists, especially literary artists, was unique. Even a literary critic like Belinsky could achieve a position of authority simply by writing about the function of art, since it was generally taken for granted, in harmony with the temper of the romantic movement, that the artist was the wonder-worker and the critic, perhaps, the priest of the upheaval in values that went by the name of romanticism.

In contrast with the Enlightenment, with its faith in the viability of patient investigation and rational explanation of all phenomena, truth was felt to be immanent in the nature of things and beyond rational apprehension; it could be perceived best by the exercise of intuition and best expressed in art. It was up to the romantic artist, in fact, to intuit the essence of national identity and convey it to his audience through the medium of poetry or some other art.

Conceived of in this sense art was, of course, a divine activity. Schelling himself had defined philosophy as a form of poetry – a 'higher' form, of course – and considered philosophic speculation to be closely akin to poetic inspiration. In consequence there was never a sharp divorce in the Russian thought of the nineteenth century between the two pursuits of literature and socio-political activity, or between philosophy and the arts in general. Because of the fusion in the minds of so many Russian thinkers between these various concepts and activities, the artist played a magical role; the quintessence of his art was a way of expressing the quintessence of his nation.

Belinsky's reputation as a critic, for instance, was a function of his fanatical devotion to the moral factor in art and life, neither of which was, of course, distinguished from the other. This anti-analytic, anti-rational approach naturally made all the arts akin as divinely inspired: poetry was the arch spanning other arts like sculpture, painting and music. A natural consequence of this was that since all artistic media were considered, by definition, to be interrelated there was no reason for an artist of one kind not to draw freely on the work of one in another.

Poetry, for some reason, was generally accorded the palm as the paramount art form, at any rate until the end of the 1830s. It was, in fact, through poetry that Russia finally caught up with the other European nations, and with the work of Pushkin especially it reached a level far ahead of anything in its own past and well up with poetic achievement anywhere. Russian literature, indeed, considered as a literature to be appreciated not only by antiquarians, archaeologists, or historians, scarcely existed at all before the beginning of the nineteenth century. Its earliest beginnings can be traced back only to the seventeenth century, to imitations of Polish imitations of French writers. Even in the middle of the eighteenth century scarcely anything existed that could be looked at with interest by anyone who was not a professional philologist, with the possible exception of the celebrated, versatile scholar and scientist Lomonosov. For the rest of the century nothing noteworthy can even be mentioned: it was at best a mere digest of something written in France, Germany or England. The writers themselves were generally teachers or translators. It was not until the early nineteenth century that Russian writers, having been provided with models taken from German or English pre-romantic literature, finally laid the foundations of contemporary Russian literature. Here, too, it was French classicism, curiously enough, that came to the fore in Pushkin's first book, which appeared in 1820.

Pushkin, with whose emergence Russian letters rose to a position of equality with the best in world literature, was himself almost wholly a product of eighteenth-century aristocratic attitudes. Just as the Decembrist conspirators may be said to have been the concluding episode in the attempts of the aristocracy to control events, so Pushkin, with contrasting success, became the model of Russian artistic expression.

In his short life of thirty-eight years his literary talents were poured into many channels – poems, plays and stories, though it was, of course, his poetry that gave him his unique position in Russian life. His most celebrated work is his novel, *Eugene Onegin*; its depiction of the life of the provincial aristocracy, with its sad ending, made it characteristic of the mainstream of Russian writing. His great poem, *The Bronze Horseman*, considered by many the greatest poem ever written in Russian, embodied the apocalyptic strain in the Russian spirit that is one of its most abiding features. Its central image, that of a deluge engulfing St Petersburg with no Noah's Ark in sight, has been found gripping by generations of Russians: its central figure, a small clerk, was also assimilated by later Russian tradition as a precursor of the 'little man' baffled by everything that happens.

Pushkin was naturally musical, both as a poet and as a man; his own poetry found a haven in the ballet, which by the 1820s had easily outdistanced every other ballet in Europe and had become the model for an art in which Russia was to achieve permanent and unique distinction.

Pushkin, killed in a casual and pointless duel, achieved instant veneration with his death: he became a national monument at once. Lermontov, a contemporary who died only several years later, attacked Pushkin's critics; in doing so he established his own pre-eminence as a poet. Lermontov, a far more sentimental craftsman than Pushkin, injected an element of emotionalism into Russian poetry that came to be reinforced by the sudden flooding of Russian literature with three great foreign names, Byron, Chateaubriand and Goethe.

The oddity of Pushkin's career is, perhaps, that he himself, though at bottom an ideally moderate, self-contained, measured, delicate, classical poet, regarded himself as a romantic and was in fact to become the utterly unchallenged incarnation of Russian artistic creativity, the Russian national spirit, and Russian romanticism. Pushkin is, of course, considered marvellously 'Russian' by foreigners, perhaps because of his untranslatability. For Russians, however, his paramount charm lies in his all-embracing universality. He established a pre-eminence, at least with respect to poetic form, that was to survive the eclipse of his artistic content through the meteoric growth of a Messianically preoccupied intelligentsia. The epoch of classical poetry symbolized by Pushkin lasted scarcely more than a decade; by the 1830s and 1840s Russian literature, despite the giant classical figure of Pushkin, had been engulfed by a torrent of Russian ethical effusiveness.

It was the triumph of Russian Messianism, in fact, buttressed by its contact with German romantic philosophy of both Schelling and Hegel, that overwhelmed literature, which from then on was to be thoroughly imbued with moral uplift. After a brief classical phase – in poetry – Russian literature was steeped in romanticism. The overriding moral purposefulness derived from an all-encompassing view of life transformed the arts, all of them tending toward the same 'large' view of mankind and Russia, into an interdependent complex that was an appendage of non-artistic ideas in general.

This interdependence or fusion of categories was to have the most fateful effect on both Russian life in general and ultimately, in the twentieth century, on the world at large, because it was just at this time, around the beginning of the nineteenth century, that Russia began to emerge with growing speed from its traditional solitude. As reflected in literature this imprint left by the Russian intelligentsia on the course of world events is reflected with remarkable vividness in the so-called

*The Modern Age Takes Root*

Portrait of A. S. Pushkin by
O. Kiprensky (1827).

Two pages from manuscripts
of works by Lermontov:
(left) The poem 'Death of a
Poet', 1837.
(right) Vadim, 1833–4.

(opposite) Portrait of Gogol
by F. A. Moller (1841).

(below) A sketch by Gogol
for the last scene of The
Revizor.

Nineteenth-century writers:
*(above left)* Leo Tolstoy.
*(above right)* Vissarion Belinsky
(1811–48), the most famous Russian
literary critic of the nineteenth century
and a pioneer of Russian radicalism.
*(left)* Turgenev.
*(opposite)* Fyodor Dostoyevsky,
painted by V. Perov in 1872.

Three city views:
(*above*) The Kremlin, by
R. Bowyder, 1815.
(*centre*) A public festival in
St Petersburg, by J. A.
Atkinson, 1812.
(*below*) The Imperial Theatre,
after B. Paterssen, 1806.

Folk print of the Napoleonic
Wars, showing a Russian
soldier defeating a Frenchman.

Russian village life in the
nineteenth century:
*(left)* A national dance, from
a coloured print by R.
Pinkerton, 1833.
*(below left)* 'In Mary's
Grove': a folk print
*(below)* A village
scene in a silhouette by
F. P. Tolstoy, *c.* 1820.

Nineteenth-century painting:
*(above left)* A. A. Ivanov: 'Christ Appearing to the People' (1837–57).
*(above right)* A. G. Venetsianov: 'Peasant Children in a Field' (*c*. 1820).
*(below)* A. A. Ivanov: 'Olive Trees near the Cemetery at Albano' (1837–57).

*(above left to right)*

K. P. Bryullov: 'The Writer N. V. Kukolnik' (1836).

O. A. Kiprensky: Self portrait (?) (1822–3).

I. E. Repin: 'Head of a Peasant', a study for 'Religious Procession' (1893).

A. G. Venetsianov: 'Peasant Girl with Calf' (*c.* 1829).

*(below)*

I. E. Repin: 'Volga Boatmen' (1872).

M. A. Vrubel: 'A Fortune
Teller' (1895).

V. I. Surikov: 'An Imbecile',
study for 'Boyarynya
Morozova' (1887).

Caricature of the composer Michael Ivanovich Glinka (1803–57), who is regarded as the father of the Russian national school of composers.

A scene from Tchaikovsky's opera *Eugen Onegin*, first produced in 1879.

The Bolshoi Theatre was rebuilt in 1856 and the photograph above shows the façade after rebuilding. The two photographs on the right show scenes from Glinka's *Russlan and Ludmilla*, which was performed there in 1890.

The Pushkin Theatre (formerly the Alexandrinsky Theatre) in St
Petersburg was designed by C. I. Rossi and built from 1828 to 1832.

The arch of the building of the former Synod and Senate, St Petersburg, built by C. I. Rossi from 1829 to 1834.

The Church of Christ the Saviour in Moscow, designed by A. K. Ton in 1839; it was destroyed during the Revolution and replaced by the Palace of Soviets.

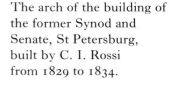

*(opposite)*
*(above)* The Academy of Fine Arts in Leningrad.
*(below)* The Museum of Russian Art in Leningrad.

The Arch of the General Staff, Leningrad, by C. I. Rossi, 1819–29.

A jewelled orange tree by Carl Fabergé.

'natural school' of literature, a striking instance of the way in which the 'two heads of Janus' – as Herzen called the Slavophil and the Westernizing tendencies in Russian idealism – were reflected in literature.

Gogol is perhaps the focal point in this 'natural school'; his early career reached its climax with a play, *The Inspector General*, which was received as a satire and has indeed enjoyed an inexhaustible reputation as one ever since. His great work, *Dead Souls*, appeared in 1842.

Significantly, *The Inspector General* appeared in the same year – 1836 – as Glinka's *Life for the Tsar*, now played in the Soviet Union in our own day as *Ivan Susanin*, and Bryullov's great painting, *The Last Days of Pompeii*, which served as the inspiration of Bulwer-Lytton's work of the same name.

Gogol's sense of mission, not to say megalomania, came to a head after Pushkin's death in 1837; with the appearance of *Dead Souls* in 1842 he became one of the towering figures in the sparsely settled world of Russian letters; praise of his work made him feel that he must do something absolutely fabulous in order to live up to his own fame. In the decade that followed he conceived a vast masterpiece that he could never complete. He felt called upon to create positive heroes, yet was incapable of transcending his own lyrical phantasy; some think that Gogol's obsession with ugliness and disfigurement – perhaps a reflection of his own self-absorption – was what inspired an equal obsession, unrealizable, with perfection: when he concluded that one had to be perfect in order to write about perfection, there was, clearly, no longer any goal he could attain, and he died, apparently disappointed and in misery, at the age of forty-three. Gogol's reputation, of course, was due to its 'interpretation' by critics, an adjunct of literature wielding even more authority in Russian than elsewhere. To an outsider it seems obvious that Gogol was for personal reasons a wholly detached alien in Russian life; his personal oddities, coupled with his remarkable lyrical gifts, enabled him to see Russia with a sort of comic quirkiness and whimsical extravagance. It really made his work essentially a phantasy, with the 'realism' he made use of no more than a background.

The talkative critic Belinsky, however, saw in Gogol's work something

9

that Gogol himself had never even dreamed of beforehand. With singular capriciousness and a sort of tendentious wrong-headedness, Belinsky interpreted Gogol's phantasies as social satire. He explained that the real point of Gogol's writing was not at all what it seemed to be, but was, in fact, quite different: it had a social 'message'. In reality, of course, Gogol's backgrounds, though realistic in some sense – in fact, precisely in the sense that there was no message at all in them – were essentially backdrops for his exuberant phantasy. The amusing part of this interaction between dedicated critic and improvising artist is that Gogol himself, very simpleminded as a person, was completely bamboozled by Belinsky: both Gogol and his contemporary audience became convinced that Gogol was a satirist of the existing order. In the middle of the 1850s he was considered a 'realist', and since the realities he was thought to be describing were obviously not very desirable, the message they contained was held to be one of socio-political dissidence.

It generally came to be agreed, among the increasingly fervent intellectuals of the mid-nineteenth century, that literature had to convey some tremendous earth-shaking truth; with this, when classical poetry yielded to prose as the accepted hub of Russian literature, the formal calm of Pushkin and his school evaporated. Writers cast about for something that would turn them into preachers; of course they succeeded, since with the stewing up of all ideas, arts, and intellectual tendencies in one cauldron of social purposiveness it was easy for a writer with any intellectual interests to become persuaded of a special mission.

Technically, to be sure, it must be recalled that aside from its actual ideational and purposive content, Russian prose owes most of its formal character to the French tradition once again, more particularly Boileau, Molière, and La Fontaine, the ultimate models of the famous Russian fabulists Krylov and Griboyedov, author of the celebrated classic *Woe from Wit* (1825).

It was the Russian realistic novel, the most massive product of the 'natural school' in literature, that not only dominated Russian literature as a whole until the twentieth century was well advanced, but also won it a place in world literature that in view of the comparatively meagre output it is embodied in can hardly fail to be amazing. When one thinks that Russian literature, insofar as it has had an effect on the outside world, is summed up by a bare half-dozen names, which are nevertheless regarded as the counterpart of the immensely rich literatures of England, France and Germany, it is clear that quantity has more than been made up for by quality.

The interplay between politics and art is splendidly illustrated in just this rise of the Russian realistic novel, for it was Belinsky's savagely one-sided interpretation of Gogol, an interpretation that to our eyes must look rather silly, that made Gogol a sort of pattern for the Russian novelists who emerged later on. If, as most people think, there is something to be said for Turgenev's witticism that all Russian novelists have, after all, emerged from under Gogol's *Mantle*, it is largely thanks to the purely socio-political axe-grinding of Belinsky, who thus may be said to have shaped a substantial segment of world literature.

The realistic novel that Russia became famous for was, despite superficial variations, essentially one literary school. Its hallmarks were a relative indifference to action in favour of character-portrayal, an aversion to style for its own sake, and the moral 'commitment' – to use a later word for the same thing – that the whole of the literature was steeped in. The impression of 'profundity' that most foreigners associated with Russian literature – which often implies, to be sure, a synonym for tediousness – is surely due to the single-minded absorption of Russian writers with the analysis of character. The reality of human beings is intended to come through the written medium undistracted by the superficialities of mere entertainment. Style as such was rather disdained, perhaps as a consequence of the authentic milieu that Russian novelists, following Belinsky's misunderstanding of Gogol, took such pains to describe. Between Gogol and the much later Symbolists, linguistic ornamentation, which in other literatures has often been a basic ingredient of stylistic distinction, was substantially lacking. Even Turgenev, considered to be a stylist *par excellence*, never revels in style for its own sake.

There is a slight confluence here between the Messianic purposefulness stemming from the social commitment of the latter-day Hegelians and ex-Hegelians, among them primarily Belinsky, and a classical

spareness of style inherited not so much from the poetry as from the
prose of the two poets, Pushkin and Lermontov. The classical school, too,
that is, contributed an essential element of 'realism' to the prose novel,
even as it went overboard into a romantic preoccupation with ethics.

The Russian obsession with the details of life, insofar as they bore on
the fundamental dilemmas of society as a whole, very naturally forbade
any stylistic fripperies, which in the face of the great commitment to
larger purposes would have seemed mere frivolity. In any case, even if
a writer had felt the urge to indulge himself in a mere *décor* he would
have been very quickly rapped over the knuckles by the literary critics,
whose role in Russia was, and has remained quite disproportionate.

Foreign influences remained cardinal in the genesis of Russian
literature; especially France, which until the Russian Revolution itself
in 1917 remained the major model for Russian creativity. Though
Dickens was widely read before the middle of the nineteenth century,
he was not generally imitated. The idols for a long generation were at
first George Sand, then Balzac; Stendhal, too, acquired a following,
chiefly in the overwhelming figure of Tolstoy, who self-consciously took
over lock, stock, and barrel Stendhal's celebrated method of literary
analysis as a way of creating and conveying character.

The first Russian novelist to make an impression on world opinion
was doubtless Turgenev, born in 1818, who for a long time was far
more celebrated than any other Russian writer, with the exception of
Tolstoy and Dostoyevsky. Later these two came to outshine him both in
Russia and abroad; the zenith of Russian literary celebrity is often
associated with their names.

It was, of course, Tolstoy and Dostoyevsky who are considered not only
the unquestioned giants of world literature – to borrow a critic's locution
– but also the most characteristic of Russian literature as such and of the
Russian obsession with the problems of existence. Though unlike each
other in most ways, they were both obsessed by God and death. In
Dostoyevsky the strong psychopathic element comes through unadorned
even by a concession to competent as distinct from fine writing: style is
almost wholly meaningless to him. Tolstoy's rather eccentric basic
personality is completely overlaid by a powerful mind and an affecta-

tion of rationalism that while seldom wholly concealing the turbulence beneath enables his analytic or polemical approach to both art and society to achieve an effective form.

It is of course possible to disentangle the various strands present in the prose of both writers; but it can be done only by disregarding the effective fusion in both of them between their fundamental concerns and their artistic performances. One is scarcely aware of the art at all – an obvious tribute to its success. The density of this fusion between interest and execution is what gives their work an intense effect of reality: some people may find this intensity tedious, to be sure, but perhaps only because so many people do not wish to confront an explicit tussle with reality.

The preoccupation with the ultimate 'point' of life, all-encompassing in Tolstoy, is even more striking, if possible, in the work of Dostoyevsky.

Dostoyevsky's obsession with 'ultimate' themes is still more passionate, since in spite of his immense energy and remarkable creativity as a portraitist of character he was fundamentally, perhaps exclusively a moralist, a 'world-wrestler'. This vital philosophic role of Dostoyevsky, the reason he has had such influence on the formation of Russian thought to this day, may come as a surprise to Western readers, who often look upon him as a 'mere' creative writer. Yet Dostoyevsky not merely questioned the ultimate Why & How of the universe, within a more or less philosophical framework, but also plumbed the depths of his own nature and thus of human nature in general. In his relentless self-analysis and self-torture Dostoyevsky was an existentialist before his time, a foreshadowing of the modern anguish with the condition of man.

Dostoyevsky himself thought of all his novels as projections of his tussle with the universe, which was, indeed, the only reason he thought them important. Because of his intense self-preoccupation he represents a peak in the alienation, or self-isolation that emerged during the nineteenth century and may surely be regarded as a hallmark of serious literature ever since. His use of a diary as a literary medium, for instance, has a compelling inner logic: perhaps his most effective impersonation in literature is that conveyed by the first person singular: his atonements, confessions, self-accusations and so on. Diaries for Dostoyevsky were no mere casual recordings of events; they were a summons to his readers to reconsider themselves and their lives.

Dostoyevsky began his career as a 'Westernizer', and was in fact exiled to Siberia as a member of the 'Petrashevsky group', a coterie devoted to the ideas of the French visionary Fournier, which was smothered by police action in 1849. Dostoyevsky had been given a lengthy court martial and sentenced to death, and was actually waiting on the scaffold to be hanged when reprieved – after a deliberate delay – by Nicholas I. He spent a decade in Siberia; during his long-drawn-out ordeal he became a changed man. Aside from the shattering of his nervous system and an intensification of the epilepsy he was plagued by all his life, he became obsessed with religion, more particularly with the figure of Christ. He identified himself ecstatically with Christ as a dazzling, remote and inaccessible symbol of the ultimate saintliness of man: as he said in a letter from Siberia: 'If Christ is not all truth, I prefer to be with Christ against truth than with truth against Christ'. He abandoned all his previous political interests; the ensuing void was filled with an ardent love of some unattainable absolute.

Yet this absolute was nevertheless soon incarnated by Dostoyevsky in an earthbound manifestation, for he came to the conclusion that Christ was incarnate in the Russian 'people', i.e., the peasantry, thus he was led to adopt a form of sentimental Slavophilism, in other words to come back to politics after all. Yet in spite of his involvement in 'national' themes he retains immense topicality even today because of his success in fusing those themes, together with his own psychic excessiveness – generally taken to be 'typically Russian' – with a broader passion for the soul of man.

In the case of Tolstoy, even before his conversion, around 1880, to his own peculiar variety of primitive Christianity, the whole of his increasingly tormented personality, even during his most purely artistic phase, was completely immersed in his preoccupation with grasping the essence of 'reality'. When he abandoned art, at least self-avowed art, after his conversion, his obsession became even more explicitly, and finally wholly, didactic. By this time, of course, he had already become a world institution.

Tolstoy was singular not only because of his talent or his impact on literature, but because of his unusual social origins. While, of course, the intelligentsia was intimately linked with many aristocratic individuals, as a whole it remained, socially speaking, to one side of the aristocracy as a class. Tolstoy, however, received a purely aristocratic education, and in fact never had anything to do with intellectuals proper at all. Though he encountered some while he was at the university, he generally avoided them then and later. Though Tolstoy entangled himself with the problems of life, death and meaning, the only point of view he was ever capable of even acknowledging was his own, that is, that of a unique individual. This is, of course, in its unquestioning self-assurance an aristocratic attitude; in Tolstoy's case it meant that as far as he was concerned the only social categories that meant anything were first himself, then mankind at large. In practice this reduced itself to the peasantry, whom he saw not so much idealistically – he knew peasant life intimately – as religiously; the virtues he chose to attribute to the peasants, not individually but collectively, were the primordial human virtue of love, and the primordial religious virtue of humility.

Despite the simplicity of his writing, Tolstoy was a remarkable stylist: the simplicity is far from accidental. Yet though in this respect he was a consummate literary artist, preoccupied in his own way, indeed, with the problems of literary style, he was possibly the least 'literary' of all Russian writers. He was really a gentleman of independent means; writing was a hobby. That it was a hobby of fundamental importance for him and for the world at large was in a way an accident due to the sheer capaciousness and passion of his personality and to his energetic disposition. Social life irritated or bored him, and he lived like a country gentleman. He was busy simply with raising a family, improving the management of his estates, and seeing the few gentlemen he regarded as friends. Artistically speaking, he wrote only about peasants and aristocrats, for him, evidently, the only real people. The odd reference to middle-class people or situations indicates only the immense distance from which he viewed them.

If one makes an attempt to free oneself from the spell of his literary powers, it would seem clear that Tolstoy's personal role is deeply embedded in his aristocratic position in society; it gave his writing a unique flavour, all the more marked after his religious conversion turned him into something far beyond a mere writer. Tolstoy became a sort of prophet, carrying his own revelation to mankind at large from out of the depths of his personal malaise, transmuted by suffering and thought into a racial paradigm of an existential ordeal. His place in world literature is of course impregnable, yet in Russian literature it is unique, combining as it does the chief features of the intelligentsia's commitment to passion-plus-purpose.

Tolstoy's conversion to primitive Christianity is an illuminating example of his individual approach. Preoccupied, on the rational level, by the need to discover just what in Christianity could be claimed to be unique, his starting-point was bound to be Christianity in spite of his dislike of the Orthodox Church. Tolstoy embarked on a study of both Greek and Hebrew, hoping to penetrate back to the beginnings of the religion in order to disentangle its characteristic message from later accretions.

In lengthy discussions with the then Grand Rabbi of Moscow, Tolstoy was presented with a close parallel in rabbinical Jewish literature to every remark attributed to Jesus in the Four Gospels, but when he in his turn presented the Grand Rabbi with the celebrated saying of Jesus – 'Resist not evil by force' – the rabbi was forced to concede a point: there was no strict parallel to this in Judaism.

Thus, on the rational level, Tolstoy felt he had won a debate, and it was, in fact, to this one remark that he reduced the totality of Christianity, dismissing all basic Christian ideas – the Incarnation, the Resurrection, the Redemption, the sacraments, the Church itself – as so much superfluous fancifulness.

This one remark attributed to Jesus coincided, very curiously, with Tolstoy's suppression in himself of certain of his own traits – namely, cruelty and brutality; he realized that these must, after all, be subordinated to love, just because he knew how strongly marked within him these traits were. This is graphically demonstrated by *Anna Karenina*, in which, when the character representing himself, Lyovin, is told by a peasant that some other peasant is a good man who does not gouge people's eyes out – if they owe him money and can't pay he gives them a few extra days – Lyovin leaps to his feet in uncontrollable excitement at this revelation that it is possible to live that way – not to gouge people's eyes out!

This comes at a point in Tolstoy's novelistic description of that stage in his life when he is preoccupied with the basic question that obsessed him and so many other Russians – 'How to live'. The fusion in Tolstoy of these two approaches, the personal-psychological and the religious-historical, led to Tolstoy's stripped-down, purely ethical Christianity, to his campaign against violence in all things, and very directly, curiously enough, to Mahatma Gandhi's own celebrated movement of 'passive resistance'. It must be regarded as one of the few crystal-clear instances of an individual's effect on history: Tolstoy's lonely self-preoccupation ultimately made him, in this round-about way, a potent political force.

Russian literature began making an enormous impact on the world towards the end of the nineteenth century; Tolstoy and Dostoyevsky were instantly accepted as geniuses, and an interest sprang up in Russian letters that has never died down. With Chekhov in the early twentieth century, however, its great, classical period may be thought of as over. At least the golden age of the Russian realistic novel may be said to have ended in the 1880s, with Dostoyevsky's death in 1881 and Turgenev's in 1883. From a purely literary point of view Tolstoy's conversion meant that his talents, applied to his prophetic mission, were lost to literature proper.

The effervescence that had begun among the nascent intelligentsia even during the police-reign of Nicholas I had repercussions throughout the domain of spiritual pursuits. In other arts, too, Russia started sending off sparks.

It was doubtless painting that was most directly affected by the Messianic effervescence and spiritual questing and confusion of the mid-nineteenth century. It was, after all, easier to portray attitudes toward ideas and states of mind in painting, a more tangible medium than music or architecture. Russian painting was always inextricably intertwined with literature; there were many intimate friendships between painters and writers and on occasion an exchange of roles, even though painting never made the same impression either on the world outside Russia or on the life of the intelligentsia.

A splendid illustration of this curious interaction between artistic expression and 'ideas' may be seen in the work of Gogol's contemporary Alexander Ivanov, whom Gogol himself, in his growing and perhaps psychopathic despair about himself, Russia, life, God and the Meaning of It All, regarded as the embodiment of all his hopes.

Ivanov, born into a secure position as the son of St Petersburg's leading academic painter, was so disturbed by the quest of Russian thinkers for some novel, arresting, and hope-giving message involving prophetic upheaval of world values, that he spent a quarter of a century working on a painting he meant to revolutionize all life. Called *The Appearance of Christ to the People*, it represented the application of titanic energies to the solution of a problem that was, of course, quite insoluble.

As a young man of twenty, when Nicholas I was crowned, Ivanov had been inflamed at the prospect of a renovation of the epoch: he thought a new age was dawning in which Russian art would play a seminal and indispensable role. To his mind, in fact, the artist bore a far greater responsibility than the political leader, since the very fate of mankind depended on the development of his potentialities.

After studying classical and Renaissance art with great intensity, he devoted himself more and more to Biblical themes; he attempted to translate into oils the subject-matter of the heroic sculptural and architectural manner of the early nineteenth century. By the end of his thirties he was ready for the *magnum opus* of his life, the celebrated Christ; but – in a way that was perhaps typical of Russian extremism – he gradually became enthralled by the delusion that there was no point in his even trying to depict Christ unless he became Christ, which unquestionably increased the difficulty of his technical problem. In growing despair over the unattainability of his self-appointed task he ultimately took an altogether different way out of the impasse: he became a Russian patriot, and chose to see in the unfolding of Russia's inevitable destiny the only hope for the regeneration of mankind.

His most famous painting was, of course, a failure, apart from its interest to the historian and its technical ability, since the depiction of God in man has, after all, been altogether beyond any artistic medium; Ivanov's final 'humanizing' of the Christ merely resulted in an attempt to portray human suffering that was made abortive by the confusion of trying to make the human simultaneously divine. This painting has an element of irony in it, when the lengthy incubation period – twenty-five years! – is recalled, since the picture itself completely subordinates Jesus, demurely remote in the background, to both the figure of John the Baptist, powerfully dominating the foreground, and a whole cluster of worldly figures.

Ivanov finally tried to reconcile art, life and Russia by a sort of portmanteau idea of having 'public artists' buttressing the universal rule of the Russian throne, venerated at 'temples of humanity'.

Ivanov illustrates the matter-of-factness with which such a quest – for the founding of a new religion – could be embarked on by any practitioner of the arts. In an epoch when ideas had to be all-encompassing and suffused with ethical content, any artist could without an appearance of embarrassing irrelevance don the mantle of world-prophet.

Both Gogol and Ivanov made a pilgrimage to Rome, at the time, under Nicholas I, when a romantic longing for exotically significant places became a commonplace among artists. There they both devoted themselves to an exploration of the same focal themes. Both men were convinced that somehow or other Russia must give the world spiritual redemption. They were both enthralled by the need to finish a 'major work', which in fact was never completed. Both were, finally, a little deranged, also quite indifferent to women; they both died prematurely, apparently by their own hands.

It may of course well be that the very reason for the special role assigned to painting in the development of general themes laid a heavy mortgage on the medium itself; if tendency was the order of the day, and painting technique was merely subordinated to the need for conveying a 'message', it was, perhaps, hampered from the point of view of innovation; the result was a certain stagnation.

Because of this, painting, despite the talent of various individuals, made a far less dramatic advance than the other artistic media. The pseudo-classical tradition was safeguarded by the Academy of Arts, which clung to a position of authority until the 1860s, when a younger generation successfully contested its pre-eminence. At a moment when realism, or some form of it, was inundating literature, the only themes thought worthy of art were exclusively Biblical, allegorical or mythological subjects, or at the least historical subjects 'illustrating' certain ideas. Only upper-class surroundings were depicted, as far as Russia itself was concerned, or, in the domain of romantic projection, bucolic invocations of 'sunny Italy'. In painting, curiously enough, with few exceptions, notably Alexis Venetsianov (1780–1847) the originator of Russian genre painting and the first to introduce, for instance, true peasant life onto the canvas (in the first third of the nineteenth century), no Russian theme was tolerated unless it was romanticized beyond all reality.

This was made all the easier since most Russian painters were trained abroad, particularly in Italy. What that meant in practice was a concentration on a servile imitation of the Renaissance, which together with antiquity became an object of cultic veneration for the Russian intelligentsia as a whole, especially in the arts, where the technical excellence of Renaissance talent made the authoritativeness of the models almost suffocating. The Society for the Encouragement of Artists, founded in 1822, remained in the grip of academic routine for almost the whole of the nineteenth century.

Because of these factors Russian painting, from the technical point of view, remained scarcely more than a reflection of Western European standards, though it is true that after the Crimean War painters too were moved by the general fever that infected the country. The artistic movement resulting from the new fabric of ideas, previously represented mainly by Ivanov, though in his day there was no question of a changing technique as distinct from content, now culminated in a general revolt.

The opposition that had long been simmering quietly against the Academy of Art's identification with the pseudo-classical tradition exploded in 1863, when the whole of the graduating class ostentatiously boycotted the traditional contest for a painting prize to be awarded a painting on a conventional theme; the dissident artists, slightly organized, broke away from the academy, founding the Association of Free Artists; this later broke up, leading to the establishment in 1870 of the Society of Circulating Exhibitions, which endured until the 1917 revolution.

The social involvement that had always been a hallmark of Russian intellectual life throughout the century now inundated Russian painting too; the Messianic fury that had inspired the arts now expressed itself in painting in the form of a social commitment taken over *in toto* from literature.

The social-message theory of literature achieved its grossest expression in the latter half of the nineteenth century, when the youthful insurgents against academic tradition began a systematic attack on all the old masters as a matter of principle. The radical wing developed the theory that the audience for a work of art had itself to be changed; they began aiming their work at the 'toiling masses', though these, of course, seldom appeared at openings. Because of this extravagant addiction to the concept of the primacy of the 'social content' of a work of art – theory that reached a sort of grotesque perfection after the revolution, with the installation of the Stalin régime – all questions of technical ability were regarded as subsumed under the general rubric of the 'message'. This entailed a total subordination of the medium to the idea, which in the event, of course, was bound to be an idea that came from somewhere else and was more or less artificially transplanted into the medium itself.

Even Ilya Repin, without question the most celebrated of all Russian realistic painters, not only because of his remarkable talents but because of an unusually long life (1844–1930), is of interest to art-lovers nowadays primarily as an example of sociological themes. Beginning as a prize-winner in the Imperial Academy of Arts in the 1860s, Repin had a successful career during the short-lived period of liberal democracy, and even managed to survive with favour into the Soviet era, though he personally left the country. The Soviet régime, indeed, because of the general penury of Russian culture and the failure of the Russian people to produce a flood of artistic innovations, was bound to make do with as many artistic monuments of Tsarist Russia as it could, simply in order to provide the government with some artistic props. Repin's career had been so long and productive that it was quite easy to find in his work enough illustrations of the hortatory motif that the Soviet régime came to be characterized by. He became a sort of godfather of the monumental, didactic themes of Soviet art, though in his own work his gift for realistic portrayal had been in the service of very general tendencies quite independent of the specific goals imposed on art by the needs of Soviet propaganda.

Fascinated like so many Russians by historical themes, Repin had given blood-curdlingly realistic portrayals of some of the climactic events in Russian history, as in his painting of Ivan the Terrible holding in his arms the son he had murdered. Repin was, of course, more than an objective portraitist; in his painting of Ivan the Terrible, for instance, the whole painting is thoroughly sentimentalized in the direction of general human tragedy by Repin's insistence on injecting an expression of grief into Ivan's face; the son's face is modelled on that of a friend of Repin's, the writer Vsevolod Garshin, thought by many contemporaries to resemble Jesus.

Repin's portraits were not merely celebrated; they actually perpetuated and fixed themes and memories in the minds of a whole people, so that Tolstoy, for instance, would be visualized primarily through Repin's famous portrait of him dressed as a barefooted peasant. Invaluable as a piece of propaganda for Tolstoy's own version of himself, the remarkably insinuating realism of Repin's technique helped fix this particular image of Tolstoy in the public mind to this day.

So too an equally famous painting of Repin's, his *Haulers on the Volga* (1870–3) became prototypical of the Russian flood of sentimentality in the latter half of the nineteenth century on behalf of the suffering Russian people. Repin's portrait of the Volga boatmen, intensely moving in its apparently simplistic portrayal of primordial human patience under suffering, inevitably became a part of the cult of the people that served the populist movement as an axis for its ideas. The painting was so powerful that it inspired Moussorgsky, whom Repin also painted in an equally famous and enduring piece of work, to create a whole new musical edifice out of chants from his birthplace on the Volga.

Repin's career also illustrates, in a rather less demented way, the Russian predilection shown by Ivanov in his quest for some all-embracing theme. Russian artists – writers, painters and musicians alike – have often felt they had to create one single masterpiece whose redemptive effect would be shattering. Repin's *Haulers on the Volga* was only one attempt at a redemptive masterpiece. Repin was obsessed, from 1878 to 1891, with the great theme in *The Zaporozhian Cossacks Write a Letter to the Turkish Sultan*. Here he managed to find a fusion of two different kinds of idea: on the one hand, the combination of a given historical incident with a genre technique; on the other, two different kinds of political identification – the elegiac treatment of Cossack liberties, endearing the painting to the hearts of a variety of Russian revolutionaries, and a simple-minded patriotism that enabled all sorts of conservatives, pan-Slavic expansionists, etc., to rejoice in the defiance of the Turks.

A curious development of the themes of the 'divine' and the 'demonic' can be seen much later on, toward the end of the century, in the work of two quite different painters, Nicholas Ge, a great associate of Tolstoy in the sort of artistic co-existence familiar to Russian intellectual life, and Michael Vrubel. One of Ge's greatest paintings is a complete antithesis to Ivanov's conception of Jesus, as indeed it was to all previous conceptions of Jesus in Russian art. Ge's *Crucifixion*, painted in 1891, shows a far-reaching abandonment of all divine elements in Jesus; in a deliberately crude, indeed almost cartoon-like sketch of an utterly worn-out Jesus, being looked at with some consternation by one of the thieves, an impression of either satire or despair on the part of the artist is irresistibly conveyed.

Towards the end of imperial Russia the influence of Michael Vrubel was quite remarkable, not only on painting but on poets and composers. Vrubel had begun as a technician in the restoration of church frescoes and mosaics, but his imagination was soon deflected from the traditional preoccupation of the Church toward a celebration of the mysteries of mundane beauty, culminating in a lifelong obsession with the figure who became his hero – Satan. The whole gamut of romanticism was made use of by him to consecrate his feelings of awe and fascination with the Devil; towards the end of his career to extend the medium of oil painting to do justice to his inner fancies led him, in his famous painting of *The Demon Prostrate*, done in 1902, when he underwent his mental collapse, to resort to the European influences of *art nouveau* and expressionism – in a slightly wild development of the semi-cubist backgrounds of his *Demon*, done in 1890–1.

It was doubtless in music, next to literature, that Russia marked itself out in the nineteenth century in an historically novel manner.

Hitherto Russian music had been something of an unknown quantity, since not many transcriptions of folk-music, the principal Russian contribution before the middle of the nineteenth century, had been available. The Russian Church had made no use of instrumental music, and since religious music had been insulated against secular influence as much as possible, instrumental music had no leeway in which to develop. Throughout much of the nineteenth century there had been little music in St Petersburg or Moscow; only private persons could learn anything from their own tutors, who were mostly foreigners.

It was not until the late 1830s that Russia developed any operatic or concert music. The native composers, who had begun by writing down vocal music, remained predominant until the late nineteenth century, when instrumental music overtook and passed vocal music.

In the eighteenth century, to be sure, a great influx of foreign composers, largely Italian, had begun flooding St Petersburg; by the time of Catherine the Great a 'Russo-Italian' style had evolved; this combination of native Russian material with foreign forms has also been called 'St Petersburg musical baroque'.

This 'Russo-Italian' style may be said to have culminated in Catterino Albertovich Cavos, considered the founder of Russian opera. Cavos arrived in Russia after the death of Catherine the Great, to work in the imperial theatre: his most successful work was an opera in two acts, *Ivan Susanin*; this may be taken as representative of the tendency toward the historical opera he thus implanted in Russia. Cavos was also the father of another principal operatic current in Russia, the 'fairy-tale' opera, with the *Fire-Bird* (1822) and *Dobrynya Nikitich* (1818).

The prototype of Cavos's style was Russianized somewhat more by A. N. Verstovsky (1799–1862), whose most successful opera was *Askold's Tomb*. This was the first work to attempt to characterize each personage in the actual composition; it also stressed the Russian motif, as an application in music of genre painting.

The ripening of Russian symphonic music is inevitably associated with the work of Michael Glinka (1804–57), who succeeded in implanting symphonism within the confines of the operatic medium, in his overture to *Ruslan and Lyudmila*, and later on in the form of impressionistic genre compositions, such as the symphonic phantasies, *Jota Arragonese* (1845) and *Remembrance of a Summer Night in Madrid* (1849–50). These last two works not only started a sort of mania for Spanish motifs in Russian music, but even exercized an influence on Debussy's *Iberia*. Glinka's masterpiece is often considered to be the Russian genre symphony *Kamarinskaya* (1848) which with its combination of two folk melodies, a wedding and a dance tune, and its use of some mannerisms of folk-singing, created a sort of 'singing game'.

Glinka's work, with its application of European techniques acquired during his studies in Italy, France, and Germany, to the folk-themes he had been familiar with in childhood, was an unusual combination of technical musical competence, originality, and talent. An opera, *A Life for the Tsar* (now played in the Soviet Union as *Ivan Susanin*), in the patriotic historical style started by Cavos, together with *Ruslan and Lyudmila*, which continues Cavos's fairy-tale genre, were, however, received somewhat coldly; Glinka was too discouraged to write any others. *A Life for the Tsar* was nevertheless integrated with operatic repertory because of its patriotic motif, though aristocratic audiences tended to look down their noses at it as 'coachman's music'.

A. S. Dargomyzhsky (1813–69) was considered the arch-realist in Russian music; he was an exponent of the Spanish mania initiated by Glinka's work, illustrated by his greatest work, *The Stone Guest*, whose libretto was taken from Pushkin's 'little tragedy', *Don Juan*.

Dargomyzhsky, called a 'musical portrait artist', was the first to introduce the downright grotesque into Russian music. He succeeded in mastering the lyrico-dramatic aria, in the *Rusalka* (The Mermaid,

1856): he turned away from the inspiration derived from Italian melody, unlike Glinka, and took up the arietta of the French *opéra-comique*. Some critics considered this opera marred by a hybrid style, and for that matter a rather hybrid libretto, a grab-bag of fairy-tale motifs grotesquely intermingled with modish social protest characteristic of the period. Dargomyzhsky, aware of the unsuccessfully heterogeneous mixture, attempted to correct it in his operatic work; he replaced the disparate elements of opera, full of ballets, choruses, recitatives, and arias, by a continuous line of melodic declamation, providing a recitative that could satisfy any demand imposed by the libretto. *The Stone Guest*, based on melodic declamation, was considered a great success with its emotionally faithful style, in sharp contrast to Wagner, who attempted much the same thing but failed.

It is Glinka, however, who must be looked upon as the most seminal influence in Russian nineteenth-century music: practically every composer can be traced back to his work, and even though Russian music was to bound forward after him, like so much else that was taking place in Russia during that period, Glinka remained a prototype of Russianism.

In 1859 a Russian Music Society was founded; this brought about an upheaval in musical standards. It set up branches in Moscow and dozens of other cities, and supported the establishment of conservatories in the two capitals and music schools in many centres. Symphony orchestras were supported and concerts and recitals by both Russians and foreigners were all generously helped. The Music Society was very successful; it was the handiwork of Anton Rubinstein (1821–94), a prolific composer as well as a famous piano virtuoso.

In the 1860s a coterie of exceptionally talented composers made a more or less simultaneous appearance: known as the 'Mighty Handful' or 'The Five', they aspired to follow in Dargomyzhsky's footsteps: Modest Moussorgsky, M. A. Balakirev, N. A. Rimsky-Korsakov, A. P. Borodin and Cesar Cui. Perhaps more important as a pedagogue, it was Balakirev who first brought The Five together; he also founded, together with Lomakin, the Free Music School in 1862, in an effort to promote musical education in a non-academic way.

Moussorgsky was considered the most advanced and most consistent heir of Dargomyzhsky's realism, also the most extreme product of Balakirev's independent school.

Balakirev's speciality was the composition of incidental music for the drama, more especially an expressive, concentrated kind of overture inherited from Glinka. His incidental music for *King Lear*, which he defined as 'instrumental drama', initiated a tendency in Russian music that culminated in the 'theatre without a stage', represented by symphonies like Tchaikovsky's *Romeo and Juliet* and *The Tempest*.

Rimsky-Korsakov, who leaned on Western European music wherever possible and owed a great deal to Berlioz, took a different direction: he was not interested in the instrumental drama, but in genre and landscape symphonies. He liked Liszt, too.

Borodin, whose energetic brightness is often contrasted, in a conventional manner, with the emotionality of Tchaikovsky, was best known as a genre symphonist. His best-known instrumental work is the symphonic tableau, *In Central Asia*. In opera, Borodin carried on Glinka's style in his only opera, *Prince Igor*, which was much praised as conveying a pagan sense of the joy of life, appropriately enough, since it is about pagans.

It was, in fact, opera in general that was the forte of The Five, except for Balakirev; even the most striking effects of the symphonists are contained within an operatic framework, such as the genre and landscape episodes of Rimsky-Korsakov's opera *Sadko*, and the entire score of *Coq d'Or*, considered his masterpiece of orchestral coloration.

Moussorgsky was perhaps the most extreme exponent of the already radical Dargomyzhsky; he never wrote music as a mere accompaniment of the emotions: his melodies were contrived to depict the actual emotions. He developed a remarkable virtuosity in recitative, unsurpassed in Russia: he was constantly searching for more and more outlandish situations and characters to write his recitatives for. His masterpiece is doubtless *Boris Godunov*, which is pure grand opera, though it contains a number of realistic portraits.

The last member of *The Five*, Cesar Cui, known as a 'water-colourist' and a 'miniaturist', wrote grand operas in a style that was generally conceded to be dainty and elegant; eventually he settled down to the composition of drawing-room music.

Generally speaking The Five all believed composers ought to use a national background as a source of inspiration; they were all fond of folk-songs and popular songs, and generally hostile to the classical school and to Italian operas; they were also, of course, violently opposed to Wagner, who was the chief rival to their all-encompassing aims. It was, indeed, fear of his influence, after a visit he made to St Petersburg in 1862–3, that had been the specific impetus for the organization of the Mighty Handful as a group.

It is curious to recall that only Balakirev, of the Mighty Handful, was a trained professional: of the others Cui was a general in the Army Engineers; Moussorgsky a Guards officer, later a government functionary; Borodin was a chemistry professor; Rimsky-Korsakov a naval officer. The group disintegrated fairly soon: after the 1860s each took an independent course. The Russian symphonic school is generally considered the creation of Balakirev and Borodin; the trio of famous operas, Moussorgsky's *Boris Godunov*, Borodin's *Prince Igor*, and Rimsky-Korsakov's *Coq d'Or* are world-famous.

Their most famous contemporaries were Anton Rubinstein and Peter Ilyich Tchaikovsky, his pupil. Rubinstein's original work puts him in the line leading from Mendelssohn; his most successful composition is conceded to be the *Ocean* symphony. It was Rubinstein who began to assimilate the principles underlying the sonata-symphony, Tchaikovsky who carried it to a successful conclusion. Tchaikovsky wrote two celebrated '*pathétiques*', one of which – the Sixth Symphony – was an advanced piece of music in the most sophisticated European style. Though critics, and to a far lesser extent the knowledgeable public, have occasionally made derogatory comments on Tchaikovsky's 'sentimentality', it is, in a way, a counterpart of Chekhov's literary work; a sort of twilight yearning corresponding to something in the atmosphere of the epoch.

Tchaikovsky's technical brilliance was inherited by his pupil Tanayev, a highly intellectual composer addicted to formal elaboration and thematic acrobatics. Tanayev, together with his more famous pupils

Scriabin and Rachmaninov, made up the 'Moscow school' of the 1890s and early twentieth century. It may be a tribute to Tanayev's flexible pedagogy that the two latter represent two antipodal points of view on composition, the 'ecstatic', and the 'pathetic'.

Architecture doubtless presents the most depressing aspect of the arts in nineteenth century Russia. It was precisely because of the collective symbolism inherent in the nature of the medium that the short-sightedness of the Tsarist authorities proved most oppressive. Government approval had to be given for all sorts of public buildings and churches, occasionally even private houses. The problem was made worse during Nicholas's reign by the taste of the sovereign himself; thinking himself infallible, he took a great interest in architecture, with the upshot that the early harmonious borrowing underlying the Russian 'Empire' style of the eighteenth and early nineteenth centuries gave way to a sort of haphazard and uninspired jumbling together of all sorts of manners, styles, and foibles lifted wholesale from Western Europe.

This was still further compounded by the régime's desire for systematization: just as the notion of 'official patriotism' had been sanctioned by the police-state of Nicholas I and imposed on the country as a whole, especially on the educated classes, so the eclecticism rampant in architecture was curbed through a system devised by Professor A. K. Ton (1794–1881), which fused together what he thought were the basic elements in Byzantine and in ancient Russian architecture. This singular alloy was imposed by the government on all church designs, public buildings, and even small cottages in army settlements. Ton's most famous works were the Grand Palais within the Kremlin and the Church of Christ the Saviour in Moscow; after the revolution its place was taken by the Palace of the Soviets.

Most students of architecture are in agreement that there was an impressive worsening of taste all over Europe and the United States during the second half of the nineteenth century; Russia easily held its own, and the unfortunate improvements in technology, which made the buildings more durable than they would have been, have left a lasting depression in Russian architecture. During the second half of the last century Russian architects produced doubtless the worst durable buildings: as an ensemble they demonstrated the failure of any native tradition to evolve, as well as the general depression of even purely technical standards. The durability of the individual buildings was supplemented disastrously by their coinciding with the general urban expansion and the replacement, on an exceptionally large scale, of the traditional wooden structures of Muscovy by edifices in brick and stone.

In the last third of the nineteenth century we can see a whole new life taking place in Russia, at least on the intellectual level that the *élite* had finally been able to climb on to. The explosion of activity in all the arts, even those that Russia was to make no real contribution to, impressed not only the imagination of the world at large, but also that of the Russians themselves. At the same time the intellectual life of the *élite*, increasingly entangled in political ideas, began to revolve around the fundamental problem of Russian society – the social relationships that gave it its structure and momentum.

Thus the effervescence in the arts, dramatic though it was, and fundamental to the establishment of a culture that in spite of everything came to characterize the Russians as a people, became more and more encapsulated within the sphere of politics.

Toward the end of the 1850s, with the humiliating defeat in the Crimean War and with the replacement on the throne of Nicholas I by Alexander II, Russia entered headlong into the modern phase of its national existence that culminated in the revolutions of 1917.

## Chapter 5

# Isolation Ended

The watershed between the traditional Russia that had developed between the sixteenth and the nineteenth centuries, and the modern Russia of the past three generations, can be located easily: it was the emancipation of the bulk of the population, the peasantry, whose bondage was brought to an end in 1861, at practically the same time as the slaves were freed in the United States.

This event must, of course, be seen in its proper historical perspective, as a measure designed to bridge, at last, the chasm between the *élite* and the population as a whole that had been instituted by the reforms of Peter the Great, accentuated by the flood of French ideas under Catherine the Great, and rendered unendurable during the nineteenth century by the ethical development of Western European ideas in the educated classes of Russia, who were small in numbers but a basic factor of change.

It was doubtless the moral factor that made serfdom more and more painful for the *élite* that had been nurtured on the philosophical and moral ideas of Western Europe; the growing anguish of the *élite* over the moral problem, however, was accompanied during the nineteenth century by the development of economic factors: economics and ethics combined on the question of serfdom to insist on a denouement of this ancient problem.

It would be difficult to understand the development of Russian culture during the nineteenth century without a view of the immense importance of its socio-economic imbalance. Though the régime was aware of the quandary it was in with respect to serfdom, it could not make up its mind what to do about it. The impasse – both moral and economic – created by serfdom might have been bypassed by an improvement in techniques, but only a tiny minority of more enlightened nobles accepted this. The basic difficulty in the situation was all-pervasive: the agricultural rationalization that might have produced enough income to ameliorate the lot of the serfs could be done only through capital investments. But the only capital most of the landowners had was in fact their own pool of serfs; hence any attempt to modernize technique collided with the stubbornness and incompetence of the illiterate and old-fashioned army of serfs. This basic inefficiency then interacted with the market place, both domestic and foreign, in which any capital investment represented a risk. The upshot was that both the peasant population and the landowning class were squeezed by the general bottleneck: this led to a condemnation of the institution of serfdom as such, at least by the more progressive landowners.

This process was accompanied by the growing pace of industrialization; though still primitive, this was going ahead by leaps and bounds; there was a shortage of labour due to serfdom and to the prevalence of cottage industries. Before machinery was applied to the industrial processes on a large scale the simple hand processes could be performed by home craftsmen just as well as by big enterprises. This gave the small but growing working-class a favourable position and led, for a time, to an increase in workers' wages. On the eve of emancipation, in 1861, there were about eight hundred thousand industrial workers, a little more than 1 per cent of the population. This was about four times as many as there had been at the beginning of the century. The mechanization that was to revolutionize Russia became an important factor toward the end of the 1840s.

But mere economic factors would doubtless have been insufficient to bring about sweeping change. Material factors had to be processed, as it were, by ideas before they could become historical agents. For this, of course, people were necessary, people who could form a social background against which ideas could evolve with potency.

The socio-economic imbalance characteristic of Russia for so long entailed just that chasm between the *élite* and the masses that has so often been referred to. It is a chasm that can hardly be overestimated. For centuries there were virtually two different breeds of human beings in Russia, with hardly any intermediaries: socially speaking they were almost hermetically sealed off from each other.

By the time of Catherine the Great, to be sure, a small new class of interstitial people had come into being, with the expansion of the government services, paltry though these were. These services were staffed by a group situated somewhat uncomfortably between the nobility and the peasantry – the government functionaries, enjoying a certain administrative influence because of their position but socially a sort of twilight category with no land, money or social influence. This primitive and somewhat diffuse bureaucratic milieu, immortalized only in the whimsical literary works of Gogol, and somewhat more depressingly in those of Dostoyevsky, exercised no real influence over Russian history.

But during the middle and later nineteenth century a different and far more important social milieu coagulated. As the Russian economy went on evolving in a lopsided, spasmodic way, it failed to develop its natural resources harmoniously; there was a delay in the generation of a functionally differentiated spectrum of social groups. The resulting social gap was filled only very slowly and gradually, as the liberal professions increased in number together with the sluggish growth of the educational facilities.

It was this class that came to be known by the curious name of 'intelligentsia', invented long before and long since assimilated into the vocabulary or at least the range of ideas of the world at large.

Socially speaking the intelligentsia was a composite coterie; though not distinguished by common roots, occupations, or even manners, it shared, consciously, a common view of the world, perhaps a common religious attitude toward life. It shared, in any case, the feeling that the world should, could, and must be changed, and that this could be done only through the force of ideas, which thus acquired a fundamental importance. It shared, that is, to say, a revulsion against frivolity, rationalism, and hedonism, and its roots may be sought in the ancient traditions of Russian mysticism as modified or channelled through the general ideas borrowed from Western and Central Europe.

The culture of the Russian summit, secularized by the piecemeal reforms of Peter the Great and still more of Catherine, had scarcely percolated through to the masses. In any case, that movement of worldly knowledgeability had impinged on the social summit alone; when commoners began trickling into the universities in the 1830s the mystical fervour that was perhaps inherent in the Russian peasantry, and that hitherto had taken on a purely religious tinge, now began expressing itself in terms of the new ideas floating around even the tightly constricted universities allowed by the autocratic régime.

The desire for world-reform, perhaps an essentially Messianic impulse, became the expression of the age-old religiosity of the people; the Messianic outlook, the determination to change the world, pervaded the intelligentsia and made it the most influential layer of Russian society. Towards the end of the nineteenth century it forged one of the most effective instruments in history – the Russian revolutionary movement, which smashed the structure of Russian society and scattered its ferment abroad upon the world.

It was the creation of the 'intelligentsia' as a distinct, self-aware social group that was perhaps the most important product of the 1860s. When the word, coined at the end of the eighteenth century, was associated with an actual group of people it summed up just that alienation in Russian society that was ultimately to shatter the old order. The nihilistic iconoclasm of the 1860s, with its proliferation of purely negative attitudes, led to various forms of political extremism and to a heightening of the social realism already embedded in Russian literature. What had been an optimism rooted in the potentialities of science was converted towards the end of the 1860s into an optimistic theory of history that could justify action.

This action was ultimately triggered, perhaps, by the governmental decision to abolish serfdom, during the reign of Alexander II; the optimism associated with his reign and its reforms proved to be the matrix for a quickening of the fermenting process.

Psychologically, Alexander II remains just as elusive as his uncle Alexander I: he seems to have been just as autocratic beneath the same sort of sentimental veil. But the social framework of Russian society had changed so much between the two régimes that it was possible, indeed imperative, because of the changed social climate, to bring about social reform. Russia had left behind enough of its backwardness, in short, to enable even an autocrat to perceive the need for and the possibility of change. The abolition of serfdom was Alexander II's chief contribution to history; it marked a turning-point in the life of Russia.

Alexander II, the 'Liberating Tsar' and architect of the 'Age of the Great Reforms', straddled an epoch in which Russian society was more or less completely, though far from systematically, overhauled. A whole series of fundamental changes, including a comprehensive reform of the judicial system that finally introduced the exotic idea of equality of individuals, trial by jury, public proceedings in legal matters, the impartiality of the courts, and so on, slowly softened the ancient rigours of Russian life.

The abolition of serfdom, the crowning achievement of his reign, was probably brought about not by the maturing of some principle in Alexander's mind, but by two unrelated reasons: the disclosure of Russian military ineptitude in the Crimean War, and the growing conviction that the peasantry was about to fly off the handle.

In any case, the reforms – cumbersome, half-hearted and defective though they were – did give personal freedom to some forty-seven million peasants; the emancipation of the basic class of Russian society, coupled with the beginnings of the modern capitalism, swiftly led to the transformation of the country.

It also led, to be sure, to a variety of social conundrums that in fact made the 'accursed questions' more accursed than ever. For the basic problem entailed by the emancipation – should the serfs be freed with or without land? – was never solved by the emancipatory decrees; the land allocations were felt to be quite inadequate, an inadequacy that was coupled with the further vexation that such land as was allocated to the peasants was not handed over to the peasants individually, but to the village commune which was imposed on the peasantry. The upshot was that the peasants were bitterly disappointed; the dual embitterment of peasantry and nobility laid the foundations of the general poisoning of social relations that was one of the radical factors in the upheaval of 1917.

It was not so much a question of the amount of land the peasants were allocated as of the inability of the allotments to provide a subsistence for a given family under the conditions prevailing in agriculture; it was another reflection, in fact, of the backwardness of Russian society as a whole. The old-fashioned agricultural technique meant that the land could not be worked efficiently enough to make it pay; since this concept was itself a sophisticated one, what remained fixed in the minds of the peasants was that they had not, somehow, been given enough land. They realized that the element of constraint implied by serfdom had, to be sure, been eliminated, but only to be replaced by the constraint of economic necessity. Since from this point of view the relations between the landowners and their former serfs had scarcely changed, the peasants' disappointment took on an increasingly political tinge that was to explode with singular violence in 1917.

The emancipation of the serfs failed to help the nobility either; the great farming units of the nobility also suffered from the general backwardness of technique and the lack of capital needed to modernize the farming operation. The transition to capitalism on the farm – the employment of enough hired hands who could use the machinery and the livestock provided by the owners – proved to be exceptionally difficult for both traditional landowners and traditional peasants.

In fact, the upshot of the Age of Great Reforms was the end of aristocratic Russia, which was swiftly to be suffocated during the succeeding generations through the rise of a new class of merchants, burghers, financiers and industrialists created by the abrupt expansion of foreign trade, the construction of a vast new rail network and new harbours, and the establishment of new mines and factories.

In the two generations between the accession of Alexander II and the outbreak of the First World War, Russia was flung headlong into a capitalist transformation. A middle class came into existence and grew rapidly; the intelligentsia that had been given a new incarnation even under the police-state of Nicholas I grew with it and became an increasingly powerful agency of social turmoil.

The artistic efflorescence noted above was both the effect and the cause of a general intellectual upheaval, rooted, of course, in the expansion of education in general and in the growth of the actual numbers of educated people, though relatively these remained a tiny minority compared to the great masses of illiterate peasants. The Tsarist régime, while politically oppressive, could not, after all, control the longing for information and self-education, stimulated and channelled by the various arts.

Despite the restrictions imposed by the régime and despite its somewhat obtuse attempts at repression, education kept gaining ground. Women began to be educated in substantial numbers; in the 1860s and 1870s a genuine beginning was made even in elementary education. Despite the small numbers involved, relative to the size of the population, the educated classes, and in particular the intelligentsia, encompassed a gigantic reservoir of brainpower and moral devotion. The progress in education and technology that began about the middle of the nineteenth century created a new younger generation and with it a new type of dedicated intellectual.

Beginning with the 1860s young Russians passionately took up the study of everything under the sun, from chemistry through geology to mathematics. Science became the watchword of all those members of the younger generation disaffected from the conventional scholasticism and religious piety of traditional upper class behaviour. The disciplines of science were attractive both as keys to the problems of the universe at large and also as a shield against the oppressiveness of the political régime. Russian scientists began distinguished careers, very often under the direct influence of their Western European counterparts. A Russian scientific tradition was established by the middle of the nineteenth century that has persisted, with notorious consequences, down to our own day. By the end of the century figures like the chemist Mendeleyev (1843–1907), the biologist Mechnikov (1845–1916), and the physiologist and psychologist Pavlov (1849–1936) had become world-famous.

The outburst of literary activity that began in the 1860s gave rise to a lively periodical press; when the extremist censorship of the police-régime of Nicholas I was relaxed after the accession of Alexander I, journalism and its parallel activities were greatly stimulated. The liberalization of the government after Alexander II, though fragmentary and vacillating, had a definite effect both on the growth of realism in the arts, tacitly understood to entail a certain degree of political radicalism, and very directly on the growth of dissident social opinion.

The fundamental social process signalized and stimulated by the major socio-political event of the nineteenth century – the emancipation of the serfs – shaped a new Russia. It was a process that was, naturally, reflected in intimate detail in literature, which itself, of course, was transformed under its impact. The aristocracy that had been the sole source of literature during the eighteenth and early nineteenth centuries was now gradually ousted by intellectuals who, whatever their class attachments may have been, were personally rather rootless. The initial division of the earlier generation into the broad categories of Slavophils and Westernizers was now succeeded by a more radical polarization, of a political nature, that was to have the most convulsive effects on Russian society and, indeed, to produce and shape the Russian Revolution itself.

The Romantic Slavophilism of the intelligentsia in its earlier beginnings gradually turned into an agency of the 'Pan-Slav' policy of the régime itself, actually a mere synonym for the political goals of the Russian State. As the Russian State became more and more densely entangled in European and world politics, theories about the kinship of the Slavs, which formerly had had something sentimental about them, gradually came to furnish mere pretexts for the political activities and aims of the autocracy. The Pan-Slavists, taking the place of the sentimental Slavophils, grew substantially in influence particularly after the Russian defeat in the Crimean War; Pan-Slavism became a cover for the ambition to expand in the south and west at the expense of other governments.

The theory underlying Pan-Slavism was both incoherent and unevenly distributed among its followers. It had both a religious and an ethnic motivation. The religious Pan-Slavs were baffled by the problem of including the substantial numbers of Roman Catholic Slavs, such as the

Poles, Czechs and Croats. On the ethnic level, it was impossible to create a myth of Slav unity, counterposed that is, to the existing order of Western, or German-Magyar Europe. Nor was there any such thing as 'Slavic' civilization in the same sense as French, Italian, or German civilization. The various groups of Slavs had evolved under differing influences; in fact there had never been any prospect of genuine union on any grounds whatever but those of power-politics. Because of its various intellectual inconsistencies, as well as its emotional insubstantiality, Pan-Slavism lacked the authenticity of its predecessor Slavophilism as an emotional magnet: it was never anything but a mythological adjunct of State policy. It achieved its fullest expression as part of the propaganda that led to the First World War.

The other, Westernizing, counterpart of Slavophilism, also began taking shape in a far more self-conscious, dynamic way.

The milieu of the intelligentsia, representing towards the end of the century a fusion between the educated elements of the gentry and self-made intellectuals of plebeian origin, with a sprinkling of disaffected aristocrats, now began carrying its various abstractions into the field of action. As political ideas became more and more organized, against a background of rapid social change, one wing of the intelligentsia embarked on the action that was ultimately to transform Russia and the world.

The movement may be said to have been launched in the second quarter of the nineteenth century, when an articulate group ready to criticize the authorities, an early adumbration of public opinion, was formed from among non-aristocrats. For the first time a divergence arose between official opinion and the opinion of a growingly disaffected stratum of society.

Herzen had left Russia for good when the régime of Nicholas I began reacting with greater rigour to the political turbulence of 1848. A little journal he began publishing in London, *The Bell*, was one of the most potent factors in the formation of radical opinion; it was regularly smuggled into Russia and reached the most varied elements in the population, including highly placed government officials. *The Bell* remained influential until the emancipation of the serfs shifted the whole movement of radicalization onto a different plane. Herzen's influence began waning as the peasant question, after the emancipation, was placed in a far more serious perspective.

This radicalization of opinion, curiously enough, was a novelty in Russia, that is, in its direction and composition. In the 1850s, for instance, Russia had no revolutionary movement of any kind. Between the abortive conspiracy of the Decembrists, which may be said to have been the last gasp of aristocratic idealism, socially isolated and purely personal, and the equally abortive salon action of the 'Petrashevsky group', a whole decade went by in which Herzen's *Bell* remained the sole mouthpiece of dissidence. The decade may be summed up, psychologically, as the decade of Nihilism, a coinage of Turgenev in his celebrated novel *Fathers and Sons*: Nihilists denied not merely political, but also intellectual authority.

From the Fourierists through the Nihilists, socio-political dissidence was expressed essentially in talk. Radicalism proper may be said to have begun throbbing in the Russian body politic with the optimism surrounding Alexander's accession to the throne. The presence on the throne of a Liberating Tsar, hailed by men of all shades, generated immense excitement; and with the mass entry of young people, largely plebeians, into the universities, as the régime relaxed the various controls of its predecessor, political and social hopefulness began bubbling over. Dostoyevsky's principal political novel, *The Possessed*, gives a realistic portrayal of the social effervescence that characterized the period. Everything was thrown up for discussion, analysis, and transformation, from the institution of phonetic spelling to the abolition of the family.

Yet though restrictions were substantially loosened under Alexander II, there was, of course, no question of permitting open opposition to the régime. Secret societies sprang up again and – what proved more momentous – an open revolutionary movement took shape. Significantly enough, the entire generation that brought about the 1917 Revolution was born between 1870 and 1880.

The Westernizing tendency of the preceding generation – by and large a very general attitude of mind – evolved with remarkable rapidity into a full-fledged revolutionary movement, with two main branches –

*Isolation Ended*

Marc Chagall (b. 1887):
'The Green Violinist' (1918).

Kasimir Malevich (1878–
1935): 'Knife Grinder'
(1912).

(opposite above) B. M.
Kustodiev (1878–1927):
'Carnival Week' (1916).

(opposite centre) Natalia
Goncharova (1882–1962):
'Dancing Peasants' (c. 1910).

(opposite below) Wassily
Kandinsky (1866–1944):
'Lyrisches' (1911).

Mickail Larionov (b. 1881):
'Glasses' (1919).

(left) Mickail Larionov
(b. 1881): 'The Head of a
Soldier' (1910 or 1911).

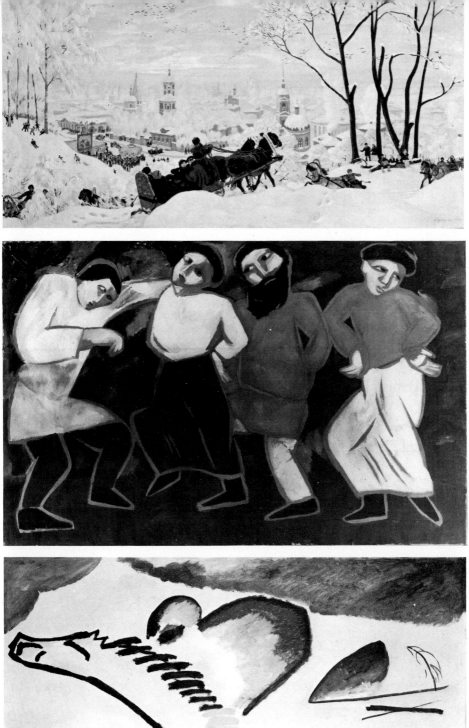

Anton Chekov (1860–1904), autographed photograph.

Chekov *(centre)* with members of the Moscow Art Theatre in 1899.

Setting for the salon in Dostoyevsky's *The Idiot*, designed by Alexandre Benois in 1924.

NIJINSKY
dans "La Péri"

Aquarelle de Léon BAKST.

Cover of Ballets Russes programme with a watercolour by Bakst showing Nijinsky in 'La Péri' (1911).

*(below)* Natalia Goncharova: costume design in watercolour for *La Liturgie,* a Ballets Russes project of 1915 which was unrealized.

*(below)* Plan for ballet lighting by Alexander A. Echter, in watercolour.

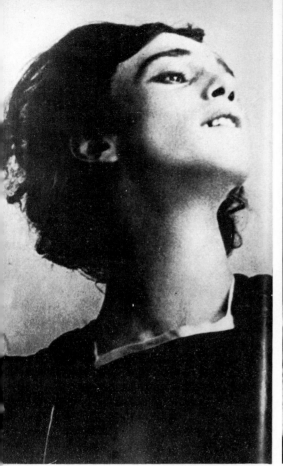

(above left and right)
The two most brilliant
dancers in Diaghilev's
company: Vaslav Nijinsky,
here seen in *L'Après-Midi
d'un Faune* and Anna
Pavlova, in *Swan Lake*.

(left) Two designs for
ballet costumes by P.
Chelitchev for Victor
Zimine's company.

The nineteenth-century
theatre:
*(left)* M. M. Sadovsky in
*Poverty is no Sin* at the Mali
Theatre, 1850.
*(centre)* M. N. Eumalova in
*Joan of Arc : The Maid of
Orleans* at the Mali Theatre,
1884.
*(right)* Tsar Feodor
Ivanovich played by I. M.
Mockvin in 1898.

Alexander Ivanovitch Bilibin: design for proscenium curtain for Act I
of Moussorgsky's *Boris Godounov ;* sepia, brown and black chalk.

Marxism and Populism. Both together absorbed the energies and minds of a whole generation of Russian intellectuals. From the last third of the nineteenth century through the period culminating in the Russian revolution these two movements came to dominate the thought of the entire *élite* insofar as it diverged from official opinion.

Populism was rooted in a perhaps sentimental attitude towards the peasantry, i.e., 'the people'; it revolved around the conviction that the spirit of the peasants would sweep away the afflictions of Russian society and usher in a new age. The idealism of a whole generation of young people, inspired by one of Herzen's last and most effective slogans, 'Go to the People!', was poured forth in an attempt to inflame the oppressed masses of Russia with a new vision of life.

In fact Herzen may have launched the Populist movement with this rallying cry of his, accompanied by another slogan of his that remained an axis of political aspiration for the revolutionary generation – 'Land and Liberty!' But his aristocratic origins, plus his merely humanitarian and reformist views, quickly caused his popularity to decline after the emancipation of the serfs. He was in fact outdistanced by the anarchist mood and the political terrorism that were soon interwoven into the fabric of the new government.

The notion of 'Going to the People' was too vague to do much more than act as a channel for idealistic fervour; because of the difficulty inherent in getting a response from the peasants who were supposed to live up to the idealism of the revolutionary generation, the movement quickly developed a violent branch that was to solve all political problems. Intellectuals were, in fact, carried into the Populist movement by two kinds of emotions: a simple-hearted adoration of The People, and a violence rooted, perhaps, in frustrated love, as The People failed to do anything.

Populism was elaborated after Herzen by a whole line of thinkers, publicists, critics and journalists, of whom the most outstanding were Chernyshevsky, Dobrolyubov, Tkachov and Lavrov. Though their ideas differed considerably in detail, they were similar in providing a Russian variation on the theme of 'moral' socialism that had become common in Western Europe. Generally speaking, the Populists believed in the moral transformation of individuals, effected by the will of the moral mind, rather than in the development of the objective forces of society. Populism, deeply rooted in the mystical ardour of the Russian people, flowered into a movement when modern education had percolated through enough non-aristocratic minds to play a role in the shaping of events toward an ideal of world-betterment.

Perhaps one of the most striking occurrences in the whole history of Russia was the so-called 'crazy summer' of 1874, when with no centralized direction, no plan or programme, a couple of thousand young students, together with some older people, including aristocrats, were suddenly inflamed by a fever of self-sacrifice. Apparently unbalanced by reports that the Russian countryside was about to burst out into flames, they rushed out among the peasants, in peasant dress, and set about installing a new order. Some of the students tried to set up permanent headquarters to agitate among the peasants, others simply wandered about giving impromptu sermons. The peasants, very naturally, thought them all quite demented even when they approved of their general ideas. In any case the police were watching them with great attentiveness: the revolutionaries were quickly arrested in droves; the extraordinary summer outburst came to nothing.

It was perhaps this massive and essentially unformulated approach to the peasant question, with its doubtless inevitable failure, that led to the growth of terrorism. As idealists despaired of sweeping masses of people along on the crest of their idealism, many of them determined to carry on the fight against the autocracy in a personal way; secret organizations were formed with the objective of conducting a campaign of assassination and public outrages as a way of electrifying public opinion and thus crystallizing the opposition to the established order.

Perhaps the most impressive thing about the Populist movement as a whole was just this idealism: though a few Populists came from the peasantry, most of them had their roots in the *élite* and the nascent middle class; they were characterized by a disinterested fanaticism that made it very difficult for the police to control them. Those with money made substantial contributions to the movement. There was, it is true, an inherent contradictoriness in the youthful idealism of people brought up on abstract ideas in a rigid and backward Russia that could not come even remotely close to applying those ideas. The children of the upper classes, as well as many individual millionaires, were torn by the magnetism of ideals; even if they did not join the actual organizations they would openhandedly give them money.

The Populist movement was, very naturally, expressed in all artistic media, in harmony with the Russian desire for all-inclusiveness and the universal feeling that all the arts were somehow an expression of the same thing. Ilya Repin was in his long career perhaps the greatest symbolization of the driving force of Populism; his canvas of *The Haulers on the Volga*, in fact, sums up in plastic form all the basic elements of Populist pathos.

The terrorist wing of the Populist movement set itself the goal of killing the Tsar, which after seven abortive attempts it finally, in the most imaginative and daring way, managed to do, in March 1881. This was its last gasp; a couple of years later most of the terrorist leaders were either in exile or in gaol, and by the end of the century the movement seemed to have completely subsided.

The Populist movement did not vanish, and was indeed reincarnated in the Social Revolutionary Party that played an important role in Russian life until the 1917 Revolution; but it was more and more overshadowed by the Marxist movement, which after making systematic headway in Europe as a whole was now, within one generation, to seize control of Russian destinies.

Marxism had arrived in Russia rather later than Populism, though Marx's *Das Kapital*, published in 1867, had its first translation – into Russian – only a couple of years later. The success of Marxism was ultimately ensured, no doubt, by the emergence of a new class in Russian society – the industrial proletariat – in harmony with the transformation of the economic process as Russia found itself entering more and more comprehensively into the development of capitalism.

Marxism may have appealed to a substantial segment of the growing Russian intelligentsia because of its unusual fusion of a dynamic Messianism with a framework of scientific methodology. The ardent determination of so many intellectuals to change the world was given an intellectual justification via the rationalistic apparatus of Marxist doctrine: the two factors together were further given a religious certitude that what was desired was also going to happen, and happen, moreover, inevitably.

The Marxist attitude on Russia was simply that since Russia was an integral part of universal history, it had to pass through capitalism in order to attain socialism in the future. Hence Russian Marxists turned aside from the peasantry as unsuited for the organization of institutions that would go counter to capitalism, since the peasants were all considered to be small capitalists at heart. They concentrated their attention on the industrial working-class as the sole channel through which a transformation of society could be effected. As a corollary of its belief in objective forces Marxism also systematically opposed terrorism.

It was in fact the Marxist faith in the 'objective' development of social forces, and its consequent hostility to terrorism, that in the beginning ensured its safety with the Tsarist authorities. The Marxist belief that Russia had to pass through capitalism to get to socialism implied, after all, that capitalism must come to Russia, therefore that progressive thinkers should help it in Russia before the succeeding stage of socialism was reached, which might take quite some time. Because of this convolution of Marxist thought, Marxism as a whole was believed to be a factor of stability in the growing turbulence of the end of the nineteenth century; many individual Marxists, indeed, found it perfectly natural to work against any disturbance that might impede the progress of capitalism. This complication led to the existence of a so-called 'legal' school of Marxism, in addition to the illegal school; in this legal form Marxism could be championed quite openly in the Russian press, until the First World War. In fact, a whole branch of legal Marxists had enrolled many of the new class of business managers and engineers that the growing industrialization of the country was engendering.

Both Populism and Marxism were at first, to be sure, confined to a rather small *élite*; neither had a mass base for decades. Among students, *Das Kapital* was the most popular book of the kind towards the end of the century, but since neither group had any authentic connections with either the peasantry or the working-class their influence on what was actually happening in Russia was nil. The great strikes that broke out in the 1880s and 1890s, for instance, were quite uninfluenced by sophisticated doctrine: they were in fact spontaneous reflections of the basic transformation of Russia that from then on was to determine events.

By the middle of the 1890s, however, the tempestuous development of capitalism was being matched by the equally rapid development of its opposition. In 1893 the Russian Marxist movement began to call itself Social-Democrat, along the lines of the German movement; in a little more than two decades it was to find itself in control of Russia. In only one decade, indeed, it managed to stage, in 1905, what was to be called a 'dress-rehearsal' for the final overthrow of Tsarism in 1917.

It was in 1895 that some twenty small Marxist coteries – discussion clubs, and literary societies – fused together to form the *Fighting Union for the Liberation of the Working Class*; by the end of the century Marxism had become a substantial current in Russian life, though in numbers it was still small. This *Fighting Union* had been put together under the leadership of V. I. Lenin (born Ulyanov) and J. Martov (born Tsederbaum); it very soon split up, and was replaced by other configurations.

Russian Marxism was even more splintered than other Marxist movements. Throughout its existence the Russian Social-Democratic movement was steeped in the most virulent factional strife; in the event, as all the world knows, it was the 'Bolshevik' wing of the movement, led by Lenin, that was to emerge victorious. The factional struggle that had led to its emergence revolved around a basic difference in the approach to revolution, a difference that in its own way reflected constantly varying attitudes towards change on the part of individuals throughout Russia's stormy history.

Idealists naturally try to link their ideals to reality; this attempt equally naturally produces two differing attitudes. One attitude is that reality will, without encouragement, bring about its own change; the other attitude is that the encouragement is indispensable, since without it reality will *not* change.

These contrasting positions were illustrated throughout the nineteenth century: the differences are best summed up in the contrast between a conspiracy and a movement. In the case of the split between the Bolsheviks and their unsuccessful rivals in the Social-Democratic movement – the Mensheviks, led by Martov – the source of the split lay in just this difference of attitude towards reality.

For the Bolsheviks it was essential to have a guiding hand at the helm of events; Lenin insisted that the Party consist of 'professional revolutionaries', who would lead the masses, or the working-class, into a revolution that would be directed or at least channelled by the Party toward the desired goals; the Mensheviks, on the contrary, were willing to accept anyone who was intellectually 'sympathetic' to the movement.

This split on the method of guiding the movement was in its turn a reflection of the general view of the transition from capitalism, once achieved, to socialism, as projected. The Mensheviks took it for granted that socialism was impossible until the society in which it was to be realized was itself ripe for it, that is, until it had enough culture and technological competence to undertake the process of industrialization without which socialism would remain a mere 'utopian' ideal. Such a society, obviously, could come about only rather slowly, as the result of the bourgeois democracy that they expected to evolve together with capitalism, and that, in accordance with the Marxist 'dialectic', they thought would automatically help the working-class evolve together with it to the point of being able, ultimately, to manage the transition to socialism.

The Bolsheviks were bound to agree in principle with these generalities, but they regarded the Social-Democratic Party as itself one of the historic factors that was to play a substantial role in shaping the aims of the working-class and so in causing events to occur.

The Party was considered to be itself one of the motors of historic progress, a sort of accelerator to the inevitable processes of history.

Thus, on the eve of the First World War we see a picture of upper-class Russians in the grip of an unusual intellectual activity, which found expression in a remarkable variety of publications and a great heterogeneity of tendencies in literature, music, painting and the theatre. Outside the specific milieu of the Imperial entourage, educated Russians were in a rather conventional way wholly critical of the existing order, without, of course, taking to the extremism of the organized political movements.

The influence of the Western European life was very profound: upper-class Russian children were as a rule brought up to be at home in a variety of foreign languages, primarily French and German, followed by English and Italian. European literature was perfectly familiar to the Russian *élite*, which regularly thronged through the various capitals, watering-places and resorts of the Continent.

By the end of the nineteenth century, in short, the educated classes in Russia had been wholly assimilated to the life of their European counterparts. It was, perhaps, this assimilation on the part of the upper classes that broadened the chasm between them and the rest of the country. Just as a century previously the result of Catherine the Great's wholesale importation of French notions had been to alienate the upper aristocracy completely from the life of the country, consummating a process initiated by Peter the Great, so by the end of the nineteenth century the upper classes, now much larger absolutely although still a rather small minority relative to the vast masses of the peasantry, were rooted in a way of life that was totally different from that of the country as a whole.

But though the educated classes were still socially isolated against the vast grey background of peasant illiteracy, in the realm of the arts the activities were varied and lively. Despite the censorship that followed the abortive revolution of 1905 the press was substantially unfettered; there was an immensely broad spectrum of opinion in the more than two thousand periodicals that appeared, for instance, in 1912. Marxist contributors found no obstacle in expressing their views; more than three thousand purely Social-Democratic publications appeared in Russia between 1906 and 1914.

For that matter the stimulation of the industrial, social, and political inflammation at the turn of the century was to have a decisive effect on literature and the arts. Russia had become famous for its realistic school of writers during the 1860s and 1870s; by the end of the century its place in world literature was more secure than ever. Tolstoy, who had by then become an international institution, was joined by a galaxy of other literary celebrities, including Maxim Gorky, Anton Chekhov and Ivan Bunin. Chekhov was taken up by the British *élite* and soon won an undisputed position not merely as a short-story writer, but more famously as a dramatist who made an enduring impression on the world theatre.

With the beginning of the twentieth century Russian painters, too, began acquiring world reputations. All the movements of contemporary art had their Russian exponents, of course, from impressionism to futurism; it is doubtless even legitimate to trace all aspects of abstract painting to the innovations of Kandinsky, accompanied as they were by a copious ideological flow of explanation and justification. In the decade preceding the First World War, in fact, Russian art was definitely on a par with that of Europe as a whole; painters like Soutine and Chagall, as well as Kandinsky, were to play an unusual role in contemporary art.

Russian music was completely at home everywhere in the world before the First World War. Not only had Stravinsky and Prokofiev acquired reputations they have never lost since, but a whole host of interpretative artists and composers – Rachmaninov, Scriabin, Leopold Auer, Ephrem Zimbalist, Jascha Heifetz, Vladimir Horowitz, Nathan Milstein – became world-famous. In the world of international music, in fact, Russia was one of the most brilliant centres. St Petersburg had four full-fledged opera-houses: Chaliapin was probably one of the most famous singers who ever lived. Stanislavsky's theatre acquired an international reputation that has come down to our own day, and for that matter started, in a characteristically Russian way, a 'school of thought' that still, under the somewhat pompous and misleading name of The Method, exercises considerable influence.

Igor Stravinsky, today surely the most celebrated of Russian and perhaps of world composers, has gone through most of the stages in modern music, both Russian and European. He effected, in fact, a transition between a purely Russian reputation and his present status as a world virtuoso. At the age of sixteen he met Rimsky-Korsakov, from whom he took private lessons in composition; up to 1908 his early works were steeped in the atmosphere prevailing at the St Petersburg

Conservatory. Until the age of twenty-five Stravinsky did not diverge much from Rimsky-Korsakov's style as current in Russia, though he introduced some Russian 'decadent' features from the period before the First World War.

Some of Stravinsky's admirers have made a point of the objectivity of his style, associated with the notion of 'pure' form in music, but all the works he composed for Diaghilev's Ballets Russes were modulated in accordance with varying conceptions, in the case of the *Firebird* by Fokine's scenario, in the case of *Petrushka* by Benois's basic idea for the production, and so on. His music was, in fact, a mere appendage to the plot in these works, as well as in *Le Sacre du Printemps*, which was dominated by Roerich's stylization.

Stravinsky went rather beyond his teacher Rimsky-Korsakov in his use of instrumental timbre, but he parallels the latter's work in his own handling of harmonic nuances. Stravinsky's early period, in fact, was linked to the harmonic era that in both Russia and Western Europe seemed to be coming to an end. In both music and painting Impressionism evolved gradually from Russian realism; and just as with painting, music underwent a growing simplification or abstraction of traditional forms and their systematic distortion, until it reached a stage legitimately called Expressionism.

By 1908–11 this process, already made familiar in the painting of the period, had reached a sort of stripped-down phase connected in Europe with the name of the celebrated Expressionist Schönberg. In Russia, however, Schönberg was thought at first to be too complicated and elusive; he exerted no influence, especially in comparison with the French Impressionists, notably Debussy. But Schönberg's authority rapidly grew.

After 1911 it was clear that Stravinsky had struck out on a new and original course. In *Le Sacre du Printemps*, which was violently reacted to when presented as part of the regular season of the Ballets Russes, Stravinsky was obliged to make some innovations in order to reproduce a genuinely savage subject. Without achieving the abstract distortions of Schönberg and his disciples – polytonality, atonality, polyrhythms, arhythms – Stravinsky was sailing with the same general wind.

Stravinsky strove for years to integrate exotic elements with his music, but eventually exoticism vanished altogether and his music, together with the Ballets Russes, became thoroughly Europeanized; it also came to exercise great influence over various French composers. In the period from 1914 to 1919, when the intellectual element in Stravinsky's work came well to the fore, his music did in fact become 'pure' in his quest of new effects through original combinations of sounds and timbres. The general trend in music had already led in this direction and Stravinsky, together with his foreign colleagues, began to concentrate on the use of instruments with a simple, clear-cut timbre, quite distinct from the slightly haphazard variations in human vocalizing or stringed instruments. The instruments in his orchestras were adapted to fit whatever experiment was being tried. This development was also reflected in the productions of the Ballets Russes, though by now the roles of Diaghilev and Stravinsky were reversed, with Stravinsky definitely the leader.

After 1919 Stravinsky's creativity took a turn backward in time: he seemed to be returning to Italian styles, then to Russian; he also adapted melodies from Russian gypsy and even American sources. His work was considered a return to classicism, with a sophisticated self-consciousness about it, however, that insulated him against a charge of mere backsliding. He even returned to Bach and to Tchaikovsky, and when in 1930 he composed a religious work he simply obliterated all his experimental innovations and went back to the colourful orchestration he mastered very early in his career.

Another celebrated Russian composer in the modern period was Prokofiev, a decade younger than Stravinsky. Prokofiev's singular productivity, coupled with a sort of spontaneous lyricism and youthful charm, reminded many people of Haydn and Mozart. When Prokofiev emerged, at the end of the first decade of the twentieth century, the innate gaiety of his work, buttressed by its remarkable harmonious uniformity and headlong flow and imbued by a strong and suffusive classicism in both form and spirit, made his work an effective protest against the various moods of nagging introspection, metaphysics and mysticism that much of Russian music of the time was subject to.

By the turn of the century the ballet itself, which had been first introduced into Russia in the last third of the seventeenth century, to become consolidated in the cultural life of the country during the reign of Catherine the Great, had dislocated its French origins to become thoroughly acclimated. Countless Russian ballerinas were world-famous. The Petersburg ballet was completely overhauled by Fokine, who managed to create a fusion between dancing and music by absorbing the work of some of the most famous Russian composers – Tchaikovsky, Rimsky-Korsakov, Glinka, Borodin, and Stravinsky – as well as Germans – Schumann, Wagner and Weber. Fokine was also instrumental in heightening the relative importance of the *corps de ballet*, by emphasizing the function of dancing as a massive element of choreography: this established a counterweight to the primacy of the prima ballerina, and increased the number of combinations possible. The Russians were thus responsible for countless innovations, all presented within a framework of original new costumes and a magnificent *décor*.

Many of the new ideas, in fact, that found expression in Russian art and music towards the end of the nineteenth century were transmitted to Western Europe by the celebrated ballet-master Diaghilev; they were presented for the first time to the international public in Paris in the summer of 1909. There they scored an immense success, subsequently evolving along their own lines.

By the end of the nineteenth century, in fact, the cultural isolation of Russia from the West had receded into the past, though naturally the cosmopolitan influences flooding the country as a whole were bound to be channelled into a very small vessel, socially in the aristocracy and the already substantial middle and upper-middle class, and geographically in St Petersburg, a thoroughly Western city. But with the exception of St Petersburg and Moscow, the life of old Russia had scarcely been touched by any of these modish influences.

Moscow itself had a certain parochial atmosphere unlike cities of a similar size in Europe; in the small towns of the provinces Europe was scarcely more than a veneer, which by the time the remoter hinterland was reached was wholly non-existent. The Russian cities in the provinces were, in fact, no more than peasant hamlets. At the end of the nineteenth century eighty-seven per cent of the total population lived in the countryside; as far as the European life of the capitals was concerned they might have been in the Middle Ages. The tiny educated class that could discuss the latest French novel or painting was quite alien in every respect; in its way of life, its ideas, and even its language. Except for the odd aristocratic landowner who indulged an interest in his farmland, there was nothing in common between the peasants and the upper classes; the same could be said of the working-class, which was evolving rapidly in conditions totally alien to the life of the small class of industrialists, while at the same time it had not yet developed a social solidarity of its own.

The literacy of the population was just what might have been expected: by the time of the First World War the country was around four-fifths illiterate; this was doubtless an underestimate, since by the standards of the government census the word 'literate' might be given to someone who could scarcely sign his name and had done nothing more than attend some village school as a child.

There was no communal activity of the kind familiar in the life of Western Europe and America, not even any organized sports. The Russian Church itself was quite indifferent to the cultural or communal activities associated in the West with the Roman Catholic or the various Protestant Churches; the numerous national and religious minorities, like Finns, Poles, Jews, and Ukrainians, to say nothing of the scores of Asiatic nationalities, heightened the disunity and backwardness of the country as a whole.

The great industrial boom in Russia just before the First World War was perhaps the most momentous event in its pre-revolutionary history: just because it took place against a background of general backwardness, it was able to transform the shape of Russia very substantially. It was precisely the belatedness of Russia's socio-economic development that made it possible for it to bypass the various obsolescent features that acted as a brake on the economic expansion of the older industrial countries. At a moment when agriculture and peasant life in general had not advanced discernibly beyond seventeenth-century levels, the technique and structure of Russian industry placed it well to the fore of international capitalism. One statistical remark may be illuminating: in Russia less than twenty per cent of all industrial workers in 1914 were employed in businesses with fewer than a hundred workers; in America the figure was thirty-five per cent. Gigantic agglomerations of men were employed in Russian textile and metal industries. The purely political importance of this fact can hardly be overestimated: in 1917 it was to give the Bolshevik Party a tremendous springboard into power.

By the time Russian capitalism was in a position to flex its muscles, its remarkable technological progress was surpassed by a quite disproportionate growth of disaffection in the *élite*. The growth of the industrial working-class was paralleled by a growth of subversive parties, so that by the time world politics had got to the point of creating the conditions in which the First World War could be kindled, the Tsarist régime, though outwardly as solid, as 'monolithic', as majestic as ever (to the public at large, indeed, it seemed an utterly impregnable edifice), was in fact quite incapable of sustaining the shock of warfare.

With the immersion of the vast country in the maelstrom of the First World War, accordingly, a whole new series of shocks was applied to the creaking, ramshackle structure of Russian society, for beneath the often brilliant layer of culture on top it was still an essentially lopsided and ramshackle structure. The vast majority of the population was still socially and intellectually backward; the cosmopolitanism of the *élite*, while genuine, was a sadly puny growth in the country at large. It must be admitted that the Russian façade of tranquillity was a mere plastering over of deeply embedded structural flaws.

Entering the war with somewhat vague ideas as to the benefits it could hope to derive from it, the Tsarist régime, utterly incapable of providing its troops even with the ammunition to fight, was equally incapable of controlling conditions at home. It managed to survive only two and a half years after the outbreak of war; by the winter of 1917 it was no more than a memory.

A revolution, which in its first phase – the winter and spring of 1917 – was quite unforeseen, unprepared for, and undirected, had spontaneously erupted. In February and March some disturbances that had begun as mere bread-riots grew, without direction, into what instantly became a major movement of disaffection. The Tsarist government proper was disregarded; some of its officials, confronted by a new situation, constituted themselves a 'Provisional Government'. On the same day, another organization, the Petersburg Soviet of Workers' and Peasants' Deputies, had taken shape, and, though reluctant to assume the direction of the State it was forced into a position of responsibility by the incontestable fact of being the sole authority for vital social services without which no organized life was possible.

The Petersburg Soviet itself was very swiftly to come under the explicit control of radical parties; of these parties the relatively unknown Bolshevik Party, still led by Lenin and with the collaboration, acquired during the revolutionary period, of Leon Trotsky, was to stage a successful insurrection some eight months later and take over the helm of the State. With the transformation of Tsarist Russia into the Union of Socialist Soviet Republics, Russia entered on a new phase of its existence, a phase in which it has, through the ideas and institutions associated with the revolution, become an historic factor of cosmic scope.

Chapter 6

# A New Incarnation

The new society launched by the tiny Bolshevik Party's triumph in the Russian Revolution of 1917 was conceived of by the party leaders as the realization of an ancient ideal – the first phase in the socialist transformation of mankind.

It must be admitted that even though the old and deeply rooted traditions of Russia were never wholly obliterated, and the new régime was to find itself organically grafted as it were onto the ancient stock of the Russian people, and was, in fact, to become increasingly Russian with time, it nevertheless basically altered, if not the actual process of government, at least the total structure of the socio-economic process.

The various catastrophes of the First World War left the country inherited by the Soviet régime substantially truncated; the old Tsarist boundaries, extended over a period of centuries, were pushed back, not to move forward again until the end of the Second World War.

In accordance with its Messianic programme the Bolshevik régime found itself trying to construct a socialist order in a country that was substantially wrecked. An initial attempt at 'War Communism' was soon abandoned, to be succeeded at first by the 'New Economic Policy', which made a brief concession to capitalist forces in an attempt to recover some economic equilibrium, and then by the titanic enterprises of the Stalin régime that emerged from the intra-party struggles of the first part of the 1920s.

In addition, and from a cultural point of view perhaps most decisively, the bulk of the educated classes vanished in the first few years that followed the Bolshevik seizure of power. Thus, when the initial enthusiasm and idealism aroused by the boldness and sweep of the Bolshevik programme, at least among the more or less socialized elements of the intelligentsia, evaporated, and the feverishness of the Russian Civil War in the early 1920s had subsided, the Bolsheviks found themselves at the helm of a ruined state, abandoned by the working classes of West Europe on whom they had been counting when they took power.

Their problem, which may be summed up as the enterprise of instituting an advanced technology and industry as the groundwork for a socialist society, was thus immensely complicated. It was exacerbated above all by the departure *en bloc* of two million Russians of the educated classes, which made the task of finding technicians and administrators for a uniquely comprehensive government programme insoluble.

It naturally took a little time for a problem of such scope even to be embarked on; in the initial period of the Soviet régime there was no time, and perhaps no inclination, to consider the arts another aspect of State planning.

Hence, during the early 1920s there was a rather permissive atmosphere in the Soviet Union with respect to the arts. Bolshevik intellectuals like Anatole Lunacharsky, a littérateur and philosophical journalist who became Commissar of Enlightenment during the first Soviet phase, were essentially old-fashioned Western European liberals, even Bohemians in their attitude toward the arts; they were delighted with the expression of all sorts of experimental attitudes. The Marxists who were in the administration took a liberal view of the arts, regarding them as part of the 'superstructure' of society rather than its material base. Thus they thought that changes in society would bring about corresponding changes in the arts rather than the other way round. Meanwhile, it was up to the artists, during the transition period, to absorb everything they could from the past.

Thus in its initial phase the Soviet régime fitted in quite nicely with the upheaval of cultural values that had been evident in Russia from the end of the nineteenth century. This cultural effervescence in Russia had nothing to do with Bolshevism at all, and for some years after the revolution it went on prospering, restrained only by the straitened circumstances of the times and not by any direct action of the Soviet State.

The intellectual effervescence in which the Russians played a role of their own was part of the reaction to the staggering technological and industrial successes that had taken place in Europe as a whole, and that ushered in the present 'age of electricity'. The fever of technological modernism had finally seized hold of the Russian intelligentsia too, and given it far deeper and stronger roots than had the ornamental aristocratic culture preceding it.

Innovation became the order of the day in all the arts. The symbolism borrowed from the French poets by the Russians gave way to practically an endlessly shaded variety of all sorts of 'isms' – futurism, acmeism, imaginism, and so on – in bewildering succession. The publicity value inherent in the performing arts gave Stanislavksy's theatre and Diaghilev's Ballets Russes enormous celebrity; Stravinsky's turn toward amelodicism helped inspire an endless array of musical novelties; the basso Chaliapin and the dancer Nijinsky became internationally celebrated personages. Russia was, in fact, swept into a preoccupation with form as such, an aspect doubtless of the shuffling around of formal elements for their own sake that is associated with abstractionism in all its manifestations. The intelligentsia turned its back, for at least a time, on the Messianic moralizing, sermonizing and earnestness that had characterized it for so many decades during the nineteenth century.

At first none of this was interfered with by the Bolsheviks, who not only indulged the many innovations they had inherited from the cultural upheaval preceding their accession to power but systematically sponsored many of its manifestations. Not only was Lunacharsky himself something of an artistic innovator and actively sympathetic to experimentation as such, but Lenin, too, though personally old-fashioned in his tastes, was wholeheartedly in favour of artistic freedom. In the early part of the 1920s it would be fair to say that cultural life

12

went on with immense verve. New forms of expression were in fact diligently looked for; the Bolshevik Party itself, in its purely social attitudes during the first decade after the revolution, showed remarkable unconventionality; the family was denounced, marriage was laughed at, sexual morality was tilted toward unbridled licence, discipline in the schools was considered preposterous, and so on. Religion, of course, became a target of systematic abuse, though the churches were never actually prohibited.

During the Civil War education had perforce been seriously constricted, but with the restoration of order it began to revive very quickly in spite of the almost insuperable obstacles imposed on it by the utter collapse of Russian intellectual life during the critical era. The intellectuals had generally belonged to the upper classes; vast numbers of them had either died in gaol or from starvation and cold; most scholars had joined the upper-class *émigrés* abroad.

During the period of the New Economic Policy, however, in the early part of the 1920s, there was a vigorous revival of education, and more importantly, perhaps, an immense artistic effervescence once again that lasted throughout the first decade of Bolshevik rule. Poets like Yesenin, Blok, and Mayakovsky became well-known; Pasternak acquired a following. Stravinsky and Prokofiev, the two great hangovers from Tsarism, enjoyed immense influence under the Soviet régime, while among the younger composers Shostakovitch was to acquire a celebrity that has proved enduring. In the theatre and the ballet the name of Russia revived very considerably, though nothing particularly novel was attempted. For a brief period those arts that had been considered decadent by the Bolsheviks beforehand were now applauded as products of the vanguard.

The Soviet cinema was doubtless the chief means of carrying the name of Russia abroad in a new artistic medium; even though the films made from the very beginning of the Soviet régime were devoted more or less exclusively to some form of propaganda.

Soviet cinema, pulsating with life for a time, had been formed by many disparate influences. In the twenties the so-called 'movie-eye' group appeared, fanatically zealous for factual precision; untrained actors and improvised scenes in the open air came into fashion for a time. A few attempts were made to implant expressionism or various kinds of abstraction into the evolving camera medium, though this lasted only until the rise of the Stalin dictatorship, which in its turn also fused together a number of disparate influences, including the ancient Muscovite tradition of the 'illustrated chronicle' that had served as propaganda for the march of the Orthodox Church Victorious. Stalinist cinematics also included a major ingredient of outsize traditional heroic painting and giant exhibitions, a commonplace of the nineteenth century as well as a sort of revolutionary mystery-play that had developed during the brief period of War Communism at the beginning of the 1920s: vast throngs took part in some of the gigantic pageants that were filmed.

If it is true that events acquire their historical meaning only through their artistic expression then it may be said that the Russian Revolution itself was imaginatively crystallized as a primordial event only through its mythical re-creation in the pageantry and symbolic re-enactment of the Soviet cinema. This revolutionary myth was itself given an immutable form in the folk imagination through the development of the cinema, an admirably suited instrument for propagandizing the masses in Russia and outside. A heroic trilogy of films appeared on the tenth anniversary of the Bolshevik insurrection: Pudovkin's *Last Days of Petersburg*, Eisenstein's *Ten Days that Shook the World*, and Barnet's *Moscow in October*. It was these films that preserved in the minds of many the heroic qualities attributed to the revolution that had created a new society.

Of all the Soviet cinema-makers it was doubtless Pudovkin and Eisenstein who achieved the most and became the most famous, exercising an influence far beyond the borders of the Soviet Union. Eisenstein's *Potyomkin* and Pudovkin's *Mother*, made from Gorky's novel of the same name, were world-famous. Eisenstein's career was perhaps stormier, since though he was bound to remain a servant of the Stalin régime his originality kept leading him into dangerous blunders he then had to make up for.

Eisenstein's career had been unusual: educated as an architect, he was quite at home in the experimentalism of various European arts. Influenced by Wassily Kandinsky, he believed that spiritual qualities could be achieved in all visual arts by the appropriate use of nothing more than line and colour; he was in the long Russian tradition that had achieved its zenith in the nineteenth century, that of believing an art to be true only insofar as it managed to achieve a synthesis of sensation. *Potyomkin*, his most famous film, was heavily influenced by the ancient Russian tradition of the open-air mass theatre; presented in such a way as to de-individualize the film, the battleship *Potyomkin* was itself the hero, with the crew as a corps of individuals constituting a vision of mankind being redeemed from both material affliction (rats gnawing their victuals) and spiritual blindness (priests and functionaries exploiting them). The film, an idealization of the abortive revolution of October 1905, merely presented a highly patheticized version of the True Revolution's precursor, and established a religious parallel between the two revolutions that was rooted in the religiosity that the régime was trying to breathe into its revolutionary myth.

Pudovkin was from the very inception of his career quite detached from the polemical ferment that followed the revolution; he was too intent on the execution of his cinematic art to bother much with politics, and never wanted to do anything but serve the régime in his own way. He wrote a good deal of theoretical analysis of the cinema, in which he emphasized, perhaps banally, the practical value of technical-innovation as a means of indoctrination: thus he had the self-avowed aim of furthering the end of the régime by means of the artistic medium instead of merely accommodating the cinema to its political encasement. He was also very receptive to the Stanislavsky doctrines of 'realism' in acting, instead of the more experimental styles that had been in vogue in the years following the revolution. It was also rather natural for him to play up the semi-dictatorial function of the film director, in contrast to the vague sentimentalities of democracy that had flourished for a time between the revolutionary upsurge of democratic optimism and the final congealment of Stalin's dictatorship.

For as we can see now, the brief period of liberalism in Soviet cultural life was a very brief honeymoon reflecting, perhaps, the idealism that had enveloped the Communist Party before its grappling with the realities of Russian life had turned it into an instrument of ferocious repression. The period ended abruptly as the régime moved on to a programme of general constraint.

As its problems deepened, the Bolshevik Party had been growing harsher and harsher; after dispersing the Constituent Assembly that had been the misty goal of Russian revolutionaries of all shades for generations, the Bolsheviks were rapidly alienated first from their former comrades-in-arms, the Mensheviks, then from the populistically minded Social-Revolutionaries, then with growing momentum from their own dissident, non-'orthodox' members.

As late as 1924, the year of Lenin's death, about two-fifths of all publishing was in private hands; only three years later only one-tenth remained, which was soon taken over by the government too. The beginnings of the homogenizing of all artistic as well as socio-economic life can perhaps be linked to the date of the founding of an official theoretical journal: *The Bolshevik*, in the year of Lenin's death; this launched a series of discussions that were to set the tone of Soviet life for a generation and more.

After Lenin's death in 1924, which was followed by Trotsky's eclipse and banishment, the Stalin faction took shape during the mid-1920s; by the end of the decade Stalin, hitherto a relatively obscure figure, was to have gathered more power into his hands than any other person in Russia or, for that matter, perhaps, in world history. Stalin may be said to have held absolute power in Russia from about 1928 to his death in 1953: his personal dictatorship came to overshadow all intellectual expression in the country and put its stamp on life more profoundly than any other institution in the history of Russia.

By 1930 the Stalin faction was firmly in the saddle, and with the suicide of the best-known poet, Mayakovsky, the formal prohibition of all private printing, and Stalin's call, put forth at a party congress, that the first Five-Year Plan, launched in 1928, be magnified into a 'socialist offensive along the entire front', the basis of the totalitarianism that has since been all-encompassing was firmly laid.

To put the matter schematically, there was an era of liberalism and freedom in the arts that lasted for a decade of Soviet rule, from the revolution to the overt consolidation of the Stalin faction in 1928. This was the beginning of a new age in the Soviet Union: from then on, or at least until Stalin's death in 1953, the Soviet State laid a paralyzing hand on every spiritual and intellectual expression of the country. The repressive activities of the régime were of course expressed as a function of Marxist theory; the cultural suffocation was based on a dogma that very soon was given formal expression in the doctrine of 'socialist realism', which came to sum up the trend that made itself felt in all the arts – architecture, painting, sculpture, as well as the cinema, the theatre, literature and poetry.

The dogma itself was an attempt to channel the national energies into activities required by the régime: the legacy of the Russian past could not, after all, simply be abandoned: nothing would have been left. On the other hand the régime had to hold out with ideological fervour the goal that had been proclaimed as the justification of the revolution to begin with – the socialist transformation of society.

'Socialist realism' was formally put into effect in 1934, in a speech made at the first Congress of the Union of Writers. The speech was made, significantly enough, not even by one of the intellectual puppets of the régime, but by an official of the secret police; Maxim Gorky's presence as chairman gave the unusual announcement a mantle of respectability.

From the point of view of the role of the State, the Stalinist harnessing of the country was a repetition of a constant motif in Russian history: the State had always played a key role in the organization of its people. The Bolshevik attempt to implement a totalitarian programme merely meant an exaggeration of the governmental role in accordance with the immense expansion of modern means. It had become possible, with modern technology, to subordinate all social and artistic, as well as economic activities, to the decisions of a small group of government figures. The heightened role of the State was emphasized by its shifting away from ideological foundations after the Bolshevik Party coup. In a short time a vast administrative apparatus had to be improvised, quite independent of the personnel of the Old Bolshevik *élite*, in order to accomplish the radically comprehensive programme scheduled by the Messianic summit.

This was doubtless the beginning of the Soviet transformation of the intelligentsia. The fetichism attached to mere proletarian origins or Marxist schooling was completely ousted by the notion of developing a new Soviet intelligentsia, as Stalin said in 1931, that would be amenable to the needs of socialist construction. This was not a mere matter of technical ability; on the contrary, the indispensable component of the new Soviet intelligentsia had to be an absolutely unswerving obedience to the Party. In this simpleminded way the new régime entered on its ideological justification of a policy of unmitigated constraint.

It is just the strait-jacketing imposed on the nation by the Soviet régime that enables us to make broad generalizations about artistic developments. For just as in literature the socially orientated themes were authorized and indeed enforced by the increasingly monolithic Soviet régime under Stalin, so in the other arts – architecture, music and painting – a wave of uniformity was imposed on all artists from above by fiat; the cringing of the artists was perhaps an inevitable result.

It would be absurd, of course, to consider the Stalin strait jacket a complete innovation in Russian history. In many ways, especially in its ideological wrappings, it seemed to be harking back to the cultural themes of the 1860s and 1870s. The rather primitive belief in mechanistic panaceas for all social ills, shown by Stalin's sponsorship of both the physiologist Pavlov and the geneticist Lysenko, was really a reflection of the somewhat catechistic chain of thought that Stalin, trained as a priest, had inherited from a long line of Russian Orthodox seminarists. The artistic vulgarizations of the Stalin era, which have since been carried abroad throughout the world, the drearily uniform injection of social content into every manifestation of art from posters to poetry, seem an echo of the 1860s. The social realism of the non-official school of painting, the ideologically motivated music of the Mighty Handful, the endless novels of social comment and criticism, all reappeared after the turbulent experimentalism characteristic of Russia around the turn of the century. Lyric poetry, satirical prose, the experimental theatre, and modern painting and music were simply obliterated by this homo-genized, streamlined, resurrection of the social attitudes of two generations before.

This whole socio-intellectual process culminated in the cult of Stalin, 'Father of Peoples' and 'Locomotive of the World Revolution'. This extraordinary phenomenon might have been adumbrated by the prior launching of the cult of Lenin, which began immediately after his death in 1924. In a celebrated 'vow' read aloud by Stalin at the Soviet Congress that year, official sanction was given to the deification of the revolution-ary Lenin, who was placed on a par with Marx in the genesis of a Soviet pantheon that very quickly came to include Stalin, too. It was doubtless the establishment of the Lenin cult that enabled Stalin to inherit its authority in his own lifetime; by presenting himself as the exclusive heir to Lenin's legacy, Stalin benefited very directly from the Lenin cult and used it to buttress his own overwhelming authority, which grew by leaps and bounds into something seldom seen in history.

As Stalin grew all-powerful, the free-and-easy bohemianism of the early 1920s was violently rejected, and replaced by the brutal, unmiti-gated authoritarianism that enveloped all aspects of Soviet life. Discipline was restored in its harshest form not only in the army, but in the school system; not only was the death sentence restored but it was applied to children from twelve on; with the elimination of the free-and-easy sexual mores even abortion was made a criminal offence. Patriotism once again came to the fore, replacing the Marxist internationalism of the early years of the régime.

This new patriotism, revolving around both the Soviet 'Fatherland' and the Great Russian people, naturally implied the massive subven-tioning of the intelligentsia as a class. As the régime consolidated itself, indeed, the intelligentsia became a vital shield and mouthpiece; it was simultaneously dragooned and pampered. It was in fact this self-conscious, systematic enslavement of the spirit, through a combination of bribery and harshness, that led to the general paralysis of the arts under Stalinism. The Bolsheviks had learned a great deal from the ineptitude of the Tsarist censors.

The effects on literature were of course the most striking, though all other media were also shackled by the dictatorship. Even science, which one might have expected to be spared by the very reason of its indispensability, was blanketed by the mystique of Stalin's capriciousness that hung like a miasma over all Soviet life.

Maxim Gorky became probably the outstanding single influence in literature, once the liberal period of the pre-Stalin twenties was over. He had of course made his reputation long before – he was born in 1868 – but as a writer who had self-consciously declared his Bolshevik sympathies he was made much of by the Soviet régime, as one of the few talents inherited by the Communist Party. Gorky had the unusual distinction of being able to be passed off as a genuine proletarian, admittedly by disguising his somewhat unresolved, though plebeian social origins. It was he, in fact, who was made a prototype, much against his will, of the 'Socialist realism' that had remained the bedrock of the Soviet State.

This slogan, whose ambiguousness if anything surpasses that of the old Tsarist slogan of 'nationhood', is a mere synonym for official patriotism – of the Soviet variety, of course. It has been successfully imposed on a wide variety of writers who may not have much else in common, from Michael Sholokhov, a Nobel Prize Winner, to Konstantin Simonov. Other Russian writers who survived into the Soviet era, like Eugene Zamyatin, author of *We*, a celebrated science-fiction precursor of George Orwell's *1984*, and Michael Zoshchenko, a popular humorist and satirist, did not survive very long.

The totalitarian homogenizing of culture that the Soviet régime has become celebrated for need scarcely be described: because of the universalization of politics in our day it has become familiar throughout the world. The principal factor underlying that homogenization is a feature of Marxist theory in general, as distorted, simplified, and iconized by the Soviet régime. The 'dialectical materialism' underlying the 'Marxist' theory of the Soviet State represents, of course, a borrowing by Marx of one of Hegel's notions 'translated' into socio-historical terms. In its nature it is bound to encompass not only all aspects of reality, including science, art and society itself, but also the very process of thought that brought it into being. The trustee of the historical process is, so to speak, the Communist Party, while its executor is the Soviet State. The coping-stone of this majestic intellectual arch is, in other words, the successful political faction of the dominant party.

The sanctification of the newly established Trinity of Party, State nd Theory led to the iconization of Stalin as the equivalent of the Godhead, for it was he who, in fact, embodied or personified the Trinity in his own personal cult. In the period between the modest, quiet, subdued celebration of Lenin's fiftieth birthday in 1920 and that of Stalin nine years later, after the tidal wave of the first Five-Year plan had smashed against the countryside, the process had been consummated: Stalin had been transformed into, almost literally, a deity.

The Stalin era proper may be said to have been launched by this fiftieth birthday celebration. The whole of the Soviet Union was smothered in reminders of his physical presence: busts and portraits of Stalin were displayed in every corner of the country. There was a quite remarkable spate of words addressed to his glorification: in politics, literature and even science he was eulogized with a Byzantine extravagance. He was praised without reserve as the superior of literally every thinker produced since time began, as the greatest genius ever produced by the human race, in short as the greatest man in history. This singular status naturally warranted the exploitation of his authority in all areas of thought, from administration to linguistics. All Russian history as well as, of course, the whole history of Marxism, culminating in the contemporary history of the Communist Party, reached its highest point in Stalin's matchless eminence.

Until his death in 1953, Stalin's position in the Soviet world was unchallenged; with the magnitude ensured by the mass media of the modern age the adulation aimed at him must be unique in history. It overlaid all Soviet culture for the whole of this period, even surviving the initial disasters of the Second World War, from which Stalin, in spite of his rather depressing role in its initial phase, emerged still more glorious.

The Soviet *élite*, trained to fawn on the new God, and simultaneously pampered and threatened, was of course the instrument of this adulation. It laid a deadening uniformity on all artistic and intellectual activities, and in spite of Stalin's dethronement a couple of years after his death, in the celebrated secret speech made at the Soviet Congress in 1955 by one of his collaborators and successors, Nikita Khrushchev, the régime has not changed very significantly in respect of the conformity imposed on the *élite* by the end of the 1920s.

The political *élite* proper, that is the ranks of the Communist Party and its satellite organisms, grew very substantially too, becoming a mass party with the great programmes of collectivization and industrialization; but it was never more than a minority of a few million against the background of the rising population of the Soviet Union as a whole. The Communist Party was itself, of course, totally streamlined as part of the iconization of Stalin; any possibility of internal opposition was systematically and ruthlessly annihilated. To a certain extent the unique position of the Soviet State as *de facto* heir of a hundred years of socialist thought forced even the political opponents of the Stalin faction to yield to the plain fact that the Soviet State was there. Since there was no possibility of organizing opposition to the policies of the successful Stalin faction anywhere in the party structure itself, still less anywhere in the country at large, all of Stalin's opponents within the Left wing were effectively hamstrung by his having pre-empted all the traditions of Marxism, 'Leninism', and the successful revolution itself. Stalin's régime was thus shielded against any principled attack arising within the Left wing camp.

The tightly knit fabric of ferocious terror, naive adulation, and political enthusiasm constituted a web that was more than adequate for the containment of the arts and sciences.

In philosophy, science and the arts a bludgeon was applied to all deviations from the official 'line'. Thus the formerly popular literary critic Voronsky and the well-known philosopher Deborin were suddenly accused of 'Menshevikizing idealism'; they recanted at once in public. Stalin abruptly announced that the traditional Marxist principle, enunciated quite unmistakably by Marx himself, to the effect that in a socialist society the State would ultimately wither away altogether, was now indefinitely suspended; not only was the dictatorship of the proletariat not going to vanish in the foreseeable future, but on the contrary the Soviet State, with its auxiliary, the Soviet judicial system, was going to be indefinitely reinforced. This rather simple-minded shelving of a treasured dogma was itself announced, of course, to be, by virtue of its very contradictoriness, a living illustration of the marvellous dynamics inherent in the Marxist dialectic.

Freud, whose school had enjoyed immense popularity in the Soviet Union during the early 1920s, was formally outlawed in 1930: his views concerning the psychic determinants of human character, a source of enthusiasm before, were denounced as running counter to the socialist potentialities of the transformation of man.

Architecture is naturally the most public, the most civic of the arts; here the Soviet authorities proceeded quite self-consciously. In a report on the award for the design of the Palace of the Soviets in Moscow at the end of the 1930s, for instance, the commission in charge of the competition said that Soviet architecture was to be a 'people's architecture, essentially humane and rich in details that must appeal to the masses'. The Report went on to say that it must also be 'based' on the past: the upshot of the so-called 'debate', run under government auspices of course, that sprang up around this theme among Soviet architects was that all experimental attitudes were rejected *en bloc*. This included the various fads popularized for more than a generation by those architects who had ceased being craftsmen and who, under various influences emanating primarily from Germany and France, began to develop theories and 'ideologies' of their own. By the 1930s the movements of 'functionalism' and 'constructivism' were definitely proscribed; technical innovations, based on function or on the formal elements of architecture itself, were discarded in favour of the architecture considered to be an integrated art, rooted in the classics and fulfilling the exalted aims of the great new society being constructed under the guidance of the Father of the Peoples.

What constituted the classics was also a subject of debate for a time, though finally the rapidly congealing dogmatism of the parvenu régime settled it: all Eastern styles, as well as the Byzantine, Romanesque and Gothic, were thoroughly tainted by their origins in religion and mystical feeling; the Gothic in addition was evidently an echo of feudalism – a conventional epithet of contemporary Marxists, whereas Renaissance architecture had been an expression of despotism, and the 'functionalism' of the period after the First World War was obviously an expression of capitalism in decadence. The selection of the classical style in architecture, accordingly, was manifestly the best solution: it was also maintained that classical architecture had been inspired by the large-scale social goals underlying the Soviet enterprise; moreover, it had the charm of a connection with the past of Russia itself, that is, of the 'Empire' style of the late eighteenth and early nineteenth centuries in Russia.

Soviet architecture has distinguished itself most clearly in the public buildings, of course, though a certain amount of attention was paid to the construction of the massive residential complexes that grew up somewhat sparsely in the midst of the general housing shortage. These buildings, remarkably banal in design and shoddy in construction, seem to have been the best response the lean and hungry régime could afford to make to the general demand for housing that had begun growing with the proclamation of the socialist goal of an economy of abundance.

The architectural monumentalities of the Stalin régime also seem to be a harking back into the Russian past even beyond the nineteenth century, in the heavy, sombre outlines of civic buildings, with their curiously unnecessary spires and frills, the leaden chandeliers and sombre antechambers. Perhaps the Moscow subway, regarded as the very zenith of Stalinist public achievement, was the greatest monument of the Stalin era. The vast, ornate, unbelievably cumbersome exterior of this subway – opened when it was a mere seven miles long – attracted the energies of officials from all over the Soviet Union, who made special trips to install elaborate stalactites and stalagmites throughout the expensive labyrinth.

In painting, the same anti-modern, anti-formalist tendencies quickly made themselves felt. The target of condemnation was any attempt to play about with the medium of painting, instead of regarding it as an historically established channel for the conveying of a social message. The ideological import of a work of art was bound to become the criterion of its excellence, even of its right to exist, the moment the régime, in the clutch of the Stalin programmes for the transformation of Soviet society, was wedded to the civic goals proclaimed by the State. The socialist realism imposed on literature was applied to art in the same primitivistic, uncompromising way. Artistic works had to mirror the great enterprises of the régime; they had to convey the titanic struggle of the straitjacket régime with the forces of nature and society in such a way as to be immediately apprehensible to an untutored public.

In and for itself, of course, there was no reason why this ideological programme could not, in the case of painting, have been associated with extreme technical talent or even artistic genius: as long as the message, ideologically, was clear, the medium itself could evolve with a great luxuriance of talent, if only along lines laid down by tradition.

Yet in the event this ideological simple-mindedness was accompanied by a thoroughly mediocre taste even with respect to the traditional standards. It was not only that the criteria acceptable to a small handful of mandarins were rejected out of hand; but the taste of the public, with all its traditional devotion to iconic simplicity, was unthinkingly and fanatically imposed on the artistic community. This iconizing tendency, accordingly, already deeply implanted within the people's hearts, was devoted to the depiction by fiat of standard episodes in the lives of the leadership, mainly Stalin and Lenin, of course, as well as to various classical episodes drawn from the endless industrial enterprises that began to proliferate during the Stalin régime.

Factories, dams, ironworks, collective farming and heroic episodes from the official version of the Civil War and the revolution became the only subjects favoured by the régime. There were, to be sure, some stylistic deviations; some painters showed a very occasional and discretely modernistic element, but by and large the slogan of socialist realism drove painters back to various traditional approaches to art, though the chorus of Soviet critical acclaim for the new realism inaugurated by the Stalin régime and continued after the death of Stalin harks back, if anything, to the old-fashioned social realism of the 1870s and 1880s in Russia, when Populist sentimentality created countless subjects for the canvas.

Music was shielded for a time from the growing pressure of the Soviet authorities, since it is doubtless difficult to deduce the ideological message of a musical composition. While the influence of Stravinsky and Prokofiev remained paramount, there was some slight experimentation, though along well-tested lines, by the younger generation of Soviet composers. What ultimately proved decisive, however, was Stalin's personal taste in music, which seems to have been of a remarkable and old-fashioned simplicity – 'something you could hum'. In the 1930s D. Shostakovitch (b. 1909) emerged as the most talented of the younger generation, but his major early work, *Lady Macbeth of Mtsensk*, put on in 1934, while enthusiastically received, fell foul of Stalin's taste later on, and afterwards began receiving the usual barrage of Soviet epithets in the area of artistic criticism – 'formalist tendencies', 'vulgar naturalism', etc., and the work was officially proscribed. To the surprise of Shostakovitch himself, who thought his opera had been steeped in social content expressed as simply as possible, he was reviled as having come under the influence of a whole group of Western 'decadent capitalists', such as Schönberg, Hindemith, Berg and so on. Stalin, as the greatest music critic in history, also added his voice to the discussion of music in the 1930s, with his remark that music in Soviet Russia was to be 'national in form and socialist in content'. Shostakovitch's career since the 1930s has been a little mottled: he was taken back into favour, fell from it, composed a patriotic Soviet symphony with the 'image of Lenin as its inspiration', and so on.

The cinema was affected far more directly, of course, by the totalitarianism of Soviet life. By the 1930s both Pudovkin and Eisenstein were completely immersed in Stalinist chauvinism; their films depicted in somewhat different styles the themes enjoined by the dictatorship. The glorifications of both Alexander Nevsky and even Ivan the Terrible – rehabilitated, very appropriately, by the Stalin régime as an essentially great and innovating Tsar – fitted in extremely well with the sombre reversion of the Soviet régime to the grotesqueries of ancient Muscovy. The career of *Ivan the Terrible* is itself illuminating: cast as a vast trilogy, the first part came out in 1945, to be hailed by the usual well-concerted praise. The second part, however, in 1946, was slightly too near the historical truth; it seems to have upset Stalin with its all-too-reminiscential relationship to his own career. The density of the intrigues, the miasma of fear in an atmosphere of impending assassination, the excessively open description of Ivan the Terrible's remarkable cruelty, as well as that of Ivan's most celebrated institutional innovation, the *oprichina*, may have conveyed overtones of Stalin's own entourage. In any case the second part was not released until five years after Stalin's death, when Eisenstein himself had been dead for a decade. The third section was never done at all; Eisenstein died half in disgrace, as he had been during the early 1930s.

The films made since the Second World War have been, almost uniformly, somewhat stereotyped romances between various kinds of heroes of socialist construction, such as dairy-maids and factory-workers, or paeans of praise to Stalin and to the Red Army. With rare exceptions they have not had much of a career outside the captive audiences of the Soviet Union; there has been no question of their exercising a stimulating effect on the art abroad.

The sole literary monument to survive the suffocation of Stalinism may be the novels of Michael Sholokhov, the third Russian writer to receive a Nobel Prize. Sholokhov's epic novels, though broadly conceived along lines acceptable to the monolithic simplemindedness of the régime, dealt with themes that were in their nature, after all, heroic to begin with: despite the implicitly propagandistic slant woven into them, their scope and depth allowed of genuine artistry in the portrayal of the grotesque, violent, and colourful social upheavals they recorded. Even Sholokhov, despite his fidelity to the Stalin régime, found himself rubbing against the grain; it was not until Stalin's death, finally, indeed, the fall of Khrushchev afterwards, that his gifts were given full recognition and he could, at last, feel secure.

The most recent flurry of spontaneous literary activity in the Soviet Union, since the publication after Stalin's death of Ilya Ehrenburg's *The Thaw*, which has given its name to the whole of the post-Stalin era, was the scandal that sprang up around Boris Pasternak's *Dr Zhivago*.

Pasternak's father, Leonid, had been well known as a painter and

## A New Incarnation

(*above left*) Illustrated page by L. Lissitsky for V. Mayakovsky's *With Full Voice*, published in Berlin in 1923 (*below left*) 'The Red Ploughman': revolutionary poster designed in 1920 (*right*) Poster by V. Mayakovsky for the Bolshevik health campaign in 1920.

(left) Portrait of the novelist Maxim Gorky, which was the pseudonym of Alexey Maximovich Peshkov (1868–1936).

(below) A constructivist set for a dramatization of Gorky's novel *The Mother*, performed by the Realistic Theatre, Moscow.

(opposite) The naturalistic acting methods of Konstantin Sergeyevich Stanislavsky, actor, producer and theatre director, have had a strong influence on acting techniques throughout the West. He is seen here as Vershinin in Chekov's *Three Sisters* in the Moscow Art Theatre's production.

The best-known film of S. M. Eisenstein is *Alexander Nevsky* (1948), officially described as 'a hymn to the combat glory of the Russian people'. This still shows the Master of the Teutonic Order, appointed by the Pope to rule Russia, asking the captured Pskov army leaders if they agree to surrender to Rome. The photograph above right shows Eisenstein editing his film *Battleship Potemkin* in November 1925.

(*above left*) The Kirov
company dancing *Leningrad
Symphony,* based on
Shostakovich's Seventh
Symphony.
(*above right*) Nureyev and
Kolpahova dancing in a
Bolshoi production.
(*centre left*) Maya Plisetskaya
and Nikolai Fadeyechev in
*Swan Lake.*
(*below left*) Two soloists
from a Bolshoi production
of *Giselle.*
(*below*) A scene from Act IV
of *Swan Lake.*

Vera Mukhina (1889–1953):
'Worker and Collective
Farmer', stainless steel
sculpture erected at the main
entrance to the USSR
Economic Achievement
Exhibition in Moscow.

V. A. Serov: 'Delegates from
the Villages visiting Lenin
during the Revolution' (1950).

The Grand Kremlin Palace, completed in 1961, is constructed of metal,
granite and glass and stands in the grounds of the Kremlin.

Monument to the Third International, designed by V. Tatlin in 1919–20.

(*opposite and above*) Both these works cannot be shown in the USSR but have been exhibited in London. The painting is Rabin's 'Church of Ivan the Terrible' (1964); the bronze is called 'Suicide', by E. Neizvestny.

'Song of the Workers' Association' (*opposite below*), a stage design of the 'twenties by Serge Soudekine, was clearly influenced by Cubism; A. A. Plastov's 'Collective Farm Threshing' (*below*) was painted in 1949.

Two photographs of the
Moscow underground
railway; it was constructed
in the 'thirties, but the
entrance to the Leninsky
Prospekt Station *(above)*
was built thirty years later.

Ernst Neizvestny: pen and
ink sketch for 'Figure of man'.

draughtsman of some distinction; he had also had a close connection with the Zionist movement. Boris Pasternak himself seems to have been converted to the Russian Orthodox Church, oddly enough after the 1917 Revolution, and though perfectly docile under the Stalin régime, confining himself to politically innocuous lyrics and translations, he seems to have suffered from nostalgia for the Russian recent pre-revolutionary past.

His novel *Zhivago*, a poetical invocation, among other things, of a pre-revolutionary arcadia, had been written out in one draft or another for years and was finally about to be published, at first in Italy, by a well-known Italian firm sympathetic to communism. Abruptly, permission for its publication was withdrawn by the Soviet authorities, and the book in fact proscribed. When it was published in Italian anyhow, in defiance of the Soviet prohibition, it achieved instant success all over the world and won Pasternak a Nobel Prize, many people thought for exclusively political reasons.

The book was a sensation for many months: it was discussed at great length by any number of authoritative critics and became, in fact, a best-seller. Pasternak's life in the Soviet Union became a little complicated as a result; he was forced to renounce the Nobel offer and in effect recanted.

His novel may illustrate the contrariness of life for a writer in the Soviet Union. Having survived the Stalin epoch almost uniquely for a person in his 'category' – a liberal, fellow-travelling Jewish intellectual – his work is a clear departure from all revolutionary themes and a harking back to something before – the lyrical, honeyed world of the pre-revolutionary intelligentsia. Though Pasternak's life under the Stalin régime had seemed placid – he was singularly undisturbed by the tempest that destroyed his whole generation of literary intellectuals – he was always, it would seem, an 'inner' *émigré*.

Taciturn about politics under Stalin, taking pains, indeed, to remain on friendly terms with Stalin personally, he could never digest the fact of the revolution itself. His book, though it might have been thought to be well-timed for *The Thaw* that took place after Stalin's death, was too comprehensive in its rejection of all revolutionary values to be

17

stomached by a régime in the throes of transition to some unknown goal.

When the authorities finally prohibited his book it seems to have been because of its historico-philosophical posture, buttressed perhaps by a reasonable distaste for the work as literature; the Nobel Prize was also given for reasons one would have thought extra-literary, and so the most celebrated instance of Russian writing in generations was itself, willy-nilly, a mirror of the curious cross-currents affecting Russian art in the post-revolutionary twentieth century.

It is clear that politics in Russia, repressive throughout its history, were even more so under the Stalin régime. It would in fact be quite impossible to understand the evolution of the arts in the Soviet Union without considering them as a function of socio-political and ultimately even economic factors.

After Stalin's death, the cult of his person evaporated so swiftly that today it is even difficult to recall how all-encompassing it once was; yet that cult provides an example, unique of its kind, of a fusion between mythology and terror that is possible only on a high level of technology, with its concomitant mass media, operating within a relatively backward milieu. The deification of the man Stalin took place, after all, in the full light of day; to understand it one must consider both the nature of the deification and the structure of the terror, seizing hold of an immense people, that made it possible.

The fusion of mythology and terror came to a head in the 'Moscow Trials' of 1936–8, surely the epitome of both the methods and the content of Stalinism. They demonstrate its character even more graphically than the great campaigns of industrialization and collectivization that will make Stalin's name an historical landmark.

In the Moscow Trials a whole generation of 'Old Bolsheviks' was simply annihilated after being 'tried' on charges of conspiring with Hitler, the Mikado, and Wall Street to destroy the Soviet Union.

In the course of three great show-trials held in Moscow, and in the accompanying and following mass 'purges' of a kind that were to become increasingly familiar, many millions of people – most conservatively estimated at seven million, with a top estimate of twenty million – were killed and executed. The trials themselves utterly destroyed the whole body of Old Bolsheviks, and as the effects of the trials fanned out through the countryside former oppositionists of all kinds – all former Mensheviks and Social-Revolutionaries, all anarchists, all Left wing sympathizers, all returned immigrants, all foreign Communists harboured in the Soviet Union, all Communists whose official duties had taken them abroad, and a substantial segment of the armed forces themselves – were simply wiped out. The whole of the population was affected, in all social strata and all professions.

The scope of the trials remains all the more incomprehensible since the 'theory' underlying them seems, in retrospect, to have been no more than a psychopathic phantasy. The vast enterprise of liquidation was aimed at the figure of Leon Trotsky, isolated in Mexico and practically powerless except for his pen; it was Trotsky personally, claimed to be the architect of the singular conspiracy, who was the target of the trials.

Every mishap in the Soviet Union was included in the comprehensive charges made at the trials; all the unprecedented hardships of the Five-Year Plans, with their incredible sacrifices in blood, all the poor harvests, the famines, and even natural disasters like earthquakes and storms, were swept within the net of the Great Purge and linked directly to Trotsky's study in Mexico.

Since the evidence provided at the trials proper was overwhelmingly based on confessions made in open court, the whole of this singular conspiracy, based on manifest fictions, was displayed to many hundreds of foreign journalists. The pages of the world press were filled with interminable accounts of the trials, which oddly enough were almost universally, except for specific ideological resistance from Trotsky's supporters and some sympathetic socialists, taken at their face value. If one recalls, moreover, that the Red Army itself was disastrously affected – with the execution of three-quarters of the Supreme War Council, thirteen out of fifteen army generals, some sixty-five per cent of all officers above the rank of colonel, and similar figures throughout the whole army structure – the Great Purge, whose effects lasted until after Stalin's death, can be regarded only with stupefaction.

It must be admitted, on the other hand, that from the narrow point of view of the maintenance of Stalin's paramountcy, the trials were an immense success. They made it quite impossible once and for all even to discuss policy; all disagreement with the decisions of the Stalin faction, in the Soviet Union and throughout the 'liberal' and 'left wing' camps in the world at large, automatically entailed a suspicion of treachery. If one assumes that a cardinal aim of the trials was the discrediting on principle of all ideological opposition they achieved that aim down to the present day. The trials were thus the centre-piece of the Stalinist façade. They are essential not only to an understanding of the Stalin régime at home, but also for some insight into its projection abroad.

A corollary of Stalin's insulation through terror against criticism was the remarkable upsurge of Russian chauvinism that took place during the Second World War and afterwards. The war itself imposed unprecedented calamities on the Soviet Union both in human suffering and in material destruction – some twenty million killed and twenty-five million homeless – but the régime itself had immense success, in the sphere of power-politics, in its contest first with the Nazis and then with its wartime allies, the United States and Great Britain. By the end of the Second World War the Soviet government had engulfed vast satellite territories, was in a position to expand its technological plant very rapidly, and had taken up a new and much more aggressive posture in world politics.

Since the Second World War was officially baptized the 'War for the Fatherland', it was only natural for Stalin to emphasize Russian patriotism, which thus specifically singled out, in the crazy-quilt of Soviet nationalities, the Great Russian people as the premier people in the Soviet Union. Thus the political theory incarnate in Stalinism, summed up as 'Socialism in one country', in contradistinction to all forms of Marxist internationalism, led to its natural consequence: Soviet patriotism became Russian chauvinism. This process, immensely reinforced during the Second World War, culminated towards its end in a savage, systematic onslaught on all non-Russian values, an extravagant campaign of glorification of everything Russian. Russians now began being given credit for all human achievements, and the old, indeed banal charge of cultural backwardness, a cliché among all students of Russian history, was now scornfully dismissed as capitalist malevolence. Soviet superiority had to be demonstrated in all human activities; even science was suddenly invaded, toward the end of the 1940s, by the famous Lysenko theory of genetics, which, because it had the support of the Party for political reasons, was imposed on all scientists. This curious form of self-insulation plus self-glorification behind a reinforced wall of censorship and cultural dragooning, lasted for about a decade, until the summer after Stalin's death in 1953. The Stalin cult, so over-powering in the dictator's lifetime, vanished overnight when the above-mentioned speech by Khrushchev, bitterly attacking Stalin's dementia, cruelty, and incompetence, interred the theory of his genius once and for all.

Khrushchev's speech may be said to have inaugurated the new era, still with us, in Soviet affairs. Contemporary events are of course beyond summary: it is enough to point out that the Russian determina-tion to modernize itself – a theme stressed so often throughout this book and summed up under the Soviet régime so pithily in the Communist phrase 'to overtake and pass the West' – seems to have been realized, at least in one or two senses.

It is undeniable, for instance, that in the field of technique, which of course may be said to include scientific thought, the Soviet Union, which only a generation ago was well down on any list of great powers, has now surged impressively to the fore: its technological establishment, including its scientific and engineering personnel, is matched by its theoretical achievements; it has developed a technical intelligentsia that may be the first in the world. With its achievements in the develop-ment of nuclear devices, succeeded by the parallel development of rocketry, beginning with the celebrated 'sputnik' of 1957, the Soviet régime has finally 'caught up' with America in rocketry alone, and may even have 'passed' it in some scientific specialities, both abstract and applied. It may thus be said that the centralized economic program-ming of the Soviet Union, a Communist version, after all, of the State planning embarked on in previous Russian generations at least from

Ivan the Terrible through Peter the Great to Catherine the Great, has at last succeeded in matching the advance of the West. It has, in fact, leaped over all intervening stages in a characteristically Russian way.

Under Catherine the Great and Alexander I the *élite* cultivated itself so quickly as to create a still wider chasm between the masses and itself; similarly, the modern Soviet régime has found it possible to catch up with the first powers of the West on the levels of technique and theory, while failing to catch up with the West in the material well-being of the Soviet people. The supply of consumption goods is still sadly short. And this material shortage itself parallels the continuing lag in freedom, still suffering from the oppressiveness of a régime that has only recently, after all, relaxed to a minor degree if not its actual controls at least its harshness in applying them.

On the other hand, though it may be said that the régime is still stretched taut between the two poles of its promethean determination to transform society radically and *en bloc* and that society's persistent failure to achieve its own goals, still the rapid progress inherent in contemporary technology creates endless potentialities.

Nor can another aspect of the extraordinary Soviet enterprise be forgotten; the political effectiveness of the Soviet régime is a novel factor in world history, precisely because of its singular fusion between ideas and institutions.

The endurance of the Soviet régime has created, for the first time in history, a political organism identified with an idea that in its nature is general enough to have acquired the power to spread to political organisms elsewhere. In this one respect the somewhat simplified State doctrine claimed as ideology by the Soviet régime has all the mesmerizing qualities of former religions insofar as they could affect individuals regardless of their previous allegiance. The purely local interests of other states can be bypassed by the magnetic pull even of the Russian version of Marxism, and new structures can be created by its influences. Whereas historically normal states have gained followers by an actual act of ingestion, such as naturalization, any régime inspired by an ideology can gain partisans merely by the spread of the ideology itself. Thus the Soviet régime functions on two planes, even though the purely ideological impulse has in the past generation, with the consolidation of Stalinism, yielded precedence to the national interests of the Soviet State.

Yet the ideology remains. The Soviet Union is both a full-fledged State, with all the attributes of a modern State – government apparatus, army, State institutions – and at the same time the embodiment of the chiliastic ideal that the Russian people were the first to attempt to realize, as a people, on earth. To the followers of this chiliastic ideal – the Communists and their various sympathizers – the ideal universalizes the Soviet régime itself. The Soviet Union is no longer a mere state as even, in a way, France with all its universalism remains, but it foreshadows the realization of a perennial human longing.

This singular *mélange* of spiritual and institutional factors allows, to be sure, of an infinite variety of alternative developments. As the various undeveloped peoples of Africa and Asia emerge into some form of nationhood, the interplay between the Soviet Union as one state among others playing power-politics and its role as the bearer of the Communist idea is bound to become complex. The abrupt emergence of China as the embodiment of its own version of Marxism complicates that interplay still further.

If Russia is thought of as a cultural complex that began taking shape some four centuries ago, and if one recalls the appalling obstacles that it had to overcome in order to sustain and expand the social articulation of its identity, it must be admitted that its progress has been remarkable.

The Soviet bloc of states – which includes Red China, despite the current points of friction with the present Soviet leadership – encompasses more than a third of humanity, and Soviet influence reaches further in a myriad of ways; it can be seen that the Russian people, still inspired by an intense version of the Messianism that has distinguished it for so long, is bound to play a crucial role in world history.

The mission of Moscow as the 'Third Rome', so long an article of faith in the Russian version of Christianity, has been reincarnated – on a higher plane, as a Marxist might say – within the framework of a technology equipped to realize physical and institutional potentialities as never before. The confrontation between Russia and the world that has been in the forefront of Russian minds for so many centuries is now taking place, dramatically enough, at a point when the technology that the Russian *élite* has been fitfully striving for ever since Peter the Great can now make mincemeat of mankind as a whole.

This increases the burden of the Russian *élite*, to be sure, but at the same time it gives the solution of the problem a more dramatic allure that should appeal to the romantic pathos still embosomed in the hearts of the people.

# Index

Note. Page numbers in italics refer to illustrations.

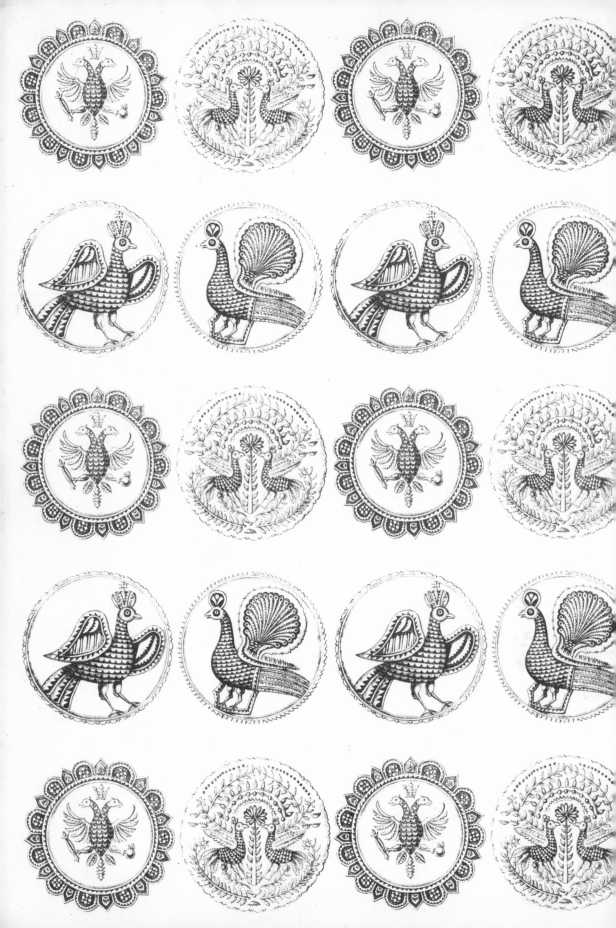